Global Software

D1521550

Dave Taylor

Global Software

Developing Applications for the
International Market

With 25 Illustrations

Springer-Verlag
New York Berlin Heidelberg London Paris
Tokyo Hong Kong Barcelona Budapest

Dave Taylor
Intuitive Systems
P.O. Box 4012
Menlo Park, CA 94026 USA

Library of Congress Cataloging-in-Publication Data
Taylor, Dave, 1962-
    Global software : developing applications for the international
market / Dave Taylor.
        p. cm.
    Includes bibliographical references and index.
    ISBN 0-387-97706-6. — ISBN 3-540-97706-6
    1. Computer software—Development.   2. Application software—
Marketing.   I. Title.
QA76.76.D47T39   1992
005.1—dc20   91-31825

Printed on acid-free paper.

© 1992 Springer-Verlag New York, Inc.

Production managed by Karen Phillips; manufacturing supervised by Robert Paella.
Typeset by Impressions, a division of Edwards Brothers, Inc., Madison, WI.
Printed and bound by R.R. Donnelley and Sons, Harrisonburg, VA.
Printed in the United States of America.

9 8 7 6 5 4 3 2

ISBN 0-387-97706-6 Springer-Verlag New York Berlin Heidelberg
ISBN 3-540-97706-6 Springer-Verlag Berlin Heidelberg New York

Dedicated to my parents, without whom my writing this book
would clearly have been a moot point.

Foreword

John Sculley

In the short history of personal computing, the task of the software programmer has been one of the least recognized—but one of the most significant—in the industry. In addition to defining the problems, and presenting the solutions, the software programmer is confronted with the challenge of having to predict what combination of ideas and technologies will move the industry forward in the most compelling way. Even though we've seen the development of tremendous applications in a surprisingly short period of time, the most difficult problems often surface when we try to elevate a successful local idea to the international arena.

In the case of Apple Computer, these challenges become especially profound when you consider that Apple sells Macintosh not just in the United States, but in Japan, China, the Middle East, Africa, Eastern Europe, and even to the United Nations itself. Of course, this means that the personal computer must work everywhere around the world. But more significantly, it also means that the software must reflect the uniqueness of a given culture, its language, morals, and even its sense of humor.

To step away from a narrowly-defined, nationally-based paradigm for software development, programmers, management, and entire corporations must learn to recognize what elements of an interface, problem solving technique, documentation illustration, package design, and advertisement are local, and which elements are appropriate for global markets.

In addition, consumers, or the software users, must learn to insist on applications and systems that are properly localized for their

needs, and fit naturally with their language and culture. The combination of these elements creates perhaps the most important job
for the software programmer: to design software that is as enjoyable—and as intuitive—to use as possible.

At Apple, we've always believed that if you can put information
into the hands of individuals, extraordinary things begin to happen.
The challenge has always been to offer tools to help users navigate
through a thicket of information in the easiest way possible.

In a global, information-intensive economy that consists of multiple languages, cultures, perspectives, and philosophies, organizations need to give individuals the tools they need to discover and
express their uniqueness. This emerging global economy is a world
in which organizations must learn to put diversity on par with their
core competencies, and a world in which the successful products
will be those that give individuals as well as organizations the power
to be their creative best.

This is exactly the point of Dave Taylor's book, *Global Software*.
He carefully illustrates that, ultimately, it is not the systems, structures or machines that represent the value of an enterprise. It is how
well these tools have been designed to allow individuals to extend
their reach, wherever they are.

Chairman and CEO,
Apple Computer, Inc.
Summer, 1991

Preface

More than any other commodity in the past decade, computer software sales have experienced breathtaking growth, with companies going from income in the thousands to income in the millions in a few years. The beginning of the 1990s signals a change in the traditional market for computer software, with the U.S. market reaching a point of technological saturation. Fortunately, outside of the U.S., the global marketplace is just opening up, with the consolidation of the European Community, the restoration of Hong Kong as a part of China, and the infusion of money into various third world countries around the world.

Targeting this marketplace can be difficult, what with the different languages, different cultural values, and even different notational conventions. Laws vary, import/export restrictions vary considerably, and even the protection offered under copyright and patent laws is very different in different parts of the world.

Learning how to target software for a foreign market, therefore, can be quite difficult, with very little information available, few programming or marketing examples, and almost no analysis of such subtleties as export restrictions. Predictions of hot future markets always seem to have a vested interest too; Japan promoting the importance of their own growing software market is a fine example.

Those topics—and more—will be covered in *Global Software*, with a significant emphasis on specific details of program internationalization, including presenting significant working code examples with detailed explanations of algorithms, actual coding details, and even the philosophies behind the code.

The main focus herein, however, is to discuss continually *why* things need to be done, instead of just *what* needs to be done. Indeed, those that are not technically inclined will find that they can easily skim through the programming section and find much to ponder throughout the rest of the book. Further, those readers interested in the actual software presented should also find the less technical portions of the book thought provoking. After all, an end-user product is considerably more than just a compilation of source code . . .

Truly international software is the result of an appreciation of the program elements that rely on the local culture and language. Armed with this information, software can be designed so that it can be easily localized for multiple languages and cultures, offering dramatically larger markets.

The sentence above offers the answer to the fundamental question that you might well be asking yourself, why should I bother? Why not let other countries either invent their own software or localize ours to work in their language and culture?

The answer is one that speaks the universal language of capitalism: profit. As you will see in the chapter entitled "Why Internationalize?" the international market for computer technology is already as large as the domestic market in the United States, and is growing at a phenomenal rate, one that should ensure that within a few years writing applications to work outside of the U.S. will be considerably more important than writing them for within U.S. borders.

As an illustration of this consider: in 1985 Sun Microsystems sold about $11.5 million dollars of equipment overseas, about 10 percent of their total revenue for that year. In 1990, however, overseas sales had jumped to $1.18 billion dollars, representing 49 percent of their revenue for the year. From 1985 to 1990, Sun enjoyed a 10,250 percent increase in their international market compared with a 2,145 percent increase domestically.

Where this will go as the European Community heads towards the much touted 1992 unification, and further as China, in 1997, absorbs the technologically advanced Hong Kong industries, is clearly difficult to predict. The continuing easing of the Eastern European political and economic situation, as well as the easing of U.S. restrictions on export of high technology, will surely add fuel to this fire, a fire that is likely to result in a multi-billion dollar software market by the year 2000. A software market that is going to absolutely require that applications "fit in" to the local culture and language so that local people can be productive.

A market that, to sum up, could easily create the next Microsoft or Computer Associates. A market that you can join once your applications are truly *Global Software*.

And *that* is what this book is all about.

Mountain View, California
July 1991

Acknowledgments

I would like to express my gratitude to the many people who made this book possible. Sheri and Daryl Orts in Norway, Bob Hepple and Jim Hanley in Hong Kong, Daniel Cordey in Switzerland, and, in the United States, Don Taylor, Nancy Louie and George Leach all offered invaluable feedback on early versions of the manuscript and insight into the subject matter. Special thanks also to Mark Hall for originally suggesting I write a book on global software, and his resulting direction, assistance, and encouragement during the initial phases of the project. Arne Thormodsen and Richard Artz, both of Hewlett-Packard, greatly assisted the writing of the chapter on HP's Native Language Support system: without them it would not have been possible. John Gilmore also aided my navigation through the Data Encryption Standard (DES) puzzle, offering insight into export restrictions and software copyright.

I am also indebted to Daniel Cordey for his assistance with the French that appears in this book, Mike Neumann for the German, and Jeff Bartlett for the Spanish. Any language errors herein are my own fault, not theirs.

The staff at Springer Verlag also greatly assisted with the production of this book, even with the many schedule conflicts and dilemmas we encountered along the way.

Grateful acknowledgement is also made for electronic correspondence and lively discussion from the following people; Dwight Aplevich, Lars Aronsson, Paul Bame, Nelson Bolyard, David Brooks, Alexander Dupuy, Adam Feigin, Chytil Georg, Jim Giles Jr., Madeline Gonzalez, Gisle Hannemyr, Kee Hinckley, Per Holm, Chris

Jones, James Jones, John Kennedy, Rob Kolstad, Wayne Krone, Tim Lambert, Frank Letts, Vincent Manis, Michael McKenna, Wes Morgan, Peter Neilson, Bill Petro, Jim Reid, Dan Sandee, Dave Schnepper, Erik van der Poel, and Al Wesolowsky.

Finally, I would like to thank my friends and long-suffering housemates Pat and Tai for putting up with my seemingly-incessant typing, and tip my hat to Plucky, Elmyra and the rest of the gang for offering much needed humor breaks each afternoon.

Contents

"What it is"

Comprising:

Before you descend into the actual specifics of creating international software, and how to localize it for a specific culture and language, there are more basic questions that need to be addressed, namely: why internationalize? What elements actually end up being internationalized? What is the difference between internationalization and localization?

Today, it is not surprising that most companies have at least tried to sell their products into foreign markets. Many have been successful, leading to powerful global corporations such as IBM, NEC and Nixdorf. Even the best intentions, however, sometime lead to gaffes and errors in the difficult niche of international product marketing. In this section you will look at some of the more interesting examples of "internationalization gone horribly wrong."

1
Introduction

In the early years of the computer revolution, the technologies, from integrated circuit design and fabrication to operating system and application software development, were mostly products of the United States. The money for these developments for a large part was supplied by the Defense Department of the United States government, a source of funding that continues into the 1990s.

While much of the push for technological innovation remains within the United States, the development and distribution of computer-based technologies has expanded dramatically, to where it now covers the entire world. From the basement of the Kremlin to research laboratories in the Antarctic to the thousands of satellites orbiting the Earth and flying out into deep space, computer technology has truly gone global.

This transition has had a cost, however, a cost that, to paraphrase a notion, could be considered a backlash of the virtual manifest destiny of English-based computer software spread throughout the global technology community. In a nutshell, people in other countries have become quite dissatisfied with having to work with computer systems that only understand English, and U.S. English at that.

The computer programming language niche is an interesting example of this phenomenon; while there have been a staggering number of different programming languages invented, they have almost all started out life with U.S. "keywords" that delineate which of the actions the user desires. It is quite illuminating to pick up a programming journal that is written in a language other than English and notice that the programs often have lines where the program instructions are in a jumble of English and other languages, and the comments are completely in the language of the programmer or readership. Software written in the C programming language within Japan often can be spotted by the U.S. keywords such as "read" and "main," the cryptic (though equally cryptic for English and Japanese readers) variable and subroutine names, and the Japanese—kanji or katakana—comments, all neatly tucked within the C /* */ comment delimiters.

There's more than just language at work, however. Consider trying to trade slang with an Australian or South African; the basic language is the same, but the cultural conventions are different. Indeed, this extends to seemingly simple things too. For example, eleven-thirty in the evening is noted succinctly as 11:30 pm, 11.30 pm, 11.30p, or 23.30. Even more surprising, things that are absolutely taken for granted in the United States do not necessarily hold true elsewhere in the world. For example, a standard piece of paper for a printout is 8.5 inches by 11 inches. In fact, that's an artifact of earlier paper developments in the U.S. In Europe and elsewhere other sizes (typically an inch or two longer—the so-called A4 pads are an example) are the rule. It shouldn't matter, but if you write a program that wants to add a page header or footer on each page of a printout, the program needs to be able to take into account the varying length of the paper.

To consider why, another illustration: have you ever purchased a consumer electronic item that was designed, built, and packaged in a foreign, non-English speaking country? One immediately notices the confusion of the dials and controls—the so-called easy-to-use VCR is an example of this—but even more, the instructions are all in terribly confusing English, and might even contain illustrations that appear insulting. When I recently purchased a new stereo receiver, the instruction sheet listed various safety suggestions in a typically Japanese manner, as shown in Figure 1.1.

Advertisements are the same way, and indeed one of the most startling realizations U.S. nationals have when in Europe is that the style of advertisements on television is dictated by local cultural and societal mores and values, not a global authority. In England, for example, advertisements might well show nude children, or news snippets might even have topless young women displayed, neither of which are likely to make it onto commercial television airwaves in the U.S. Even in print, advertisements can vary surprisingly. Figure 1.2 gives a style of advertising that is unlikely to be effective and visually appealing outside of Japan, where it was designed.

3. **Avoid placement of the unit where it will be exposed to the direct rays of the sun, or where ventilation is inadequate.**
Don't place this unit in a bookcase or between cabinets, or where curtains or furniture may obstruct the ventilation holes.

Figure 1.1. Safety Suggestion #3 is accompanied by a typical Japanese illustration.

To be successful in the international marketplace into which computer technology is now sold, applications and the underlying operating system need to work *in the language of the user, not the developer.*

In the United States, software developers have been imposing their own values and ideals upon the foreign cultures where the applications and operating systems are sold. How much better things might be if, as a program was written, the programmer could isolate and mark the cultural and language dependencies, then easily translate them, en masse, into a target language, allowing for Spanish, German, Arabic, or even Chinese editions to be released!

That is what this book is all about. Starting with a discussion of cultural, social, and language dependencies, the main body of the book will discuss how programs can be easily designed and implemented to ease the challenge of internationalization, and then subsequently allow for straightforward localization. Continuing with this theme, the second part of the book presents a small, exemplary C program that demonstrates many of the issues faced by an international software developer, and chapter-by-chapter expands portions of the program to illustrate key concepts in internationalization.

The book concludes with a look at some existing packages to aid in the development of international software, some of the key standardization organizations and how they are trying to help devise a standard and consistent solution to this challenging problem area, and some thoughts on export restrictions and the global marketplace for computer software.

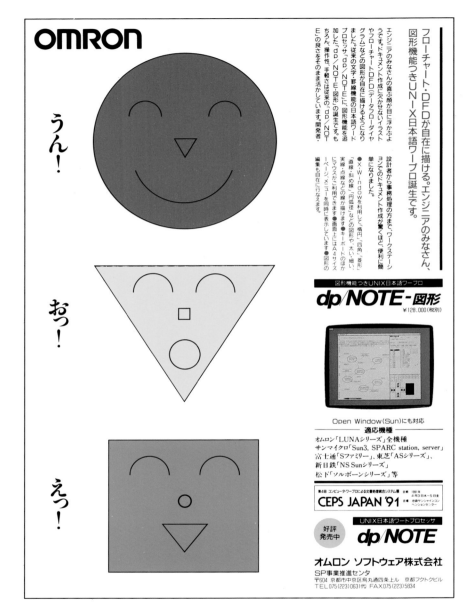

Figure 1.2. Cartoon-Style advertisement for Unix workstations.

1.1 Obtaining Source Code

For those who have programmed, either for their own edification or as part of their employment, this book should also prove a worthwhile reference. The examples are all written in the C programming language and, though developed and tested on a laptop DOS computer and a high-end Unix workstation, they have few features specific to the operating system. The solutions should be interesting and helpful to programmers in any environment, and using any programming language or system.

If you have a C compiler, you might well be interested in obtaining the actual source code on a disk. If so, check Appendix B entitled "How to Obtain Source Code." Appreciation of the information presented, however, is not reliant on having the source code available on your computer (or even having a computer), so do not be too concerned if you do not have a Unix machine or C compiler available for use.

2

Why Internationalize?

Computer programming as an art is unusual in that it naturally lends itself to exploration of technologies along the way while solving the specific problem at hand. Indeed, it is the rare software engineer who does not on occasion solve an intermediate problem or—more typically—unrelated problem while trying to meet a project deadline.

With a highly active programming community, an operating system designed by and for software engineers, and a system oriented more towards programmers than users, the Unix environment is perhaps one of the most powerful and, simultaneously, most esoteric to the common user.

Recognizing that programming is a continually more complex task, it is clear that adding any level of complexity to the process must be justified, especially if the change results in products having a longer time to market. If you are a bit cynical about things (as engineers often are) the obvious question to ask about this internationalization issue is, "Why bother?"

The answer is simple: profits.

2.1 The International Marketplace

Ten or twenty years ago, the computer marketplace could be typified by the observation that the United States had the top computer technologies and that if other countries could afford them, they ended up with what amounted to technological slices of Americana. If the Spanish wanted to obtain computer systems for their government or universities, they would more likely than not end up with a computer that worked in English.

Not surprisingly, this spawned a number of European and Pacific Rim software companies, each trying to duplicate the software found in the United States, but in the local language. In parallel to this, chip, board, and cabinet manufacture migrated into the local countries to aid in attaining the power, aesthetic, and other criteria demanded by the local market.

An example of this is the strict ergonomic limitations imposed by the German government upon manufacturers that desired to sell their technologies in Germany. Although a specific company might want to get, say, an IBM mainframe, they were prohibited unless IBM qualified under the German rules and regulations concerning that class of equipment. Primarily oriented around the hardware itself, and even more specifically to do with the human factors (such as the height and tilt of the keyboard, the level of VDT emissions from the display consoles, and the ease of access of the toggle switches or buttons on the main units), these regulations encouraged hardware vendors to offer special versions of their products for specific international markets, while simultaneously offering a level of protectionism for national businesses.

A fragmented community, the European nations spawned a surprising number of different, country-specific, restrictions and requirements for those hardware vendors that desired to sell their products overseas. The logical and most cost-effective solution to these difficulties was for companies to open local branches of their manufacturing and sales facilities, and the 1980's have witnessed an unparalleled expansion of U.S.-based companies into the international marketplace.

This may all be well and good, but what does it have to do with software, and the quest for international, or localized, applications? A little reflection should point to the fundamental realization; if you are a French national and desire to have a computer on your desk, are you more likely to purchase one with software that works in French or English?

The key here, of course, is the word *purchase*. While it may be nice to discuss the global community, of the contributions that the U.S. melting pot approach to cultures can offer to world peace, and similar, the bottom line is that creating international versions of software is just good business.

How good? In this section sales figures from national and international distribution and marketing branches of a number of global computer concerns will be examined, including Lotus, Compaq, Microsoft, Apple, Digital Equipment Corporation, and Hewlett-Packard.

2.2 Lotus Corporation

Lotus Corporation is best known for their flagship product, Lotus 1-2-3, a PC-based spreadsheet that is widely viewed as one of the most important factors in the explosive growth of individual computing stations in the industry. First shipped in 1983, 1-2-3 has gone through a number of revisions and been joined by a considerable number of different products from Lotus, including Symphony, Notes, and FreeLance. Expanded beyond the initial PC MS-DOS platform exclusivity, Lotus products are now available on a wide variety of operating system platforms, including the Apple Macintosh and Sun Microsystems' Unix machines.

As might be expected, Lotus has enjoyed impressive growth, growth in a manner that is common for the success stories in the computer industry. In particular, Lotus has spent considerable attention on the international marketplace, and has been rewarded handsomely.

"A company like Lotus," Michael Kolowich, Vice-President of Marketing points out in the Lotus 1985 Annual Report, "cannot sustain itself on technical wizardry alone. The only way to develop successful new products and business lines is to listen to customers, study what they do, and how they do it, and then make it easier, faster, simpler—more economical—for them to do it with Lotus products."

Chuck Digate, Vice-President and General Manager of the International Division, explicitly addressed the challenge and reward of properly internationalized software. "Software products must mirror the local business culture as well as the language. The Japanese version of 1-2-3, for example, reflects not only the complex nuances of a 7,000 character language, but also Japan's tradition of collegial versus personal decision making. For us, Asia and Europe represent phenomenal opportunities: to create tools that are uniquely suited to the local language and culture."

More recently, Lotus commented about the success it has enjoyed with the international economists community: "We have learned, too, from our huge success in the international market, that 1-2-3 is becoming the new lingua franca of international business. When the International Monetary Fund goes on an economic mission to member companies, the economists take 1-2-3 on portable personal computers."

Indeed, in the 1989 Lotus Annual Report, David Gurteen, Manager of the Systems Technology Group/International comments upon the history and outlook for internationalization at Lotus:

"I manage a small team that is part of the Systems Technology Group here at Lotus. We work with all the Lotus development groups to help develop better international products. We help these groups collaborate with our international development teams in Dublin, Staines and Tokyo.

"Through our 'think globally' task force, we are helping to spread the news that all products, unless otherwise specified, should be designed as international products from Day One. To design an international product, you first need to understand the requirements. Before 1989 these requirements were not specified very well. But no longer. Our team here, in conjunction with our teams in Dublin, Staines, and Tokyo, worked very hard to specify these requirements and to document additional technical information in an 'International Toolkit' that was distributed to all development and quality assurance engineers last year.

"Then a single, integrated documentation system was developed here at Cambridge. Prior to 1989, each development group would adopt whatever documentation system matched its needs. This was not a major problem for Cambridge, but it was for International since they needed to purchase all the different systems and train their people on each one. Through this new system of documentation, it was obvious that Lotus was committed to thinking globally. The success of Freelance-3J in Japan is proof of it. And proof too, that we view graphics as one of our core business products. Global success, of course, depends on the proven quality of the U.S. products, and on strong marketing and sales organizations, which we already have.

"In 1984, the year Lotus set up its international organization, 9% of our revenue came from international sales. By 1989, it had grown to 41%. Over the next several years, we expect our international sales to be well over half of our total business. We have learned a lot in a very short time. And it shows."

There's no doubt that for Lotus, at least, the international market is a hot one, growing at a much faster pace than the domestic market. With growth rates like the 70% expansion the Japanese Lotus group enjoyed in 1989 with the launch of Freelance-3J, a localized version of the popular Freelance product, Lotus' international market is hard to match. Further, if they continue their growth, over half the sales of Lotus products will be from outside the United States within two or three years.

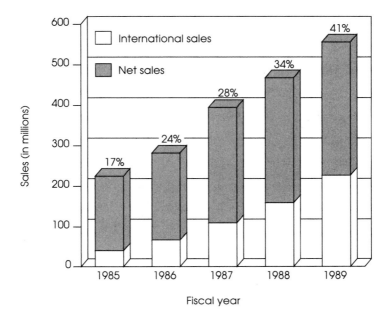

Figure 2.1. Growth in sales, Lotus.

2.3 Compaq Corporation

Explosive growth in the international market is not limited to software companies either; Compaq Computer in many ways is a typical high-tech hardware success story. Founded in 1982 by Rod Canion, Jim Harris, and Bill Murto with a $1000 investment from each, the sketch for their first computer design was done on a paper placemat at a pie shop in Houston, Texas. Securing venture capital from the same group that aided Lotus, the first version of Compaq computer—a fully functional, 100% compatible portable PC—was being shipped in 1983, with the company earning over $110 million that first year. In 1985, Compaq broke $500 million in sales and was placed in the "Fortune 500" list, the first company to ever accomplish that in less than four years of business.

Only a year after its first computer was introduced, Compaq started targeting the European market, with the introduction of wholly-owned subsidiaries in Germany, France, and the United Kingdom in 1984. Since that point, they've also established subsidiaries in Australia, New Zealand, Norway, Singapore, Spain, Sweden, and Switzerland. All in all, Compaq products are sold in 63 countries.

With more authorized dealers outside of the United States than within the borders (1,661 in the U.S., and 1,827 in Canada, Europe, Asia, and elsewhere), Compaq Computer Corporation is clearly one of the new global market computer companies.

Indeed, market research firm Dataquest Europe notes that in 1989, the company attained the Number Two market share position in the European business PC market niche, with their overseas sales surpassing $1 billion worldwide that year (93% of that from Europe).

Rod Canion, then President of Compaq, noted in the 1989 Annual Report:

"Compaq has invested heavily in people and resources in Western Europe since 1984 when we authorized our first dealers in the UK, Germany, and France. That investment has paid off handsomely in recent years, enabling us to become in 1989 the second leading supplier of business personal computers to Western Europe. Compaq was in fourth place the year before.

"Our coverage of the market includes more than 1,650 Authorized Dealers supported by twelve wholly-owned sales and service subsidiaries. We strengthened our position during the year by authorizing over 300 new dealers, opening subsidiaries in Norway and Denmark and expanding our manufacturing and service operations.

"We are well-positioned for the approaching single European market of 1992 at which time Western Europe will begin to discard decades (in some cases centuries) of regulations that have kept it economically fragmented. The market will begin to take on the appearance of one giant trading bloc, much like the U.S., but with 70 million more people. Its GNP of $3.5 trillion, while slightly smaller than that of the U.S., is growing at a considerably faster rate.

"The impact of this change is already spurring economic growth in Western Europe. From French banks and London insurance companies to Italian fabric makers, the operative words now are "productivity" and efficiency". Businesses everywhere are restructuring, trimming costs and seeking to join other companies in their own industries. This activity has led to increased demand for high-performance PCs. We are seeing more and more of our computers used in European-wide PC networks. We expect this demand for personal computers to remain high for some time."

He continues, discussing the Pacific Rim and Latin America:

"We see substantial opportunity in the Pacific region because of the growing demand for PCs among businesses and the limited penetration of computers into the white-collar workforce. Several of the countries, such as Thailand, Malaysia and Indonesia, have very fast growing economies.

"Indonesia is a case in point. Its GNP of $86 billion is growing at a healthy 6% rate. Its 190 million people live on a vast archipelago of 13,500 islands, making it the fifth most populous country in the world. For a number of Indonesian businesses and the government, PC networking is of growing importance. For example, at one of the government's largest banks, Bank Rakyat Indonesia, 600 Compaq Deskpro 286e Personal Computers are used in a network linking island branch offices with the bank's mainframe computer in Jakarta. The bank chose Compaq computers because of their reliability.

"During 1989, we also began shipping our computers to Latin America. Authorized Dealers carry our products in Chile, Colombia, Venezuela and Mexico. Substantial PC penetration has just begun in these markets and we expect them to grow rapidly."

The international political climate is of utmost importance to global corporations—indeed, Hewlett-Packard even includes a graph showing the value of the U.S. dollar against a conglomerate of different world currencies in their annual reports—and upcoming changes in the world market are critical. Of course, they can also represent tremendous opportunities, as Canion points out; "We see excellent opportunities developing in Europe. In 1992, several trade

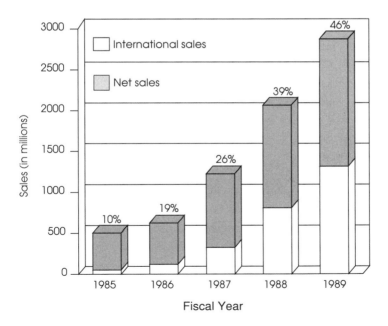

Figure 2.2. Growth in sales, Compaq.

barriers will be lifted between 12 European countries in accordance with plans adopted by the European Economic Community. More open trade should add new vigor to an already prosperous market of over 300 million people."

2.4 Apple Computer, Inc.

As far back as 1985, Apple has been enthusiastically working in the international market. John Sculley, President and CEO, commented in the 1985 Apple Annual Report that, for Apple, "one of the brightest views ahead is overseas. Apple is now a truly international company, with operations in 85 countries in all parts of the globe." Even more forward thinking, Sculley notes "To build strength abroad, we are looking to export Apple products to trade-restricted areas, including the Eastern Bloc. We have signed an agreement with the state-owned distributor of computers in China."

Founded by Steve Jobs and Steve Wozniak in 1976, Apple grew dramatically as the Apple II computer became the *de facto* standard in the primary and secondary educational market, as well as a popular machine with hobbyists and small businesses. In 1984 Apple introduced the Macintosh.

By early 1987, Apple had sold over a million Macintosh computers, initially to the educational market, but increasingly into the business and home markets. Just as Lotus succeeded because of its vision of spreadsheets as embodied in the 1-2-3 product, and Compaq succeeded due to its foresight in designing reliable 100% compatible personal computers, Apple has been successful because of its own compelling vision, as outlined in its Annual Report each year:

"We place the individual—not the organization—at the center of the computing universe.
"We believe that an organization can only be as productive as its individual members, so improving the computer user's experience is at the center of everything we do.
"We build tools specifically designed to increase personal productivity."

Sculley comments:

"In 1986, Apple made significant progress in its major international markets as well. Our largest markets continue to be France, Canada and Australia.
"Primarily because the computer revolution is still just beginning in many countries, Apple sales are growing faster internationally than they are in the U.S.
"In the UK, we introduced a new concept called Apple Centres^sm that shows great promise. Apple Centres are satellite stores dedicated exclusively to sell-

ing Apple desktop solutions. This program provides business dealers with showcase locations in high traffic areas.

"On the other side of the globe, we introduced KanjiTalk in Japan. KanjiTalk is systems software that gives Macintosh the three traditional Japanese alphabets, in addition to English, providing Japanese users immediate access to a powerful library of Macintosh software.

"What we learned developing KanjiTalk puts us far ahead in developing Macintosh systems software for other languages with pictographic alphabets. Rather than behaving as a multinational corporation, our goal is to become 'multilocal'—which means that we provide products tailored to our markets, wherever they may be.

"International sales now account for 26 percent of Apple's total revenue, a figure we intend to increase steadily."

Del Yocam, former President of Apple Pacific, the group responsible for marketing software and hardware into the Pacific Rim, noted in the same Annual Report:

"The Pacific will be the economic and cultural hub of the 1990s. And Apple will be right there, providing the kinds of tools to fuel this growth and prosperity.

"We are already successful in Canada and Australia. In the coming year, the goal of Apple Pacific is to lay the foundation that will also make us a player in Japan, in the rest of the Far East, and in Latin America.

"Apple is uniquely positioned to succeed. Because the Macintosh is a graphics-

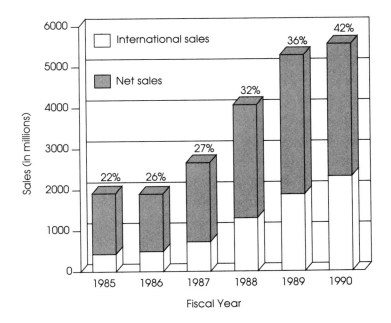

Figure 2.3. Growth in sales, Apple.

based computer, it can be adapted to practically any language. Currently, our
computer can display 17 languages in 27 dialects. That's a huge advantage
for businesses and organizations in a region as diverse as the Pacific."

Continuing the theme, Sculley recognized in 1989 that "In the
1990s, there will be no such thing as an *American* computer company. The only real competitors will be global in scale."

With possibly unintended echoes of Chairman Mao and his five-
year-plans for expansion and growth in post-revolution China, Apple Pacific began in 1989 to execute what the company refers to as
a "five year plan" to build their infrastructure throughout the Pacific
region.

Sculley pointed out that in 1989 for Apple, "our business is truly
global. International sales now account for 36 percent of Apple's
revenues, compared to 32 percent last year. It also proves the value
of our reorganization into three geographic divisions and one global
products group. Apple products are consistent around the world.
But the way we sell and support our customers is localized."

Shigechika Takeuchi, Vice President and General Manager of the
subsidiary Apple Japan, adds that "to compete successfully in markets outside the United States, you have to do business in ways that

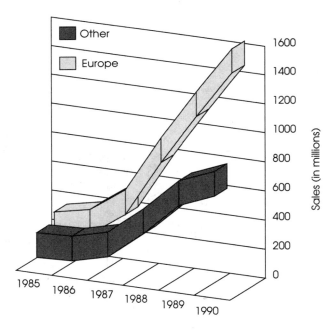

Figure 2.4. International sales by region, Apple.

make sense for those markets, even if it is different from what you do elsewhere. In Japan this meant establishing an R&D facility in Tokyo to develop products for the Japanese market, as well as listing our stock on the Tokyo Stock Exchange."

2.5 Microsoft Corporation

Another software success story, Microsoft Corporation was the first software company with the specific target market of microcomputer products. Indeed, their first set of products, released shortly after the company was founded by Bill Gates in 1975, revolved around the BASIC programming language, for the MITS Altair, Apple II, Commodore and Tandy personal computers. Six years later, 1981, IBM released the IBM Personal Computer, starting the PC revolution. Microsoft had an important part in that revolution; they supplied the operating system itself, MS-DOS. In 1985 Microsoft arrived on the market with their initial public offering of stock.

In the Microsoft 1990 Annual Report, Chairman Gates notes that "Microsoft products are designed for quick localization, so we can

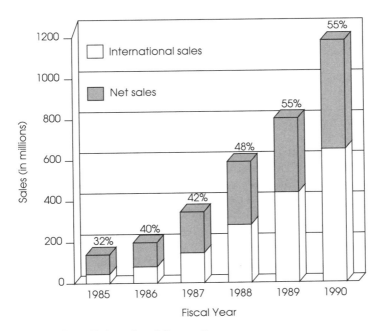

Figure 2.5. Growth in sales, Microsoft.

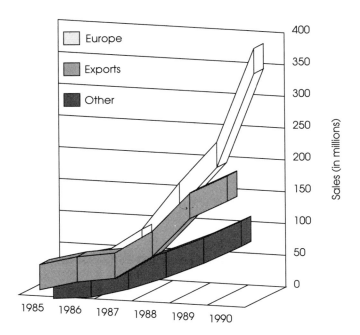

Figure 2.6. International sales by region, Microsoft.

quickly get new versions of products into the international market."
With over 25% of their business due to value added resellers (or
VARs), and a wide variety of software packages, Microsoft had to
learn quickly that being able to offer their products for global markets is critical to their continued international growth.

Among the many products Microsoft offers are a number of office
productivity applications including Excel (a competitor to Lotus' 1-
2-3 spreadsheet), Word, Project, and PowerPoint, a number of Macintosh titles, a local area network management system (LAN Manager), development tools and compilers (for FORTRAN, Pascal, C
and the language that launched the firm, BASIC), the phenomenally
popular Windows graphical user environment for PCs, and two different operating systems: MS-DOS and OS/2. Additional small
amounts of revenue are garnered by sales of their own mouse and
books published by Microsoft Press.

Similar to Apple, Microsoft also has a number of guiding principles
that give an excellent insight into the firm:

1. Products are designed to work together, simply and intelligently.
   Thus a customer can easily take information from one program
   and insert it into another.

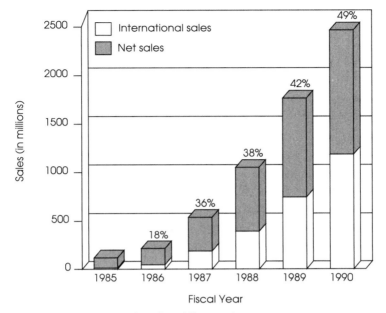

Figure 2.7. Growth in sales, Sun Microsystems.

2. While each product is designed to be individually excellent, they are even more powerful when two or more of them are used in tandem.

3. Their products are designed to be at the leading edge of what people need and want. Their applications products anticipate new advances in hardware technology, offering the average user access to the power of that new technology as it becomes available.

By 1990, overseas sales accounted for well over 50% of Microsoft business. In 1988, however, when slightly more than half their income was from domestic sales, Gates offered this insight:

"The international market is such an important part of our business—representing nearly half of total revenues—that any steps we take to advance the state of the art must also be examined in terms of how they will affect the state of technology abroad.

"That's one reason, for example, that we made the technical decision that Windows and OS/2 Presentation Manager would separate how commands are displayed on the screen from the main core of the program. So translations to those commands can be made simply, by changing a special "resource file", rather than requiring the programmer to go into the heart of the software and make changes in the core code.

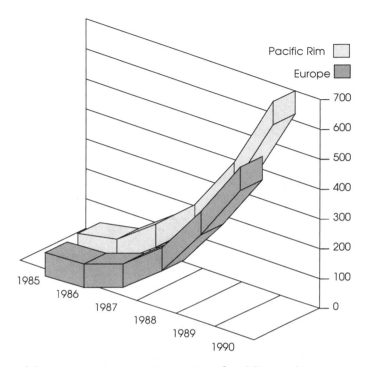

Figure 2.8. International sales by region, Sun Microsystems.

"At Microsoft, our International group plays an integral role in all our product decisions—right from the start. Products are developed with an eye to how they will be received abroad, as well as how they will perform in the American market.

"U.S. sales of personal computers now represent only 40% of the total world market. What's more, international sales are increasing at an ever-faster rate, creating major opportunities for growth and making this an important market in which to position our company for the future.

Microsoft is the only software company we will examine that prompts the question "What if they end up with most of their sales overseas?" It is an interesting dilemma, not unlike the situation many Japanese auto makers find with their vehicles; while it is clearly cheaper to shift production to the foreign locale, the location of the design and development groups remains critical for overall product success. Indeed, Toyota, Nissan, Honda, and many other Japanese auto makers continue to lead the hotly contested auto mar-

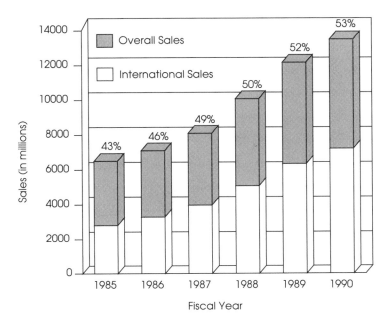

Figure 2.9. Growth in sales, Hewlett-Packard.

ket with their designs researched and completed in Japan, even if
the vehicles are actually built in the United States.

With software, it is not an unlikely scenario that a firm could end
up with their R&D facilities in the United States, and the vast majority of their market actually overseas. Certainly with some of the
more basic commodities—petroleum comes to mind—the companies
and countries that produce the commodity consume a relatively
insignificant portion. If everyone on Earth had a computer, the U.S.
marketplace would represent just over 4% of the installed base; so
while there are complex economic and geo-political reasons why
the vision of a "computer in every home" could not occur, the
prospect is nonetheless intriguing.

2.6 Workstations, Minicomputers, and Beyond

Although the personal computer market has the most compelling
story to tell regarding internationalization, other sectors of the computer industry are also indicative of the globalization of the market.
In particular, the fast growing Unix workstation marketplace is an

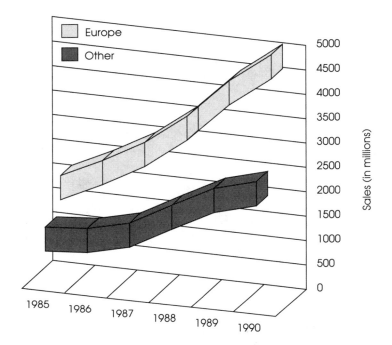

Figure 2.10. International sales by region, Hewlett-Packard.

area where a number of companies have been fighting for market share, revenues, and installed-base overseas.

2.6.1 Sun Microsystems

The brightest of these stars is undoubtedly Sun Microsystems. Founded in 1981 by Vinod Kholsa, Scott McNealy, and Andreas Bechtelsheim, the Silicon Valley company continually bucked the trends as they lead the blossoming market for desktop Unix-based engineering workstations, and ultimately personal workstations. In the hotly contested workstation niche, analysts such as Dataquest Corporation estimate that Sun has over 35% of the market.

Sun's growth in the European market has been rather gradual. But Sun unquestionably exploded onto the Asian computing scene, getting up to a half-billion dollars revenue within four years since the introduction of its products to those markets.

More so than with personal computers, the Unix customer demands a product that is localized appropriately, requiring companies to internationalize as they develop. Initially, Sun took a common

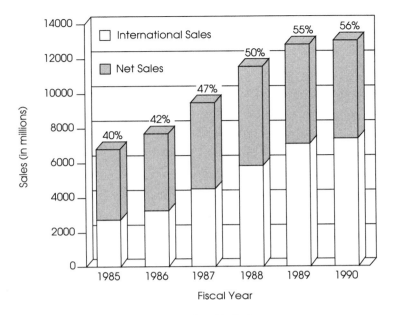

Figure 2.11. Corporate growth rate, Digital.

approach; they licensed vendors in the foreign markets to translate
and localize their software, without significant assistance from the
domestic development teams. Within two years, however, the corporation realized that a streamlined process could reap significant
benefits and now ensures that products can be internationalized (and
localized) during design and development.

2.6.2 Hewlett-Packard Company

The oldest of the companies examined here, Hewlett-Packard is also
the most diversified, with a product line that ranges from stetho-
scopes and medical equipment to calculators, to discrete electronic
circuitry, to printers and personal computer accessories. All told, this
over fifty year old corporation founded by William Hewlett and
David Packard has in excess of 10,000 different products bearing
their logo. One thing all these products have in common, however,
is that they all have technical sophistication and are all destined for
the global marketplace.

   Although many business analysts view excessive diversity as a
dangerous strategy, it is interesting to note that HP, one of the most

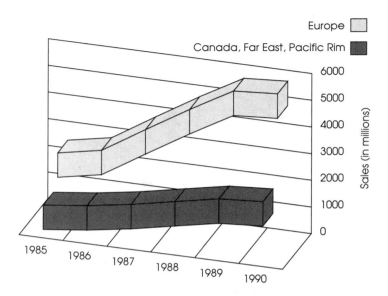

Figure 2.12. International sales by region, Digital.

diversified companies in the computer industry, has had almost half their sales overseas for over a decade now.

Within the software universe, Hewlett-Packard has been the dominant force in developing internationalization and localization software and tools for the entire industry. Indeed, the run-time internationalization library presented later in this book is modelled after the HP Native Language System. HP has always been a conservative company, carefully monitoring its growth and expansion, but has nonetheless managed to build a highly successful sustained global business.

John Young, Chief Executive Officer of Hewlett-Packard, outlines recent international growth as follows in the 1990 Annual Report: "During 1990 HP's already strong global presence grew significantly. We moved the headquarters of our PC business to Grenoble, France. We opened a branch of our corporate laboratories in Tokyo. We established new subsidiaries in Thailand, Turkey, and Portugal, and are rapidly putting sales organizations in place in Central and Eastern Europe."

2.6.3 Digital Equipment Corporation

Unlike Hewlett-Packard, Digital Equipment Corporation derives all of their income from computer, and computer-related products. Founded by Kenneth Olsen, the company first gained fame by supplying machines to the MIT AI laboratory in the 1960s. Since then, their VAXen line, and proprietary VMS operating system, have become common fixtures in companies throughout the world.

Digital is also distinguished by their aggressive attitude towards expansion into the international arena including ventures in Hungary, Yugoslavia, Czechoslovakia, and other Eastern Bloc areas. While other companies talk about venturing into new territory, they are likely to find Digital already there.

Kenneth Olsen, President of Digital, comments in the 1990 Digital Equipment Corporation Annual Report, "Digital's strategy is being implemented worldwide. We derive 56 percent of our revenues from the 81 countries outside the U.S. where Digital does business. During the year we opened our most advanced semiconductor manufacturing plant in Scotland. We established a joint venture in Hungary to kick off what will be a growing presence for Digital in the emerging markets of Eastern Europe, and business is already exceeding expectations."

2.7 The International Market

Each of the companies considered in this chapter are at the top of their markets, with not only excellent products, but a tremendous history of success in the international market, even as the marketplace changed from year to year. The most important lesson is that while companies with a national scope and perspective can often be reasonably successful, the companies that really lead the computer industry are those that see the *world* as their marketplace, not just the country that is home for the corporate headquarters.

Further, none of these companies have become leading members of the international computer marketplace overnight; they have all had the foresight and savvy to target markets, work with local and foreign representatives of these markets, and then give the marketplace time to mature and become profitable. If there was one generalization that could be made about internationally successful companies, it is that they have the patience to view the long term profit and potential of a market, even if a short term loss may ensue.

Indeed, one of the most important challenges facing successful companies is the tradeoff between long term and short term goals, results, and profits. Companies can manage for either extreme, but it is those companies that find the appropriate middle ground, and offer their individual teams the leeway to navigate within those constraints, that truly find success on a global scale.

3
Internationalization versus Localization

Whenever a software program is written, it is *localized* to the culture and language of the programmer. That is, it has the cultural context and culturally appropriate notational conventions of the local culture and language, simply because that's what the programmer is familiar with.

The process of extracting the cultural context from a package, be it software, hardware, documentation, or even packaging, is *internationalization*. The end goal of internationalization, then, is to be able to have a sort of generic package, with an appendix or attachment that details all the culturally specific items. As a useful analogy, think of a complex piece of audio equipment, with basic circuit boards, metal casing, power supply and so on in the *international* corner, and a panel of buttons, controls, and, most importantly, labels, cover plates, and even packaging and documentation, in the *local* corner.

The separation of product elements, into *culturally dependent* and *culturally independent*, is what internationalization is all about.

By contrast, localization is the opposite process; taking something that is designed for the international market and adding features and elements to better match the target culture and marketplace. Continuing with the audio equipment analogy, the localization company would be the one to which the parent corporation sends all *international* parts and items, the local company then being responsible for appropriate *localized* versions of the dials, buttons, cover panel, packaging, documentation, and so on.

To internationalize a product successfully, the people involved need be aware of their own culture, language, and social values and expectations. To successfully localize a product, the people have exactly the same requirements. Confused? After all, didn't you just agree that localization was the opposite of internationalization?

Consider the consumer electronics manufacturer again to better understand this curious similarity.

When the parent corporation designed the new stereo equipment, it knew that the product would have to work in not only the company's home market, but overseas as well. Internationally, the company has a lucrative business selling to original equipment manufacturers (or OEMs), who repackage the product and sell it in the foreign marketplaces. To make this as easy as possible, one of the primary design criteria for the new unit was to isolate all local elements, and design in support for certain international features.

Based on what we have previous discussed in this book, there are a number of things that you can imagine might be culturally dependent, including the display format for tuning the stereo (e.g., the radix point) and which words (or pictures) show up on the display for different actions. Further, more subtle differences have to be designed, including the variation in tuning and radio station frequency assignment throughout the world. In the United States, for example, FM radio stations are assigned frequencies that are two-tenths of a megahertz apart, all being on odd numbered values (e.g., 101.3, 96.5, and so on). In England, however, the radio stations are broadcast on a completely different frequency, and are separated by different increments too; thus a tuner customized for the U.S. market by automatically skipping past the even-numbered fractional frequencies might completely miss stations in a foreign marketplace.

In addition, the new stereo would require a set of specification sheets and other supporting documentation, detailing the actual features of the unit in as culturally independent a way as possible. Localization efforts, then, could focus on transforming the generic, highly-flexible international product into a more specific localized product, perhaps even including the "skip even numbered frequencies" feature for the United States.

Along the way, the localization firm could also better tailor their marketing, sales, and distribution channels to fit into the local culture and values. This "local agent" approach is incredibly predominant in business, with local agents representing foreign producers of just about any product imaginable, from computers to cars, from beers to carpets, even from clothing to video games.

Clearly, then, both sides of the coin are vital for the international success of a product. Internationalization is the preparatory stage,

FAST COMFORT!

Sport Seat by **DEE**

Finally. . . Sport Seats that combine quality workmanship, style, price and ease of installation. Available in popular colors, fine vinyl, plush Sport Cloth™ and combinations. Sport Seats by **DEE** feature molded urethane foam construction, multi-position recline with forward tilt for rear seat entry and a large rear map pocket. All mountings incorporate stock locations and are designed to 'Bolt-in' with no drilling or cutting required. The best features. . . the highest quality . . . All at an extremely affordable price!

DEE *Engineering* inc.

Dealer Inquiries Invited.

3560 CADILLAC AVE., COSTA MESA, CA 92626
714/979-4990 • FAX 714/979-3468

Figure 3.1. Ostensibly advertising car seat covers, but selling sex?

where products have their embedded culture and language extracted and generalized, while localization is the completion stage, where the product is fine tuned for the specific market niche that is targeted.

It is interesting to note that certain elements of products are often localized differently, even within a single geographic region. For example, many products have different types of advertisements in high-brow, high-income magazines than lower-income magazines. Further, an advertisement that might be seen in a ritzy Manhattan spot would be quite different than one passed on a billboard driving through Kansas, even though they are selling the same product.

If that fine tuning of market requirements and needs can be done successfully, it certainly seems to make sense. Just as a Greek man would not want the English word "page" to intrude on his Greek printout, a San Franciscan banker would not find an advertisement lauding a product's ability to save having to buy new shirts after a long day on the prairie particularly important or relevant either.

To internationalize a product you need to be able to identify not only the language-dependent elements, but the culturally dependent elements too. For example, many companies that sell sheepskin auto seat covers have advertisements featuring attractive young women dressed quite scantily, as shown rather explicitly in Figure 3.1.

In the United States and the U.K., this type of advertisement can be effective in certain markets, catching the eye of the (predominantly male) target audience, and helping to sell the product. In the Middle East, however, if the company wanted to distribute its product into a new market, these advertisements would be completely inappropriate and wouldn't even be allowed in local newspapers or magazines.

Another interesting approach to advertising products in foreign locales is to offer multilingual advertisements, as shown by the excellent Aldus advertisement in Figure 3.2.

To localize a product, you need just as much knowledge of the local cultural context, if not more; if you miss a subtle feature when internationalizing, the localization teams will likely find them later and point them out. When localizing, though, that's the end of the line for the product. Once it is localized, it is out the door and done, so "cannot grok" error messages absolutely must be fixed before the customer sees the product (as shown in the "grok" anecdote on page 49).

Figure 3.2. One advertisement; two languages.

To summarize:

Internationalization is the process of isolating and extracting all cultural context from a product.
Localization is the process of infusing a specific cultural context into a previously internationalized product.

4

Elements of Internationalization

The abstract question of different markets and profit margins is certainly interesting, but the real fun starts when specific elements requiring translation or modification to fit into a foreign culture are identified and isolated. Ranging from the obvious—such as the language of the error messages—to the subtle—such as how many lines fit on a typical printout—the specifics of international software ultimately represent slices of the culture for which they are targeted.

4.1 Cultural Context

The general idea here is one that sociologists call *cultural context*. Cultural context refers to the realization that all elements of a particular culture or society must be viewed from the point of view of that culture, rather than that of the viewer. Examples of this abound, with some amusing ones being in the area of cuisine. How many times have you heard horrifying stories of the parts of animals that people eat in remote locales? Surely people in other parts of the world find it quite shocking to find that U.S. residents commonly eat products fried in lard, which is just boiled animal fats, for example?

Clearly, then, to fit into a culture, software must also be designed to fit in to the cultural context of the user. A difficult task, this implies a comprehensive understanding of far more than simply the language and notational conventions. Indeed, because of this complication, many of the most successful international products end up being localized in the target country, rather than at a central facility in the United States or elsewhere.

This approach to international markets can be seen with the Pacific Rim consumer electronics products as well; while the units themselves are primarily designed in the home countries (Japan, Korea, Taiwan, etc), they are custom fit for the target market cultural context. Japanese telephones, for example, have U.S. phone digit/letter equivalents shown, as well as packaging and documentation in English. Of course, therein lies a pitfall too; many of the documents for consumer products are written in English by Japanese native speakers, rather than U.S. or English native speakers, leading to obfuscated, awkward prose. It is easy to extrapolate and imagine someone in a non-Western nation looking at an error message from a program such as "line 40: cannot grok 'k++' here," without any clue whatsoever about the meaning of the message.

What then needs to be encapsulated in this concept of cultural context? Just about everything, from the basic language to the slang and colloquialisms, to various notational conventions, and more. Let us take a closer look.

4.1.1 Transliteration

When first learning how to write, I was puzzled over why certain words got the first letter capitalized while other words did not. If I talked about a specific person, for example, his Mother, the upper case is used, but the more vague someone's mother stayed as all lower case. Of course, what we are talking about are proper nouns, which now rarely present a problem in my writing.

There's a subtle activity that was taught while learning what proper nouns were, however; how to capitalize a letter. Seems pretty simple, doesn't it? You just hold down the *shift* key on the keyboard and type, right? Well, not really. Similar to many other facets of international software, shifting case, or transliteration as it is more formally known, is fraught with pitfalls.

Many languages simply do not have the concept of upper and lower case letters at all, such as Hebrew and Arabic languages, as well as many of the Asian languages. Other languages have subtle constraints involved with transliteration, constraints that aren't likely to be known outside of that country.

An example of this is French versus Canadian French. If you have the word *école* and want to transliterate it to all upper case, is it the same in both languages? Logic says "yes." Canadian French is almost completely identical to the French they speak and write in

France. But the languages are *not* identical. In France, the notational convention would be to retain the accent when the first letter is transliterated, leading to ÉCOLE, but in Canada, the French speaking population simply drop diacritical marks, such as the grave, when transliterated, leading to the French Canadian ECOLE. Ironically, most French speaking people drop the accent on capitalized words because they're not available on typewriters and computers, even those manufactured in France.

Another interesting example is the name of one of the largest cities in Switzerland: Zürich. In German, the word is correctly capitalized ZÜRICH, retaining the umlaut, but in Swiss German, they capitalize it as ZUERICH instead.

4.1.2 Hyphenation

Although only used in a small subset of applications, justification of text is a feature that your product might well have. If so, how do you hyphenate words in a foreign language?

Originally hyphenation arose as a way to align the right columns of textual information, in an identical evolution to proportional spacing. The idea was since words naturally broke at syllabic boundaries, they could then be split at those boundaries and shown on two lines. For example, a typesetter coming across a document that contained "antidisestablishmentarianism" might well break into a cold sweat thinking about how to crush that into a two-inch-wide column in a newspaper. Being able to split it into syllables, however, gets us to "an-ti-dis-es-tab-lish-men-tar-i-an-ism", which now has ten different possible spots to break the word gracefully. While many hyphenation programs use simpler rules to figure out where words can be broken (rules such as "double consonants can always be split; 'comment' to 'com-ment' ") all hyphenation capable software inherently uses English-based hyphenation rules.

These rules do not work globally. An interesting example is in German, where the word for cuckoo "kuckuk" is not hyphenated as "kuc-kuk" as one might expect, but rather as "kuk-kuk". The actual spelling of the word changes because of the presence of the hyphen. Imagine how complex that algorithm needs to be.

4.1.3 Spelling

Another area that is more difficult than it initially may seem is spelling. Most modern computer operating environments offer a wide variety of document spelling checkers, from those incorporated into sophisticated packages such as Microsoft Word to the Unix *spell* command.

Yet spelling is another cultural context-specific facet of internationalization. Even in English, spelling rules are more complex than simply: "is it in my dictionary of correctly spelt words?" For example, should that last sentence have the word "spelled" or "spelt"? It depends on which dictionary you use.

More subtle examples are when slang and colloquialisms creep into use, especially nonsense words such as "cowabunga" and speech-imitating phrases such as "fer shure," rather than the correctly spelt "for sure." The point is that "fer shure" might be correctly spelt, or spelled, for a possible cultural context.

Capturing this knowledge in a spelling checker is almost impossible, and is shown by the proliferation of spelling packages. Options available in spelling checkers now include being able to ignore words in all uppercase and words that are abbreviations (a facet that is not going to be explored herein).

With other languages it is even more curious. For example, on December 18 of 1990, Portugal, its former African Colonies—Cape Verde, Angola, Mozambique, Guinea-Bissau, and Sao Tome e Principe—and Brazil agreed to adopt identical spelling for their local dialects of Portuguese. Their hope is that the accord will create a unified market for Portuguese-language books.

4.1.4 Collation

Sorting, or collation, is something that almost all software packages bump into at one point or another. This can show up in surprising places too. Would you have guessed that the Unix *ls* command, which lists files in a directory, requires a sophisticated sorting algorithm for it to work correctly?

Collation is a fascinating problem with many languages, ranging from the relatively straightforward addition of letters such as the ñ in Spanish* to the formidable challenge of sorting proper names in Japanese.

What's even more confusing is that many languages actually view two-character pairs as a single character. In Spanish, the 'ch' in

---

*Ironically, Spain has been arguing with the rest of the European Community over the retention of the ñ character; the EC wants to abolish it as unnecessarily locale-specific, and the Spanish, as might be expected, are highly unhappy with the turn of events. In mid-1991 Spain agreed to drop the ñ, but later rethought their idea and continue to petition the EC to retain the additional character.

"chico" is viewed as a single letter, which should correctly collate between 'c' and 'd' in a Spanish program. Similarly, ñ should collate between 'm' and 'n'.

English isn't bereft of these curiosities either. Where do numbers sort to in a list? The top? How about upper versus lower case words? That is, where should "Smith" collate to; between "small" and "smythe" or before them both, since it is upper case? (In this particular example, numbers and upper case letters almost always sort before lower case letters due to ASCII character ordering. The simple rule used in most sorting software is that if the ASCII representation of a letter is a smaller number than another, the letter is bibliographically lower, or earlier, in the alphabet.)

The new lexical ambiguity of non-alphabetic characters has led to an interesting phenomenon where lists, such as the indices of books, are now sorted differently than they might have been a hundred years ago when the ordering would have been done by hand. The reason for this change is simply that sorting algorithms on computers have not adequately modelled the lexical ordering of earlier indices.

Cultural context jumps into the fray, with subtle requirements of international software. In Japan, tradition has it that lists of names are sorted by the rank or importance of each person, as well as alphabetically within each rank. To properly fit in, then, an electronic mail system for a Japanese firm should properly sort the list of names in the distribution list by their rank and importance in the company. An impossible task for a traditional collation algorithm.

4.1.5 Notational Conventions

Of all the different elements of internationalization, the most obviously different are notational conventions for date, time, numbers, and so on. Indeed, the simple move to metric can be quite jarring. When travelling throughout the world notational conventions can prove confusing too. If you are in England and you see "11/10/90" written down, is it November 10th or October 11th?

At the same time, the difference in notational conventions is one of the most exciting facets of international software, where correctly matching a particular cultural context can reap immediate rewards regarding the international look and feel of a software package. Indeed, there are many programs that change the notational conventions for different countries, but ignore the more subtle (and more difficult) variations examined in this chapter.

4.1.5.1 Numbers

Almost all countries in the world use Arabic-based numbers, namely 1, 2, 3, 4, 5, 6, 7, 8, 9, and 0. Further, numeric values are "base 10" too; 124 is $1*10*10 + 2*10 + 4$. Numeric notational differences come in when numbers are extended to fractional values or add break characters or punctuation to help understand very large numbers.

In the United States, the 'radix' point, or character between the whole part of a number and the fractional, by convention, is a dot. Seven-and-a-half can then be represented as "7.5" and understood. The radix changes in Europe, however, where "and" becomes a comma; "7,5" isn't a list of two numbers as you might expect in the United States, but rather is another way of noting seven-and-a-half.

In the U.S. the comma is used for numeric notation, as breaks within very large numbers. For example, two-million might well be represented as 2,000,000 in the U.S., with it commonly understood that the commas are there as a notational convenience and have no actual numeric value. In much of Europe, however, since they use the comma as a radix point, they clearly cannot also use it to separate very large numbers because the result would be ambiguous. Occasionally, very large numbers might have quotes as separators: 2'000'000, but there remains ambiguity with numbers such as 3,443: is that approximately three and a half, or over three thousand? Instead, the European notational convention is that dots are used in this context, resulting in a complete reversal of the notation. The number 3,000.50 in the U.S. would be represented as either 3.000,50, 3'000,50, or 3000,50 in Europe.

Although this notational difference may seem straightforward, there are some subtle problems that can be caused here. For example, if you want to market a spreadsheet in France, not only do you need to take into account the differences in numeric notation, but you might well have to relabel some output features too (it doesn't make sense to talk about "lining up the decimal point" on a column of numbers if the decimal point isn't a point, does it? Interestingly, the French translation of 'decimal point' is *virgule*, which literally means 'comma.')

Another interesting variation between the U.S. and European convention is what a "billion" represents, numerically. In the U.S., a billion is a thousand million, or 1,000,000,000. In European countries, however, a billion is a million million, a significantly larger quantity: 1,000,000,000,000.

As with much of the varied cultural context involved with international software, numeric notation is straightforward to cope with, but the tendrils of the U.S. culture can be embedded deeply in the design of software, interfaces, and even documentation. A straight translation is rarely, if ever, an appropriate solution.

4.1.5.2 Currency

Just as numbers have different notation based on cultural and language context, so does the notation to represent amounts of money vary throughout the world too. Even in the U.S., in fact, there is a fair amount of difference; consider 50¢ versus $0.50. Not only are you seeing a decimal point radix on the latter, but you are seeing examples of both a postfix and prefix currency delimiter (after the value, as in 50¢, and before the value, as in $0.50).

Throughout the world there are a wide variety of different notations for currency, including prefix notation—£5 representing five pounds British—infix notation—5$50 representing five and fifty in Portugal—and postfix notation—50¥ representing fifty yen in Japan. Confusingly, some countries try to adapt similar notation to others, with subtle differences. For example, Australian currency is denoted in Australia as 500$AU and Canadian money, in Canada, is referred to as CD$500.

4.1.5.3 Time and Date

One of the first sets of nouns learned in a new language seems to be the days of the week and months of the year. Indeed, this is a very useful item of information, learning that if *a la casa en Sabado* refers to being at the house on Saturday. More than just the names of the days of the week and months being different, though, the actual notation representing dates can vary widely too.

You've already seen, for example, the difference in simple abbreviated month-day-year notation; again, does 11/12/90 represent November 12th, 1990, or December 11th? In fact, that varies based on interpretation, with the common U.S. notation being Month/Day/Year (leading to November 12) and common European notation as Day/Month/Year (December 11). Even with this simple numeric notation, however, there are further variations. For example, official U.S. Government documents typically are dated Year/Month/Day. For example: 90/12/11 (or was that 90/11/12?).

In the United States, there are a wide variety of date formats that could be needed in a software program, including: August 3, 1990, Aug 3, 1990, Aug 3 '90, 3 Aug 90, Friday, Aug 3, and so on.

Even more confusing, some countries traditionally use non-Western (Gregorian) calendars. Japan, China, and Israel all have their own way of keeping track of the date. For example, Israeli dates might well refer to years in the 5700 decade (known in the U.S., Europe, and elsewhere as 1900).

Time notations are equally varied, with some cultures encouraging the inclusion of seconds—11:40:33—others preferring 24-hour, military time—21:30—and yet others using a different delimiter between times—11.30. Adding to the confusion, notation also includes 11:30.40 to represent seconds added to a time.

When combined, the date and time formats can result in quite a tremendous variety of forms, which is especially troubling for software that must read user input and extrapolate the specified date or time entered. Spreadsheets, for example, often are required to offer this feature, allowing users to add time/date information to their numeric information. Clearly, adding language and cultural support for Spanish in a spreadsheet is quite a bit more than simply changing the prompts.

4.1.6 Other Culturally Dependent Elements

In addition to all the different notational elements, other features of software and hardware interfaces can require modification to fit in with a foreign culture too. For example, individual colors have widely different meanings; white represents purity and hope in the U.S., but in Japan, white is the color of death. Red, by contrast, represents danger in the U.S., but happiness in China.

Graphical elements are also subject to local interpretation. On the Apple Macintosh, the trashcan icon that we are familiar with would have a completely different meaning to people from an African or Middle Eastern culture, to the point where they might not understand the symbolism, making the interface considerably more difficult to use. By the same token, many consumer electronics from the Pacific Rim come with instruction booklets that feature illustrations Westerners find offensive or overly cute. For example, consider Figure 4.1, where the manufacturer is warning the consumer not to plug the unit into an inappropriate power outlet.

While it might be an accepted and enjoyable method of conveying information to customers in the Japanese culture, cute cartoon-like illustrations are not as widely appreciated and accepted in the United States.

With internationalization, even the most subtle features can prove to be culturally sensitive. When looking at a printout, it is clear that the words and typeface will change to reflect the local culture (you wouldn't want to print Chinese using a Cyrillic font), but even where the page number is placed can vary. Indeed, I recall talking once

9. **Concerning the power outlet(s) of this unit**
If this unit has a built-in electric power receptacle, be sure to connect only equipment with a power rating not exceeding that indicated by the receptacle of this unit. (Only connect audio equipment to this outlet.)

Figure 4.1. Another typical Japanese illustration— ensure correct outlet!

with a purveyor of international software who boasted about page numbering from their product always being in English. When it was suggested that customers might want the word "page" in the appropriate language, the response was "I doubt it."

Even the size of the paper can vary, with 8.5 × 11 being the U.S. standard, and 8 × 13 being a British/European standard. If your program must be able to add a page number (in the right language, please!) half an inch from the bottom then it clearly needs to know where the bottom of the page actually is.

Actually, while that is true, it really glosses over one of the most annoying features of most word processing and desktop publishing packages; everything is oriented and computed around the inch measure. Point size on fonts, for example, are computed as $1/72''$. Outside of the United States, paper size is rarely stated by measurements, so 8 × 13 paper is referred to as A4, and if size is mentioned, it is in terms of centimetres.

Finally, a challenging cultural variance is the order that characters are displayed. In Western languages the standard method is reading from the top to the bottom, left to right, lines of text. That is not consistently true for all written languages. Changing the order of text can prove tremendously difficult for software packages. Hebrew and the Arabic languages, for example, are line oriented similar to English, but read right to left (which has the interesting result that books are 'printed in reverse;' one starts by opening up what you would consider the 'back cover' and reading towards the 'front cover').

Chinese and Japanese, sharing a written language, can be written in almost any direction, but are most often written left to right or top to bottom, column oriented rather than line oriented. Imagine figuring out how to prompt a user for input with *that* notational convention. In fact, these cultures have moved towards a more tenable middle ground, with the Japanese having a number of different language variants including Katakana and Romaji, which are Japanese words line-oriented rather than column-oriented, and Japanese words phonetically spelt out in Roman (English) letters, respectively.

It should be clear that the task of successfully internationalizing either software, hardware, or even documentation is challenging. With differences in language, notational conventions, word ordering, color cues, and even variation in icons, the amount of knowledge required is substantial.

5
Pitfalls

Although much of internationalization is serious and complex, with millions of dollars riding on making the correct decisions at the correct times, there is nonetheless an amusing side. Companies that have tried to break into the international market (and foreign companies that have entered the U.S. market) have committed an almost infinite number of gaffes, from product naming to packaging, to advertisements, to even the location of manufacturing plants.

It is important to remember, however, that while these stories can be quite amusing, they demonstrate the exceptional difficulties facing a company moving into an international market. Further, as with any report of failure, companies prefer to brush these experiences under the proverbial rug rather than admit to any failures, so ascertaining the veracity of some of these tales is very difficult, as will be seen in the similarities between anecdotes.

• • •

The first, and perhaps most well known story is that of Chevrolet introducing their "Nova" automobile in Spanish speaking countries. Stories have it that the car sold very poorly because 'nova' means "doesn't go." In actuality, 'nova' means nothing in Spanish at all; 'va' is the verb 'to go' in Spanish, so "no va" is Spanish for "doesn't go." 'Nueva,' however, means 'new', so many people have in fact suggested that the original Chevrolet name for the car was tied in with the Spanish nueva, or new.

That explanation seems unlikely, given the astronomical meaning of 'nova' in English. On the other hand, that meaning itself strikes one as a curious name for a car; 'nova' is defined as "a star that suddenly becomes more brilliant and then gradually fades," not an obviously good name for an automobile. The confusion is particularly illustrative.

Indeed, articles have been written on the strange apocryphal story of "nova" being interpreted as "doesn't go" in Spanish speaking countries. David Garrison, a professor of Modern Languages at Wright State University, notes that "Spanish speaking persons easily recognize 'nova' as a word relating to Spanish 'nueva', meaning *new*." Donald Ball, however, a professor of International Business at the University of Texas Pan American, makes no note of 'nueva' in his book, noting that "nova" and "no va" are pronounced differently anyway. Further, he notes that Pemex, the government-owned oil monopoly in Mexico, offers an unleaded petrol called "nova."

The theory of naming comes into play again too here; Ball states in his endnotes that "Most native Spanish speaking people connect nova with the star or with nuevo, which is probably what General Motors had in mind." Again, though, it seems difficult to believe that the car is named in the U.S. for a word that is 'similar to' a couple of different words in Spanish.

Finally, Juan Jorge Schäffer, Associate Dean of the Mellon College of Science, points out that 'nova' as "doesn't go" is clearly an anecdote, because the idiomatic translations for "doesn't go" would be "no marcha," "no funciona," or "no camina."

Similar to much of internationalization, there are glimmers of truth in the story, yet upon further examination, it is difficult to see how much is misunderstanding within the market, and how much is more of a misunderstanding of the marketplace. David Rickes, however, notes that General Motors did in fact change the name of the automobile to "Caribé," with a resultant increase in sales.

• • •

International marketing is often more subtle than simply getting things to fit into the local marketplace. An example of this is the question of which side of an automobile the steering wheel should be on. Many analysts believe that it is vital for the wheel to be on the same side as the rest of the vehicles in the country (e.g., on the left in the U.S., on the right in England and Japan). Yet most Japanese who buy a Mercedes or BMW prefer the steering wheel to be located on the left—or wrong—side, because it is a status symbol. Further, according to Japanese reports, Honda quickly sold out of U.S.-made Accords that were brought into Japan, even though the steering wheels were, again, on the wrong side. In fact, a Japanese writer reported that the automobile "captured the hearts of young people with its left-hand steering wheel and luxury interior, unlike other cars found in Japan."

• • •

Naming of products is another spot where marketing can get in the way of success in a foreign marketplace. Just as French names add prestige to U.S. products, notably perfumes, foreign companies will often give U.S.-sounding names to their own products. Visitors to Japan, for example, are amused by a pre-moistened hand towelette called "Pocket Wetty," a lawn fertilizer called "Green Piles," "Cow" brand shampoo, "Shot Vision" televisions, a soup mix called "Kitchy," "More Ran" tea cakes, "Creap," an artificial coffee creamer, and even "Trim Pecker" trousers.

Some take a turn to the bizarre too; "Calpis" is not, as *Advertising Age* gleefully points out in an article on the subject, a bovine urine, but rather a popular Japanese soft drink. And "Nail Remover" isn't something to aid torturers, but rather a way to remove nail polish instead. Further, while "Taverna" might be an acceptable name in European countries for an eatery, it is surprising to find it used in Japan, as "taverna" translates, roughly, to "Do not eat."

When the Japanese beverage "Pocari Sweat" was brought to the United States the import company learned this cultural lesson first-hand. While the connotations of sweat in Japan are not a detriment in Japanese marketing—since the Japanese believe that it represents a healthy, hard working body—the connotations proved a significant problem in the U.S., and the manufacturer was forced to drop the second word before the product was successfully marketed in the U.S.

• • •

Another interesting situation is when a company anxiously spends considerable time and money to ensure that not only are their products appropriately named for each of the foreign markets they compete in, but that the company name itself is free of negative implications in any marketplace. Perhaps the most well known example of this is the series of name changes that Standard Oil have gone through in their decades of business. After concluding that Standard

Oil sounded too much like a U.S. company, they changed the corporate name to "Esso." Esso, however, has some significant negative connotations in the Japanese market: it translates phonetically to "stalled car."

Using modern technology, Esso spent great amounts of money studying the language and slang of dozens of languages, enabling them to feed the data into a computer which then generated inoffensive non-word names suitable for an international corporation. This list of words was then given to numerous linguists who ascertained that "Exxon" was the best of the choices. Ironically, Exxon is similar to an obscure obscenity in Aluet Eskimo.

Richard Carr of the Carr Group notes that for all the effort spent by Exxon to devise a pristine name, they then changed their advertising slogan from "the sign of happy motoring" to "the sign of the double cross." The company has again revised their slogan, however, since 'double cross' has significant negative connotations in English.

• • •

Vehicles seem to be particularly prone to difficulties in naming for the international market, as has already been shown with the Chevrolet Nova. In the U.S., Daihatsu sells a vehicle called "Charade," which clearly has more negative connotations than positive in U.S. culture. "Cressida," a high-end Toyota sedan, is an allusion to the character of the same name in a Shakespearean play *Troilus and Cressida*. Problem is, in the play the character of Cressida is quite perfidious.

When General Motors Europe (Opel), introduced their popular European Corsa into the UK, they changed the name to, ironically, "nova." Research indicated that "corsa" was too close to "coarser," which was viewed as a detriment to successful sales.

Mitsubishi Motors of Japan tried marketing their popular Pajero car in the Spanish market but were baffled by their lack of success. The reason? Pajero is slang for "masturbation." The name was, well, withdrawn.

In a similar way, Fiat, a sporty Italian auto manufacturer, found that they had to rename their "uno" when selling it in Finland. "Uno" means garbage in Finnish.

• • •

Another common gaffe with software in particular is the use of obscure references or jargon to the confusion of the customers. An employee of Tandy Computer Corporation relates a tale of this nature; upon shipping a Unix system to Germany, it seems a customer there tried to rewind a tape. A slip of the finger resulted in them typing "rewund" rather than "rewind," however, and they got the error message "cannot grok rewund." Confusion and chaos ensued; no reference to *grok* was found in the documentation, English-German dictionaries had no entry for the word, and the European headquarters for Tandy Corporation had no idea either, being staffed with Europeans. The problem was ultimately escalated to the point where engineers back in Texas at Tandy headquarters saw it, to their amusement. In fact, 'grok' is a bit of computer jargon introduced by Robert Heinlein in the science fiction novel *Stranger in a Strange Land*, where *grok* means "to understand fully and completely."

Another example of this can be illustrated through considering a recent advertising campaign from Data General Corporation. As shown in Figure 5.1, the idea of the campaign was to poke fun at their competitor Sun Microsystems, with its popular "pizza box" profile Unix workstation. Instead, they ended up with an advertisement that is difficult to understand, and certainly would be baffling to those not having grown up in a culture that had pizza "to go," in the omnipresent flat cardboard boxes.

•   •   •

Graphical interfaces are also prone to some confusion. In particular there are numerous stories about how the Apple Macintosh "trashcan" icon (a cylindrical bin) confused Britons; it looked much more like their postal boxes than a waste bin, and one can imagine the havoc ensuing when they delivered electronic mail to the box. In the same way, Sun Microsystems found that the icons they had for their electronic mail package under SunView (a graphical interface) confused those not in the U.S., who had never seen mail boxes on posts with small flags indicating whether new mail had arrived or not. (Further, the metaphor is incorrectly implemented anyway; physical mailboxes in the United States often have flags that are raised as a sign to the postal carrier that there is outbound mail therein. When mail is delivered, the flag is then lowered, giving an easy way for people to ascertain at a glance whether the mail has been delivered or not. On the computer, however, the meaning of the raised flag is reversed; a raised flag on the mailbox icon indicates that mail has arrived, not that it is queued to go out.)

The Free Software Foundations' GNU Emacs editor has a com-

Figure 5.1. Data General advertises via pizza, but is delivery cold?

monly used iconographic representation with graphical interfaces that represents a small (Western) kitchen sink. Why? Because the programmers and the user community have a running joke about how the editor is so powerful and complex that it is "everything but the kitchen sink." Needless to say, this type of graphical representation can prove tremendously confusing to users unaware of the joke, let alone those that are from a different culture and language completely.

Using animals for product imagery is fraught with dangers too. A U.S. deodorant found great success in the U.S. with their witty advertisement showing an octopus using the product under each of its eight "arms." When translated and shown in Japan, however, it was a flop, quite vilified by the locals; the Japanese consider octopus to have eight legs rather than eight arms.

In a similar manner, a U.S. marketing firm found that while a deer was a sign of masculinity in the U.S., it conveyed a slightly different image in Brazil, where "deer" is Brazilian slang for homosexual. In a similar manner, another company erred when it chose an owl as part of its promotional efforts in India. Problem is, Indians view the owl as a symbol of bad luck.

•   •   •

Product names that translate into obscenities represent a surprisingly large category of internationalization gaffes, many of which tend more to slang or colloquialisms than more formally defined words. For example, a while back Rolls Royce was planning on adding a new vehicle to their successful Silver Cloud line, tentatively named the "Silver Mist." Things were fine until someone pointed out that in German "mist" means manure.

Similarly, a Prime Computer engineer relates the tale of the renaming of their technical publications due to an unfortunate set of letters for the French market. Documents from Prime are denoted with a specific alphanumeric identifier in addition to a title, the identifiers indicating what type of release the document is associated with. For example, "IDR5595" might refer to "Initial Document Release," or "FDR48" would indicate "Final Document Release." Everything was fine until a Major Release Document was sent to France, much to the amusement of the locals; MRD was pronounced as merde, which translates to "shit."

Indeed, when Toyota Motor Company released their popular MR2 sports car in France, they encountered the same obscenity; MR2 was pronounced as "el merdeux," which loosely translates to the phrase "hey little shit man," a famous joke in France for years!

A member of the Multics group at Honeywell relates the story of how they were completing an on-line conferencing system called "continuum," with an abbreviated name of "con." Bull of France, however, a firm that often marketed Honeywell products overseas, sent an urgent plea back to the development group when they heard about the product; "con" in France refers, rather crudely, to a particular portion of the female anatomy. The program was therefore renamed "forum."

This type of mistake can occur with products imported into English speaking countries from foreign corporations too. In particular,

Olivetti of Italy introduced a product in the 1970s by the awkward name of "Square Holes in Tape." The acronym didn't work too well in English and the product promptly was given a different name in the English speaking market.

Canadians often encounter bizarre product names, since their products are required to be labelled in both English and French. In particular, people report boxes of cookies whereupon the English phrase "without preservatives" has been translated into the French "sans préservatives," which means "without condoms".

Speaking of prophylactics, in England a well known brand is called Durex. Australians, however, are used to Durex referring to cellophane—or Scotch—tape, so one can imagine the look of consternation when an Australian visiting England innocently walked into a chemist (drug store) and asked if they had any Durex with Father Christmas pictures on it, for a package he was wrapping to send home to Australia.

In the U.S., "BS" often is used as shorthand for "bullshit." In Australia, however, bulls (and steer) aren't as commonly a part of the cultural mythos as in the U.S., so instead they refer to rats (in particular, it is reputed to refer to kangaroo rats which are extremely common there) with the acronym "RS." Companies unaware of that are surprised when products are met with amusement by the local community. An early example of this was the Hewlett-Packard calculator line, where a key labelled "R/S" was a source of some chuckling in Australia (R/S is the "run/stop" key). More recently, IBM has been quickly renaming their RISCstation/6000 computers, since the original name of "RS/6000" was not too popular.

In Taiwan, a popular toothpaste used to be called "Darkie," a name that is clearly quite inappropriate for English speaking markets. Recently, they renamed the product to "Darlie," though the corporate logo remains a grinning black minstrel.

•   •   •

In the United States, perfumes typically keep their exotic, French names, but that can sometimes backfire. Yves St. Laurent found that out when they introduced a fragrance into the market called "Opium." It was believed to be in poor taste to name the fragrance after an illegal, and dangerous drug. The original French slogan for the product only exacerbated the situation: "Pour celles qui s'adonnet à Yves St. Laurent" or "For those who are addicted to Yves St. Laurent." When introduced into the Asian market further difficulties were encountered, as the Chinese viewed the use of the word "opium" as a racial slur.

• • •

A more general case of being unaware of foreign cultural traditions often also leads to amusing and bizarre situations. Gerber found this out in the African market rather the hard way; in many parts of Africa, because there are so many languages spoken, the custom is to illustrate the contents of a product on the label, ensuring customers are aware of what they're purchasing. Not knowing that, Gerber was quite surprised when their line of baby food products did so poorly; yet one can only imagine the horror an African must have experienced seeing a small glass jar with the picture of a baby on the label.

Japan has always been a fertile marketplace for U.S. entrepreneurs, often without sufficient research into the cultural differences there. In the early 1980's, for example, a baking firm spent a considerable amount of time inventing and perfecting a cake mix that could be made in the traditional Japanese rice cooker, an extremely common household appliance in Japan. Trials were quite successful, with people praising the company on how tasty and easy to make the cakes were. When introduced, however, no-one would purchase the product. Why? Rice, and the rice cooker, have a special significance in Japanese culture, and the Japanese were aghast at the possibility of sullying their rice cookers with another food, regardless of how tasty.

IVAC Corporation of California produces intravenous infusion pumps—to deliver intravenous drugs to hospital patients—and electronic thermometers. In the mid-1980s, they introduced a product into the market called "neomate," targeted at neonatal intensive care. In Spanish, however "neomate" translates approximately into "fresh kill", so, needless to say, they chose a different name for the Spanish product.

• • •

A particularly well known example of the difficulty in packaging a product for the overseas market was encountered by CocaCola Corporation when they introduced their flagship beverage into the Chinese market. Choosing glyphs in Chinese that sounded similar to the English words Coca Cola, they ended up with a product with the rather peculiar name of "bite the wax tadpole." (Other versions of this indicate that the translation was "beat the dead fish," a phrase sufficiently similar that they could both well be true.)

Their arch rival, Pepsi Corporation, has also proven prone to similar mistakes; the marketing slogan "Come Alive with Pepsi" was first translated into the Chinese phrase "Pepsi brings your dead ancestors back to life," a rather poor approach to selling soda. The same slogan was also translated into an interesting German approximation; "Come out of the grave with Pepsi."

• • •

Sometimes internationalization mistakes are more subtle, violating basic cultural mores and values. Ashton-Tate found this out the hard way when they introduced their FrameWork I and II PC software products into the Scandinavian market; the tutorial that was shipped with the program was humourously entitled "SpyMaster," and included students applying to "Spy School." What had gone over quite well in the U.S. market was flatly rejected by the Swedish, and eventually Ashton-Tate shipped FrameWork into Sweden without any tutorial at all.

Even within a corporation, information can be difficult to prepare for the international market. Nancy Foy, in her book on International Business Machines, relates the tale:

One Asia/Pacific veteran told of a visitor from headquarters who asked "How do you like the training stuff we are sending out from New York these days?"
"Some of it is okay"
"What do you mean 'some'? We are putting a lot of work and money into that stuff. Do not you appreciate it? How about our September selection of aids for the Fall Kickoff Meeting?"
"First of all," responded the weary countryman, "the word in English speaking countries out here would be 'autumn', not 'fall'. And below the equator, it is coming up to spring, not autumn. Finally, the word 'kickoff' relates to a uniquely American sport."

• • •

When Lotus first translated their best selling 1-2-3 spreadsheet package for the Japanese market, they found that they had to remove all beeps from the program; audio feedback upon making a mistake was viewed with a great deal of hostility by the Japanese who didn't want to broadcast to the entire office when they had made a mistake. The same translation yielded another cultural error; Lotus 1-2-3

Japan not only allowed users to add the common imperial date (or Emperor's Reign), but they also allowed users to change the name of the Emperor too. The Japanese were appalled, because the existence of this feature signified that one was planning for the Emperors' death, a concept fraught with cultural taboos.

Cultural differences can occur at any point in international product marketing, as two tales from Ferranti International Controls illustrate. In the first, the U.S. company was trying to sell automation systems to the Soviets and found difficulties with the translator. In particular, an engineer describing the remote telemetry equipment and the accompanying "infant mortality" caused the translator to look quite somberly at the engineer and ask "what do dead babies have to do with computer systems?" to the great amusement of the U.S. nationals present. To simplify, the engineer rephrased it as "setting a flag in the operating system on power failure", which gained a puzzled question from one of the Russians present; "Flag?"

More recently, Ferranti was working with a client in Venezuela on a power control system. The president of Ferranti ended a sentence rather emphatically by noting "And that is all we provide, period." Later, one of the Venezuelan engineers came up to the president and asked discretely whether people from the U.S. often used references to a woman's menstruation when swearing.

The Unix operating system, being primarily developed by researchers at Bell Labs, then significantly enchanced by a variety of U.S. university students, is full of curious cultural anachronisms that are not understood by non-technical U.S. residents, let alone foreign speaking cultures. Unix has countless references to "daemons", "killing processes," "zombie processes," "parent and child processes," and so on. With this nomenclature, it is easy to believe anecdotes such as the one relating that the first translation of "a child process was killed" (which means that a process spawned by the current process was terminated) into Japanese resulted in the more horrifying error "we just murdered your first-born child."

•   •   •

Cultural differences encompass more than just language translation and iconographic variation. A number of anecdotes refer to cultures that read from right to left, as opposed to the Western left to right ordering. In particular, billboards and advertisements that attempt to demonstrate the value of a particular product can backfire quite dramatically.

Consider a billboard that had three pictures:

a dirty shirt
the dirty shirt being dipped into a tub of laundry soap
a clean shirt

The consequences of reading that in the opposite order to what the advertiser anticipated are clearly disastrous for the product in question. A similar billboard was used for a headache remedy in the Middle East, with the illustrations being a sad man with a headache, a man taking a pill, and a smiling man without a headache. Again, not too successful.

Interestingly, another aspect of billboard advertisements in the Middle East is that they often demonstrate that the company is not familiar with the local environmental conditions more than anything else; because of the extreme heat, many billboards deteriorate to a point where the advertisement is unreadable within two or three weeks, especially during the hotter summer months.

•   •   •

A significant difference between cultures is the role that women have in cultural and social activities. Indeed, the differences can sometimes become dramatic and unacceptable for the local market. In particular, the Canadian state of Quebec created an advertising review board to ensure that women were appropriately portrayed. The group has issued a number of "awards" for sexism since its formation. In 1981, for example, Sony and La Place stereo jointly created a television advertisement where a big busted woman, with her nipples clearly showing through her T-shirt, roller skated while listening to her Sony tape deck. The review board found that because there was absolutely no connection between the product and the image being shown, the advertisement was inappropriate and offensive.

Another "award" from the review board was given to the U.S. giant Proctor & Gamble for an advertisement featuring their household cleaning product "Mr. Clean." In the TV advertisement, a young girl is shown cleaning up her brother's mess as he watches, without any attempt to assist. The board noted that it reinforces stereotypes that are unacceptable in Quebec, including that housecleaning is solely womens' work, and that women should serve men.

•   •   •

A U.S. company that hired an Arabic speaking translator to help it prepare a product for the Arab market was surprised to find out— after the fact—that the translator had mis-translated the electronics phrase "dummy load" to the Arabic term for "false pregnancy." In a similar vein, another company hired an exchange student from Indonesia for some translation work. Unfortunately, the student did not understand computer terminology, and in particular did not understand the word "software." The result? The word was translated as "underwear", which no doubt made for amusing reading.

•   •   •

The international market for commodities, goods, and technical products is quite varied, with the different cultures and languages offering not only the opportunity for new sales, but the chance to make some embarassing and awkward gaffes. While there is an amusing side to the tales related in this chapter, the lesson to be learned is that international marketing is much more than the simple translation of a program into another language, or the documentation into a different format.

Properly localized software applications, just like properly localized automobiles, toasters, beverages, and magazines, reflect the values, ethics, morals and language (or languages) of the nation in question. Similarly, properly internationalized applications are those where the development team has a sufficiently broad understanding of their own culture to be able to isolate and remove not only the language, but culturally specific items.

After all, mistakes are amusing, but not when you and your company are at fault.

How to Internationalize

Comprising:

With an understanding of why to internationalize, as well as what to internationalize, the next question is how to accomplish not only the internationalization of software, but the subsequent localization too. In this section we will consider the three primary approaches to internationalization, compile-time, link-time and run-time, as well as introduce and develop the sample C program "salary.c".

Once the different approaches are considered and demonstrated, we will close this section with a brief look at some of the more complex elements of internationalization that were not covered previously due to the added complexity and space requirements they entail, including multi-byte language support (such as Chinese and Arabic), color, graphics, and documentation.

6

Three Approaches to Internationalization

As computers have become a pervasive element of modern culture, no group has become more curious and mysterious than professional programmers, people that have the patience to teach the machine laboriously, in astoundingly fine detail, to perform all the feats that it is capable of accomplishing. In that sense, then, the job of a programmer is similar to that of a teacher, though perhaps with a less unruly audience.

The similarity is that the computer, as has oft been said, is quite stupid by itself, can only do what people tell it to do, and only then when in sufficient detail to avoid confusion and mistakes. Programming is simply the formalized art of teaching at this level of detail.

Further, and not at all surprisingly, as computers have become more and more widespread, the tools available for programming, or teaching, the computer have dramatically improved too. In the first days of programming—the 1950's—programmers were constrained to either flipping switches on a panel or otherwise learning the language of the computer by using machine code or other very low level, purely numerical languages. In that type of environment, a program that would print "hi" on the printer might look similar to:

456F4	05945	FF454	849C4
9567A	000B0	3214C	47098

Clearly that level of detail was exceptionally complex, and quite got in the way of developing even mildly sophisticated software. Further, as computers continued to spread into the commercial, government and educational marketplaces, it became obvious that the reliability and accuracy of the computer programs was more and more important too. After all, if you have a computer running a nuclear reactor, an error of 1% could result in exceptionally bad results (as indeed happened with the Three Mile Island Nuclear Reactor in 1979, when a computer sensor failed to recognize a faulty valve and failed to automatically cool the reactor core when it began to overheat).

The result of much thinking about how to teach computers was the innovation of language translators, or compilers. Initially very simple—assembly language—it still allowed for significant improvements in programming technology:

```
STO      R1,08CFF
STO      R2,"hi"
MV       @(R1),R2
```

In a dizzying succession of developments, computer programming languages, as they became known, quickly evolved to the flexible, easy to read and understand, portable languages used today. The heritage of early computer programming is still present, however, and indeed even today the "source" to a program will go through the transformations shown in Figure 6.1.

Starting out as a human readable "source" code, a compiler translates that into a form not dissimilar to assembly code, though typically without any human readable comments included. The final step is when the object code is combined with pre-programmed "libraries" referenced by the programmer into an executable, again not dissimilar to machine code. The last step is accomplished by a linker, a reasonable name for a program that links object files together.

If you think about this transformation process for a minute, it will become clear that there are three different places where a program can be modified, corresponding to the transformations discussed above. One could make alterations within the source code, allowing change at compile time, by linking different libraries during link

Figure 6.1. Code transformations.

time, or by actually accessing different computer instructions during execution of the final program.

These, then, are the three possible types of internationalization that can be utilized: Compile-time internationalization; Link-time internationalization; and Run-time internationalization. Like any technology, each of these approaches has significant advantages and disadvantages.

One of the key ideas with internationalization is that most software has a core of algorithms, or instructions, that are the real heart of the program. Look and feel is important, and well designed programs that work in the appropriate language and cultural setting are a clear win, but fundamentally most successful software is worthwhile to the user because of what it does, not how it looks.

With that in mind, all approaches to internationalization absolutely must allow software developers to isolate and protect the central algorithms from the interface alterations. The reason should be straightforward; protection of the investment in program development. Needing to continually poke about inside the central portions of the program is expensive and disruptive at best, and can introduce not only unnecessary delays in shipping the product, but also spurious flaws or "bugs" in the program that can be quite damaging and costly to track down and remedy.

6.1 Compile-Time Internationalization

Of the three approaches, this is probably the most obvious and easy to understand for programmers. Basically, it takes the approach of "if you want it in French, then write it that way!"—a reasonable approach to the situation. Consider a sample printing program; this version could be used in English or Spanish:

```
void print_hi(void)
{
   /** say "hi" on the printer, in the appropriate language **/
   FILE *printer;          /* need a file descriptor for the printer */
   /** open printer for writing, if we can **/
   if ((printer = fopen(PRINT_DEVICE, "w")) == NULL) {
      fprintf(stderr, "Couldn't open printer for printout.\n");
      exit(1);
   }
#if LANGUAGE=SPANISH
   fprintf(printer, "hola");
#else
```

```
    fprintf(printer, "hi");
#endif
    fclose(printer);        /** close printer when done **/
}
```

Notice how the program contains a series of statements preceded by "#" characters, as if-else-endif commands. Recognized by a program called the preprocessor, these statements instruct the computer on which actual instructions to consider or ignore. For example, if you had a statement of the form:

```
#if condition
    action1
#else
    action2
#endif
```

then action1 would take place (or at least be recognized by the compiler in this case) if, and only if, the specified condition was true. In exactly the same way, the sample program demonstrates how a variable called "LANGUAGE" can be checked, and if it is set to a specific value, can cause different instructions to be compiled.

Notice also that we have made a mistake in this program too; if everything occurs without incident, the word in the appropriate language will be printed out. If there is an error encountered (perhaps the printer was offline and could not be used), the error message will be in English, not the language of choice. While quite obvious in this example, this problem will come back when you consider larger programs.

A glimmer of one of the most significant problems with compile-time internationalization should start to shine about now, too. To see it more clearly, let us expand the example to support a few more languages:

```
void print_hi(void)
{
/** say "hi" on the printer, in the appropriate language **/
FILE *printer; /* need a file descriptor for the printer */
/** open the printer for writing, if we can **/
    if ((printer = fopen(PRINT_DEVICE, "w")) == NULL) {
        fprintf(stderr, "Couldn't open printer for printout.\n");
        exit(1);
    }
#if LANGUAGE=SPANISH
    fprintf(printer, "hola");
```

```
#elif LANGUAGE=FRENCH
    fprintf(printer, "bonjour");
#elif LANGUAGE=GERMAN
    fprintf(printer, "wie gehts");
#elif LANGUAGE=ITALIAN
    fprintf(printer, "bonjourno");
#else
    fprintf(printer, "hi");
#endif
    fclose(printer);        /* close printer when done */
    exit(0);
}
```

Clearly the complexity of the program is expanding by leaps and bounds here. The problem is that the last thing you want to do by internationalizing a program is to dramatically increase the complexity. Why? Because more complex programs take longer to design, and the final software is more prone to errors.

A more subtle problem is at work here too; the programmer must either be working on the internationalization personally, or working in close conjunction with the people localizing the software. In fact, a little reflection will show that this approach really bypasses the whole two-stage process of extracting the cultural context (internationalization) and then adding cultural contexts for specific geographic markets (localization).

Approaching this problem slightly differently, the programmer could at least isolate all the language and culturally sensitive elements into different portions of code, improving modularity:

```
void print_hi(void)
{
    /** say "hi" on the printer, in the appropriate language **/
    FILE *printer;              /* file descriptor for printer */
    printer = open_printer();   /* open the printer */
    say_hi(printer);            /* actually say "hi" */
    close_printer(printer);     /* and close it too */
    exit(0);
}

FILE *
open_printer(void)
{
    /** opens the printer, exiting program if failure **/
    static FILE *printer;
```

```
    if ((printer = fopen(PRINT_DEVICE, "w")) == NULL) {
        fprintf(stderr, "Couldn't open printer for printout.\n");
        exit(1);
    }
    return( (FILE *) printer);
}


void close_printer(FILE *printer)
{
    /** close the printer, flushing print queue **/
    (void) fclose(printer);
}


void say_hi(FILE *fd)
{
    /** output "hi" to specified device, in the right language **/
#if LANGUAGE=SPANISH
    fprintf(fd, "hola");
#elif LANGUAGE=FRENCH
    fprintf(fd, "bonjour");
#elif LANGUAGE=GERMAN
    fprintf(fd, "wie gehts");
#elif LANGUAGE=ITALIAN
    fprintf(fd, "bonjourno");
#else
    fprintf(fd, "hi");
#endif
}
```

This has the advantage that you can now easily isolate the language-dependent portion of the code into a separate file, for example, allowing the programmers to work on the main algorithms—the heart of the software, as we have already discussed—without worrying about the complexity of the program being internationalized.

Nonetheless, the problem with having to go into source code to localize the program cannot be overemphasized; if some time after the fact your company chooses to sell the program into a foreign market that you have no experience with, the most likely route is to find an individual or organization in that marketplace that can assist with the localization process. Yet, if they are good at that, are they going to be good enough to work with your code, without damaging it, altering command flow, and generally mucking it all up?

A more subtle problem is that since software is legally recognized as worthy of copyright and patent, the source code therefore becomes quite proprietary and confidential information. Indeed, few people have ever seen the actual IBM-written basic input/output system (BIOS) software source, the cornerstone of the entire multi-billion dollar personal computer marketplace. To offer localized versions of the program, then, you really do not want to have to send source code, of any nature, to a foreign localization expert and distributor. It is just too chancy, especially when many countries refuse to recognize international patents and copyrights, and instead freely distribute licensed and non-copyable software throughout their organizations.

Further, there is the question of whether the programmer should be spending time developing internationally structured software, rather than the more fundamental algorithms anyway. Also, as more and more of the burden of internationalization is placed on the programmer, more and more of this task also ends up being reinvented time and again, a significant waste of time for any individual or organization. In fact, link-time internationalization offers more productive utilization of prior programmer effort, and run-time internationalization offers the best opportunity to actually let programmers focus on the software, not the methodologies.

Another down side to compile-time internationalization can be best illustrated by stepping back a bit from the printout example and imagining the sequence of commands required to compile the program and create an actual executable:

```
$ tcc -DLANGUAGE=SPANISH print.c
```

The end result of this command, which will include a separate stage to link all the appropriate libraries with the program, will be to create a program called "print" which will actually work in Spanish, rather than English.

What if you now want one that knows English? And another for French, perhaps? There's only one solution; you end up with three different executable programs—print.english print.french and print.spanish. The user is then required to remember which suffix is appropriate and instead of just remembering "print" as the command, must deal with a considerably more complex command mnemonic.

There are some interesting schemes that could be used in this situation to alleviate some of the complexity, including a command interpreter (or "shell", in Unix parlance) which automatically looked for any command with a ".language" suffix first, but they do not change the fundamental problems of this approach to internationalization.

This also points to another problem, one which will be familiar to anyone with too many files and too little disk space; if you want to have both French and Spanish versions of the program available, you will end up taking twice as much disk space.

Worse, while in the United States a single language and cultural context is sufficient, in Europe, Asia, and elsewhere it is quite common to find an organization with different people more comfortable in differing languages, so even a simple 700K executable for, say, a spreadsheet, might rapidly expand to requiring multiple megabytes of storage to meet user requirements. A cost that must be paid again and again; even backing up the file system would be more expensive, slower, and require more resources.

So what are the advantages of this approach, then? From a programmer point of view, it offers the ability to be in complete control of all aspects of the software; no mysterious invocations of routines that might or might not work correctly (engineers' zealousness to use only their own tools is known in the business as the "not-invented-here" syndrome,* and we will encounter it again when we consider different standard-based solutions).

Additionally, this approach requires no assistance from the vendor or manufacturer of the computer itself; again, it is a completely self-contained approach to internationalization that can just as easily work on a small DOS laptop as a large Unix minicomputer, or even a massive proprietary-OS supercomputer.

Yet fundamentally, it should be clear that mucking about with the source code as a way of internationalizing, then later localizing, a program is a poor solution to the problem. And you have not even begun to consider the logistical problems of distribution, packaging, and support, which we will look at in much greater detail later, in the final chapter of this section.

6.2 Link-Time Internationalization

If you take the ideas presented in the last example program shown in the previous section and generalize them just a bit, we will move into the territory known as link-time internationalization. The key

---

*Not-Invented-Here (or NIH for short) is a surprisingly common phenomenon at software companies, wherein they create all their own software development and production tools rather than use applications from third parties, "invented elsewhere".

to getting there is to move all the language and culturally dependent features into their own separate files, which then compile into their own object files.

Linking, as we have already discussed, is the process of putting all the appropriate object files together into a single executable image, or sequence of instructions. To understand how this moves us into a different type of internationalization, let us take a closer look at just what the linker program really does.

Imagine that you are reading this book with a poor understanding of English, and absolutely no knowledge of computers, or anything even vaguely computer-related. Not surprisingly, each time you see a word such as "executable" you become quite confused. Further, imagine that you have a dictionary by your side, and as you find words you cannot fathom, you quickly swap books and look the heinous phrase up to ascertain its meaning. Stretching the analogy just a bit, imagine that you are actually writing a new version of this book without any of these pesky "look up" words. It will be longer, of course, because instead of saying "megabyte of RAM" you would have to actually explain the concept in non-technical terms, but that is an acceptable price for the improved clarity.

That process is exactly what the linker does. If you spin the words around a bit and restate the onerous book rewriting task as one of "resolving the external word references", then we have arrived at the actual definition of what a linker does; it resolves external references so that all needed instructions are contained within the space of the single executable file. Just as the book without technical jargon would be considerably longer, so are executable files dramatically larger than the object files that the programmer contributes to the link process.

To accomplish this recasting of the program to a completely re-solved set of references and a single executable, the linker refers to a number of different "libraries" of subroutines. For example, in the "print_hi" routine shown in this chapter, the following instructions are actually external references that would need to be resolved by the linker before an executable could be created: *fopen(), fprintf(), fclose()* and *exit()*. Not included, because it is built in to the C programming language itself: *return()*. Without the linker referencing other libraries to resolve these procedures, as they are known, the end user would find the executable would stop in the middle of being run, unable to ascertain what *fopen()* meant, for example, and how to proceed.

Software development environments typically include hundreds, if not thousands of pre-defined and pre-programmed utility procedures, ranging from the simple to the exceptionally complex. Indeed, the simple call to *fopen()*—to open a specified file for future actions indicated—actually invokes a library that involves hundreds upon hundreds of lines of previous designed, written, and tested source.

If you can have libraries offering useful procedures, then you can also borrow that idea for your own programming, and write your own libraries of useful internationalized procedures.

To understand how that could work, let us delve back into the printing example and look at another way of structuring the program. With this version, you will explicitly separate the main program from the culturally dependent procedures, in different files. The main program would then be:

```
void print_hi(void)
{
    /** say "hi" on the printer, in the appropriate language **/
    FILE *printer;          /* need a file descriptor for the printer */
    printer = open_printer();    /* open the printer */
    say_hi(printer);             /* actually say "hi" */
    close_printer(printer);      /* and close it too */
}
```

which could then be compiled into an object (or intermediate) file. Meanwhile, we will add two new libraries; a printer-interface library and a say-something library. The printer interface library might look similar to:

```
/** printer interface library **/

FILE *
open_printer(void)
{
    /** opens the printer, exiting program if failure **/
    static FILE *printer;
    if ((printer = fopen(PRINT_DEVICE, "w")) == NULL) {
      fprintf(stderr, "Couldn't open printer for printout.\n");
      exit(1);
    }
    return( (FILE *) printer);
}

void close_printer(FILE *printer)
{
```

```
/** close the printer, flushing print queue **/
(void) fclose(printer);
}
```

and the say-something library is where you will finally see the difference between the different internationalization approaches:

```
void say_hi(FILE *fd)
{
    /** output "hi" to specified device **/
    fprintf(fd, "hi");
}
```

What has happened here is that you have completely removed any sense of different language from the source. Seems a step backwards, but what you have gained is the ability to partition the program into more reasonable files. Remember the anxiety about shipping proprietary code? Well, now you can keep the source code to the main program secret—shipping the object code instead—and include source to the various libraries for localization.

Indeed, at this point you should be able to start seeing how the differentiation between internationalization and localization will prove to be a powerful concept.

From this point in the sample program, to create an English version of the program you could type:

```
$ tcc main.c printer-lib.obj say-some.obj
```

which would compile the source code and link it with the previously compiled object file libraries.

To create a Spanish version, you would simply rewrite the say-something library to have "hola" instead of "hi," then rebuild the library itself with a similar compiler instruction:*

```
$ tcc -c say-some.c
```

Some of the disadvantages of source-level internationalization have been eliminated by this change in strategy, but there are still quite a few obstacles with this methodology, including source-level localization (and the subsequent errors and complexity introduced) and the continued requirement for unique executable files for each language supported (the ".spanish", ".french" suffixes).

---

*The "-c" option to the compiler informs it not to try to create an actual executable, but to stop when an intermediate, object file has been created.

6.3 Run-Time Internationalization

Now that we have a reasonable idea of what is actually involved with internationalization of the sample program, the question is rapidly becoming "What's the best way, then?" The answer, not too surprisingly, is run-time internationalization. Allowing for a single executable to work with an arbitrary number of different languages, run-time internationalization offers freedom from almost all the shortcomings of the prior methodologies.

To understand how this approach differs, let us again step backwards from the specifics for a minute and think about what the ideal solution to the problem of just how localized software might appear. In Douglas Adams' *Hitchhikers Guide to the Galaxy*, there are "Babel fish" that magically translate all spoken words into a language understood by the listener. A perfect computing universe would be like having the fish living in your computer, so all software would just magically 'know' what language and cultural context you required, and would work in that context. Without fuss, without bother, and without having dozens of different versions of the program on the computer.

Surprisingly, that's almost exactly how end users perceive the result of run-time internationalization; they tell the computer what language they prefer and all the commands suddenly work in that language rather than English.

At some point in the process from what the programmer types to what the user sees, with any form of internationalized software, a decision must be made—programmatically—about which language to use. With compile-time it is the programmer who makes the decision when the initial compilation is completed. Link time pushes that decision off to the link stage. Run-time internationalization pushes the decision as far as it can go; to the actual invocation and execution of the program by the end user.

The chair you are sitting in is part of a larger environment, including staples like air, a livable temperature, gravity, and more optional elements, like the art on the wall (or not), the clothes you are wearing, and even the color and style of the chair itself. Most computer operating systems have an analogous concept of user-based environment. Within DOS, for example, my environment includes:

```
ROOTDIR=C:
EDITOR=
COMSPEC=c:/command.com
PWD=C:/home/writing/book
```

```
BUFFERS=20
PATH=C:;C:\BIN;C:\DOS;C:\BIN\TC;.
TZ=PST8PDT
FILES=25
```

Without getting lost in the complexities of the DOS world, it suffices to note that while some of these values are set by the operating system itself (such as ROOTDIR and PWD (present working directory)), others can be modified by the user at run-time (such as TZ (time zone) and PATH).

Run-time internationalization exploits the user-defined environment on a computer operating system and actually chooses which language to use at run-time by examining a particular environment variable. Commonly, this variable will be "LANG", so to work in Italian, you could then simply type "LANG=italian" at the command line and then, voila! Next time you invoke a particular program, it'll be in that language rather than English.

The actual run-time libraries might well look similar to the following:

```
void say_hi(FILE *fd)
{
    /** output "hi" to specified device **/
    if (getenv("LANG") == "spanish")
      fprintf(fd, "hola");
    else
      fprintf(fd, "hi");
}
```

What has just been presented, though, is clearly not too useful an approach, because while it offers run-time choice of language, it has all the problems of both source-level internationalization (since the programmer still must know all the languages) and link-time internationalization as well (since the foreign language and culture knowledgeable libraries would still need to be explicitly linked in with existing source files).

A few moments thought might well suggest the step in methodology needed. Before explaining further, imagine if you could use a function that performed word to word mapping and translation. If it were called, say, "translate", then you could rewrite the previous example as:

```
void say_hi(FILE *fd)
{
    /** output "hi" to specified device **/
```

```
    fprintf(fd, translate("hi", getenv("LANG")));
}
```

The code is certainly getting a lot closer to what you want; the translate program could be run in parallel to the actual application, and could then free the programmer from ever worrying about what "hi" is in Greek, Swahili, or any other language ever again.

What is being presented here, really, is an external database of words, phrases, and cultural context information for the target languages and cultures, accessible at run-time by the program. And that, finally, is *exactly* what run-time internationalization really is.

Having the database external means that foreign distributors who are busily localizing the package can focus on external language and culturally dependent data, completely (and probably blissfully) ignorant of the basic software itself. It also allows languages to be added independent of the original software developers.

Using numeric indices into the external program database, the final "say hi" program might be:

```
void print_hi(void)
{
    /** say "hi" on the printer, in the appropriate language **/
    FILE *printer;          /* need a file descriptor for the printer */
    choose_language();          /* get LANG variable */
    printer = open_printer();   /* open the printer */
    say_hi(printer);            /* actually say "hi" */
    close_printer(printer);     /* and close it too */
}


void say_hi(FILE *fd)
{
    /** output "hi" to specified device **/
    fprintf(fd, get_message_from_db(1));
}
```

The database might look as simple as:

```
## language = English
1     Hi
```

or

```
## language = Spanish
1     Hola
```

and the internationalization support code would be written:

```
void choose_language(void)
{
    language = getenv("LANG");        /* save user lang */
    open_language_db(language);       /* open right db file */
}

void get_message_from_db(int index)
{
    rewind(db);
    while (read_line(buffer, db) != EOF)
    if (indexof(buffer) == index)
     return( (char *) valueof(buffer));
    return( (char *) NULL);       /* specified index not found! */
}
```

This example is a bit simpler than would actually work as production code, but it does not really matter, in some sense, because all the internationalization support code would be supplied to the software project by a third party, probably based on the pioneering work done by the X/Open consortium* or a specific vendor.

What is best about this solution is that not only can new languages be added without modification to the source code, and not only does the amount of disk space required equal the space for a single executable plus the database files (which are typically quite small) but programmers are now almost completely freed from the complexities of having to internationalize their code, per se. Instead they call international-knowledgeable routines—*int_strcmp( )* rather than *strcmp()* to compare two strings—and can focus on the development of the key algorithms for the product.

In actuality, the database of international support becomes split into two pieces; the "static cultural data," notational conventions, collation data, transliteration data, and so on, and the "active program-specific data," which the programmer is responsible for creating and utilizing. This split allows vendors to include not only internationalization libraries, but the static cultural database to sort, output date and time, and accomplish similar tasks.

Finally, we have reached a point where support for the error message can be added with almost no work:

```
FILE *
open_printer(void)
```

---

*Composed of most of the largest international computer vendors, X/Open is discussed in considerably more detail later in the book, in Chapter 14.

```
{
/** opens the printer, exiting program if failure **/
static FILE *printer;
if ((printer = fopen(PRINT_DEVICE, "w")) == NULL) {
 fprintf(stderr, get_message_from_db(2));
 exit(1);
}
 return( (FILE *) printer);
}
```

The appropriate language data files (or message catalogs, in the parlance of the internationalization community) would then read:

```
# language = English
1    Hi
2    Couldn't open printer for printout.\n
# language = Spanish
1    Hola
2    No se podría abrir el impresor para impresión
```

7
Elements of Internationalization

Theory and discussion are all very well, but if you are a typical engineer, you are itching to actually get your hands on some real source, and see how things really work. That is what we will be doing in the next few chapters; this chapter will introduce the "salary" program, a simple employee database, which we will then internationalize (and localize) in subsequent chapters.

The salary program works with a disk-based data file containing, for each employee, their full name, date of hire, current salary, and the date of their last raise, if any. That file will remain identical across the different versions of the program. Since you are interested in being able to manipulate the data, the format chosen for the data file is quite simple; each field is separated by a single space, and lines prefixed with "#" are considered comments and are ignored by the actual program.

New employees can be added to the database from within the salary program, but, being eternally optimistic, the program will not allow employees to be deleted from the database; another reason to leave the file in "flat ASCII" format (e.g., allowing direct manipulation via traditional editors such as "vi" on Unix, or "Word" on DOS).

Initially, the data file, "salary.dat", is written:

```
# Employee name/earnings database
#
# format : name hire-date salary last-raise-date
#
```

Richards,Mary 10/5/88 4500 12/1/90
Davidson,James 4/8/89 5600 12/1/90
Bishop,Patrick 2/24/90 1200
Holland,Xaviera 7/7/89 2200 1/15/90

Note that the dates are currently in U.S. "slash format", a month/day/year ordering. As you change this for different regions, you will find that the order of these fields might change too, but for now it is just a simple program and you can ignore that issue.

Notice also that the last-raise date is an optional field and that employee Bishop has never received a raise. The program will be required to work correctly when that field is missing, but the other three fields (name, starting date, and salary) will be required.

Before looking at the source to the program, let us look at how the program works, with user input in bold face:

Salary database program: read in 4 entries
Please select: Add, Find, List, Print, Stats, Quit: **list**
Current Employees as of 22 Dec, 1990 at 17:50
Bishop,Patrick:
        salary $1200, hired 24 Feb, 1990, (no raise recorded)
Davidson,James:
        salary $5600, hired 8 Apr, 1989, last raise 1 Dec, 1990
Holland,Xaviera:
        salary $2200, hired 7 Jul, 1989, last raise 15 Jan, 1990
Richards,Mary:
        salary $4500, hired 5 Oct, 1988, last raise 1 Dec, 1990
Please select: Add, Find, List, Print, Stats, Quit: **add**
Adding an employee. Name: **Anders,Becky**
Salary: **$950**
Start date MM/DD/YY: **1/8/91**
Date of last raise (ENTER=none):
Please select: Add, Find, List, Print, Stats, Quit: **list**
Current Employees as of 22 Dec, 1990 at 17:53
Anders,Becky
        salary $950, hired 8 Jan, 1991 (no raise recorded)
Bishop,Patrick:
        salary $1200, hired 24 Feb, 1990 (no raise recorded)
Davidson,James:
        salary $5600, hired 8 Apr, 1989, last raise 1 Dec, 1990
Holland,Xaviera:
        salary $2200, hired 7 Jul, 1989, last raise 15 Jan, 1990
Richards,Mary:
        salary $4500, hired 5 Oct, 1988, last raise 1 Dec, 1990

Please select: Add, Find, List, Print, Stats, Quit: **stats**
There are 5 employees in the database.
 Davidson,James is paid the most ($5600)
 Anders,Becky is paid the least ($950)
 and the average salary is $2890
Please select: Add, Find, List, Print, Stats, Quit: **find**
Find what employee? **anders**
Name: Anders,Becky
Starting Date: 8 Jan, 1991
Salary: $950
(no raise dates recorded)
Please select: Add, Find, List, Print, Stats, Quit: **quit**

Seems a pretty straightforward program, doesn't it? Now let us go back and analyze the interaction and algorithms to see just how much ethnocentricism is actually embodied in the program.

Before you even get to the program though, consider the data in the datafile:

Holland,Xaviera 7/7/89 2200 1/15/90

We are assuming a name ordering, a certain number of names (since we are separating fields with a single space, what if a Maria Juanita Lopez was entered? The format would presumably be last name, first name then middle name, or "Lopez, Maria Juanita." But with the data format as we have specified, "Juanita" would be read as the starting date, the actual starting date would be read as the salary, and so on, messing things up completely). Further, the date format, as we have already mentioned, is clearly cultural context dependent; if we are not familiar with reading it as month/day/year, then while the first entry neatly works out, the second refers to the 15th month of the year? Most confusing.

One nice feature is that we have avoided specifying currency notation in the datafile, so that is okay. Or is it? Since we are working with single-precision integer values (which, of course, you do not know yet unless you have read forward and glanced through the program listing), the maximum value is 32767. More than that and you bump into integer overflow situations and end up with unknown results. Since we are specifying a monthly salary it is not likely anyone in the company is going to be earning more than $30,000/month. But if we are talking about a company in New Delhi that pays employees in rupee, or an Argentinean company that pays in austral, then the numbers will be woefully inadequate; 30000 austral/month is a very low salary—about $6/month!

Suffice to say, while it may have seemed initially a reasonable format for the datafile layout, the field separator is inadequate, the date formats are probably going to be trouble, and we will need to remember that numeric values can be quite considerably larger than they are in the U.S., by factors of thousands or more. (The U.S. dollar to Argentine austral, as of January 1991, is about 5500 austral to $1.00, by the way, representing one of the most dramatic differences in international currency.)

The program interaction itself also exhibits a great deal of ethnocentricity. Consider the main selection menu:

Please select: Add, Find, List, Print, Stats, Quit:

While it is obvious that we would need to change the language of the prompt, what might not be so obvious until the actual source code is examined is that each command has a unique first letter, and that in fact the program only looks at the first letter typed in by the user. That is, "a", "add" and "aardvark" will all suffice as a way of requesting the addition of a new employee. In computer circles, this type of input processing is known as "minimum distinguishable abbreviation" and is more common than you might think. The problem, then, is that if you change language, what happens if two commands end up with the same first letter? Then not only will the prompt itself have to change, but the actual algorithm used in the program will require modification too.

When listing the current database, the first line of the output is of the form:

Current Employees as of 22 Dec, 1990 at 17:50

This is where the culturally dependent date format shows up; you can read this and understand that "Dec" is an abbreviation (even though there is no period) for "December." Further, 17:50, though not otherwise qualified, is understood as the time, by a 24 hour clock. This implies that the ':' is known, and that skipping the seconds is acceptable and understood too.

Each line of the listing is of the form:

Richards,Mary:
    salary $4500, hired 5 Oct, 1988, last raise 1 Dec, 1990

Again you can see the culturally dependent date format, and can see that the monetary notation is also culturally dependent. Not just the '$' currency symbol, note, but also the convention of having a large number without any separator (e.g., not "$1,200") and without any fractional value indicated either (e.g., "$1200.00").

7.1 The "Salary" Program

As with any piece of software, the "salary" program requires some fundamental building block programs. In this case, however, the development environment contains a number of sophisticated libraries, so you find that every routine in the final program contains cultural context sensitive information. Let us look at these, one by one.

7.1.1 THE_DATE—Date and Time as Printable String

The first function that the program requires—*the_date*—gets the time and date from the system and formats them presentably. The library calls required are *time()* and *localtime()*, the first returning the current time, and the second breaking that numeric value into its component parts: month, day, week, year, hour, minute, and so on.

```
char *
the_date(void)
{
    /** return current date and time as a printable string **/
    struct tm *timeptr;
    long     thetime;
    static char buffer[SLEN];

    time(&thetime);
    timeptr = localtime(&thetime);
    sprintf(buffer, "%d %s, 19%02d at %d:%02d\n",
        timeptr->tm_mday,
        monthname[timeptr->tm_mon],
        timeptr->tm_year, timeptr->tm_hour,
        timeptr->tm_min);
    return( (char *) buffer);
}
```

When this routine is internationalized later, the only significant modification will be to the *sprintf()* statement. Unfortunately, though, we will see that simply changing the format string will not suffice, since the data given to the statement is still in the presentation format: day-of-month, month, year, hour and minute.

7.1.2 SHOW_DATE—MM/DD/YY to DD Month, YY

The second date-related subroutine—*show_date*—accepts the date format used in the actual database file (Month/Day/Year) and returns it in the more readable Day Monthname, Year format.

```
char *
show_date(char *date)
{
    /** given MM/DD/YY date, return it as; DD Mon, 19YY **/
    int     mon, day, year;
    static char buffer[SLEN];

    sscanf(date, "%d/%d/%d", &mon, &day, &year);
    sprintf(buffer, "%d %s, 19%d", day, monthname[mon-1], year);
    return( (char *) buffer);
}
```

This time almost the entire subroutine will be replaced when the program is internationalized; not only does the output format possibly change, but the actual format of information stored in the datafile—and therefore given to this routine—is based on the ordering popular in the United States as well.

7.1.3 LOWERCASE—String Into All Lower Case

One of the simplest routines in the program is the *lowercase()* routine, which simply rewrites the given string to be in all lower case characters.

```
lowercase(char *string)
{
    /** translate string, en situ, to all lowercase letters **/
    do {
    if (isupper(*string)) *string = tolower(*string);
    } while (*string++);
}
```

At this point, however, you should be thinking to yourself "Aha! This isn't going to be easy at all!"—and you are right. As the program is internationalized and then localized for different countries, the question of transliteration of characters will prove to be a rather thorny issue. Not only are there languages that do not have the concept of upper and lower case, but there are also languages where case is transliterated based on not only the character, but the diacritical associated with the character.

Actually, the way this particular subroutine is designed, the issue of transliteration is shunted off to the definition of the routines *is-upper()* and *tolower()*, both of which are traditionally defined in the included system file "ctypes.h", shipped with most C compilers. Unfortunately, as you move into other languages you will not be able to use these built-in subroutines, but it is interesting to see how they are actually defined:

```
#define islower(c)   ((c) >= 'a' && (c) <= 'z')
#define isupper(c)   ((c) >= 'A' && (c) <= 'Z')
#define toupper(c)   ((c) + 'A' - 'a')
#define tolower(c)   ((c) + 'a' - 'A')
```

This is a straightforward solution, though clearly one that is going to be difficult to translate neatly into other languages.

7.1.4 COMPARE—Compare Two Strings

Similar to the task of translating a word into all upper or lower case letters, the function to compare two words for lexical equality is really a rehash of a built-in function, and in fact calls that function—*strcmp()*—directly.

```
int
compare(char *word1, *word2; int minlen, case_sensitive)
{
    /** Compare the name in both list elements, returning < 0 if
       list element 1 is lexically less than element 2, =0
       if they're the same, and >0 if greater than. Stop
       comparison at "minlen" characters if appropriate, and
       use a case insensitive search if "case_sensitive" is TRUE.
    **/
    char our_word1[SLEN], our_word2[SLEN];

    if (case_sensitive) {
    strcpy(our_word1, word1);
    strcpy(our_word2, word2);
    lowercase(our_word1);
    lowercase(our_word2);
    return( strncmp(our_word1, our_word2, minlen) );
    }
    else
     return(strncmp(word1, word2, minlen));
}
```

The only real work done by this routine is to ensure that it is a case insensitive comparison; both given strings are copied into local temporary buffers and then those are mapped into lower case. This is a bit of a chore, but as neither of the development environments used offered a case-insensitive comparison operation, the programmers are presumably required to do the task themselves. It is okay in this case, however, since this explicit separation will reap great benefits when you get into the more complex aspects of supporting other languages.

7.1.5 SORT—Sort the Employee List

One of the most popular areas of algorithm design is the challenge of sorting data, quickly, and without an excess of external memory. Rather than choose one of the exotic algorithms available, however, we will use a straightforward and easy-to-understand sorting approach called "bubble sort." Simply explained, the program takes each element in the list and "pushes it down" until it is at the appropriate spot in the list. This cycle will continue until the program makes an entire pass through the list without any changes.

```
void sort(void)
{
    int sorted, index, ptr;
    do {
    sorted = TRUE;
    for (index = 0; index < entries; index++) {
     for (ptr = index; ptr < entries; ptr++) {
      if (compare(names[index].name, names[ptr].name,
                      -1, FALSE) > 0) {
       swap(names[ptr], names[index]);
       sorted = FALSE;
      }
     }
    }
    } while (! sorted);
}
```

Notice that the call to *compare()* indicates that the entire string lengths should be considered (the third parameter, "-1"), and that the entries should be compared in a case-insensitive manner (the fourth parameter, "FALSE").

Exploiting the macro preprocessor available in the C programming language, the *swap()* procedure is actually a macro function:

```
#define swap(a,b) { struct namelist tempentry; \
                 tempentry = a;      \
                 a = b;              \
                 b = tempentry;      \
              }
```

The advantage of this approach is that it gives slightly better performance (since each invocation of *swap()* actually is *en situ* expanded as in-line code, rather than the added overhead of yet another subroutine call in the program) and also allows the program to be slightly more succinct.

An important aspect of the *sort()* subroutine, actually, is that because it uses the included compare routine it can be left alone as the program is internationalized and localized. Indeed, the *sort()* routine is internationalized already, and is one of the few routines in the "salary" program that will require no further modification to change languages and cultural contexts.

7.1.6 LOAD-DATABASE—Read in Database

To understand why earlier you used a simple datafile format it is necessary to look at the subroutine that reads in each entry, adding it to the programs internal data structure:

```
int
load_database(void)
{
    FILE *fd;
    char buffer[SLEN];
    int index = 0, i;

    if ((fd = fopen(DATAFILE, "r")) == NULL) {
    fprintf(stderr, "Couldn't open database %s\n", DATAFILE);
    exit(1);
    }

    while (fgets(buffer, SLEN, fd) != NULL) {
    if (buffer[0] == COMMENT) continue; /* skip comments */
    names[index].lrdate[0] = 0; /* optional data field */
    sscanf(buffer, "%s %s %d %s\n", names[index].name,
            names[index].sdate,
            &(names[index].salary), names[index].lrdate);
    index++;
    }
```

```
    entries = index;
    fclose(fd);
}
```

While this may initially seem complex, the two parts of this sub-routine are straightforward. The first step is to attempt opening the datafile (the call to *fopen()*), failing if the file isn't available. The second loop reads each line of the file, skips those that are comments (e.g., that have "#" as their first character, as defined—#define COMMENT '#'—in the header section, presented later in this chapter), then uses the C library function *sscanf()* to break down the line into specific fields for the program.

Without going into incredible detail about how *sscanf()* works, it will suffice to note here that "%s %s %d %s" instructs the program to look for two (space delimited) series of characters, a numeric value, then a final series of characters, loading them into "name", "sdate" (starting date), "salary", and "lrdate" (last raise date) respectively. Typically *sscanf()* does not work gracefully with non-space delimited character sequences (e.g., having spaces be an allowed part of a field, with each field separate by, say, a ":" or other punctuation character), a limitation that will come back and haunt us later when the program is internationalized, forcing an almost complete rewrite of this routine.

7.1.7 ADD-ENTRY—Add New Employee to Database

The other half of interacting with the disk-based database file is the ability to add employees to the database, and that is what *add_entry()* performs.

```
void add_entry(char *name, *start_date; int salary; char *last_raise)
{
    /** append this entry to our database. **/
    FILE *fd;

    if ((fd = fopen(DATAFILE, "a")) == NULL) {
      fprintf(stderr, "Cannot append '%s' to database %s\n",
          name, DATAFILE);
      exit(1);
    }
    fprintf(fd, "%s %s %d %s\n", name, start_date,
          salary, last_raise);
```

```
        fclose(fd);
}
```

Notice especially how the format string for the *fprintf()* call, which actually adds the data to the file, is identical to the format string used for the *sscanf()* call in the subroutine *load_database()*. In this case, however, modifying the format to use ":" as a delimiter would be as simple as changing the *fprintf()* format string to "%s:%s:%d: %s\n". This will also be helpful later when the program will have to accept spaces as a valid part of the database entry.

7.1.8 ADD—Add a New Employee

Since *add_entry()* expects all the information to be in memory before being invoked, there needs to be another routine which actually prompts the user for the name, salary, starting date, and date of last raise (if any) directly. That is where the *add()* subroutine will prove useful:

```
void add(void)
{
        /** add a new employee! **/
        char buffer[SLEN];
        output("\nAdding an employee. Name: ");
        gets(names[entries].name);
        output("Salary: $");
        gets(buffer);
        sscanf(buffer, "%d\n", &(names[entries].salary));
        output("Start date MM/DD/YY: ");
        gets(names[entries].sdate);
        output("Date of last raise (ENTER=none): ");
        gets(names[entries].lrdate);
        printf("\n");
        add_entry(names[entries].name, names[entries].sdate,
                names[entries].salary, names[entries].lrdate);
        entries++;
        sort();
}
```

Since most implementations of C use a line-buffered input and output buffering scheme, characters sent to the screen without an end-of-line aren't displayed until an end-of-line does show up. To circumvent that, C includes a standard subroutine called *fflush()* which forces all pending characters in the specified file to be output, whether with or without an end-of-line. The routine call "output", then, is yet another macro function:

#define output(s)   printf(s); fflush(stdout)

This causes the neat "output("Salary? $");" to be actually rewritten as "printf("Salary? $"); fflush(stdout);" before being compiled.

This routine clearly has a number of aspects that will require modification when it is internationalized, not the least of which are all the actual prompts for information from the user.

7.1.9 LIST—List all Employees to the Specified File

One of the peculiar characteristics of C programming is that input and output are done to files, conceptually identical to other devices, and even to specific, named files on the disk. As a result, input comes from "stdin" (standard-input), output is sent to "stdout" (standard-output: see the *fflush()* statement above), and so on. Some C environments go further, offering a variety of other predefined file descriptors. Turbo C, on DOS, offers one that you will use, in particular—"stdprn" (standard-printer)—when you want to add the ability to actually print out the employee list.*

```
void list(FILE *outfd)
{
    /** list employees in database **/
    int i;
    fprintf(outfd, "\nCurrent Employees as of %s\n", the_date());
    for (i = 0; i < entries; i++) {
    fprintf(outfd, " %s:\n\tsalary $%d, hired %s,",
            names[i].name, names[i].salary,
            show_date(names[i].sdate));
    if (strlen(names[i].lrdate) > 0)
     fprintf(outfd, " last raise %s\n",
                    show_date(names[i].lrdate));
    else
     fprintf(outfd, " (no raise recorded)\n");
    }
    fprintf(outfd, "\n");
}
```

---

*Printing by opening up the printer device driver rather than invoking an external printing program does present some difficulties with portability, but is common nonetheless.

Clearly this contains a number of elements that will require modification when the program is internationalized, including most obviously the textual portions of the strings. Additionally, however, more subtle changes will be required with the currency display format. What if, for example, we are talking about lira, where traditional notation includes a fractional portion? That cannot be displayed using a single "%d" numeric integer format.

Further, when listing the employees, we will need to include the date and time for tracking purposes (which can be done by using the subroutine *show_date()*, already presented).

7.1.10 STATS—Compute and Show Some Statistics

A traditional feature of database packages is the ability to analyze the data for interesting trends and characteristics, and "salary" is no different; the *stats()* routine shows the lowest, highest, and average salary for the employees on record.

```
void stats(void)
{
    /** output some statistics about the current employees **/
    int lowest_id, highest_id, lowest = 32767, highest=0;
    long int sum=0;
    int i;

    for (i=0; i < entries; i++) {
    if (names[i].salary < lowest) {
     lowest = names[i].salary;
     lowest_id = i;
    }
    if (names[i].salary > highest) {
     highest = names[i].salary;
     highest_id = i;
    }
    sum += names[i].salary;
    }
    printf("\nThere are %d employees in the database.\n",
            entries);
    printf(" %s is paid the most ($%d)\n",
            names[highest_id].name, highest);
    printf(" %s is paid the least ($%d)\n",
            names[lowest_id].name, lowest);
```

```
    printf(" and the average salary is $%d\n\n", sum / entries);
}
```

While single precision integers were sufficient in the database to allow monthly salaries to be entered and displayed, notice that once the chance of larger numbers arose with the summation of salaries, you had to go to a long int variable, offering much more than 32767 as the maximum value.

Again, as with the previous routine, this one has a number of features that will require modification for internationalization, including the phrases output to the user, and the currency notation.

7.1.11 FIND—Find a Specific Person in the Database

Having large bodies of data available is only useful if there are methods available for choosing specific items, and with the "salary" program, *find()* offers the ability to type in a person's last name (or portion thereof) and find that entry in the database.

```
void find(void)
{
    /** look for a specific person in the database **/
    char buffer[SLEN];   /* a working character buffer */
    int i;        /* and a int for looping */

    output("\nFind which employee? ");
    gets(buffer);

    for (i=0; i < entries; i++)
    if (compare(names[i].name,buffer,strlen(buffer),TRUE)==0) {
    printf("\nName: %s\nStarting Date: %s\n",
            names[i].name, show_date(names[i].sdate));
    printf("Salary: $%d\n", names[i].salary);
    if (strlen(names[i].lrdate))
     printf("Last Raise Date: %s\n\n",
                    show_date(names[i].lrdate));
    else
     printf("(no raise dates recorded)\n\n");
    return;
    }
    printf("I couldn't find that employee in the database.\n\n");
}
```

By this point you should be able to look through that listing and identify which elements will require modification in the internationalized version.

7.1.12 SALARY—The Main Program

Finally, hooking it all together, the *main()* routine initializes the internal database, then loops waiting for input until the user enters the "quit" command.

```
main(void)
{
    char command[SLEN];   /* space for user command input */
    load_database();      /* initialize ... */
    sort();               /* ... and sort the database */
    printf("Salary database program: read in %d entries\n\n",
        entries);
    do {
    output(
    "Please select: Add, Find, List, Print, Stats, Quit:");
    gets(command);
    switch (tolower(command[0])) {
     case 'a' : add(); break;
     case 'f' : find(); break;
     case 'l' : list(stdout); break;
     case 'p' : list(stdprn); break;
     case 'q' : exit(0); break;
     case 's' : stats(); break;
     default : printf("I do not understand. Try again.\n");
     }
    } while (1); /* loop: must exit by "quit" command */
}
```

Notice this time that, as was noted earlier, the program actually is only choosing actions based on the first letter of user input, rather than checking the entire word. This is not a bad approach, allowing experienced users to type abbreviated commands such as "s" and "f", while users learning the program can use full word commands such as "stats" and "list". However, when you translate the program into different languages, you will no doubt find that this entire switch statement will have to be rewritten to check for specific words rather than the first letter. Not only will this avoid the problems of redundancy, but it will also allow multiple commands to cause the same action (such as "exit" as a synonym for "quit").

The headers for the program define most of the constants and capitalized identifiers used in the program. The first part indicates which system-level include files are needed by the various routines:

```
#include <stdio.h>        /* standard I/O utils library */
#include <ctype.h>        /* character classification lib */
#include <time.h>         /* clock manipulation library */
```

Then a number of constants, including the name of the data file and the maximum number of entries in the database, are defined:

```
#ifndef TRUE
# define TRUE      1         /* not FALSE */
# define FALSE     0         /* not TRUE */
#endif
#define DATAFILE   "salary.dat"
#define LISTSIZE   20        /* max database size */
#define SLEN       80        /* string length     */
#define NLEN       20        /* short string length */
#define COMMENT    '#'       /* comments in data */
```

Finally, the global variables are defined. First is a complex structure "namelist", which ends up as a variable "names" which is an array of LISTSIZE entries, each of which is comprised of the name, starting date, salary, and last raise date of the employee.

```
struct namelist {
        char name[SLEN];         /* persons name */
        char sdate[NLEN];        /* starting date */
        int  salary;             /* salary */
        char lrdate[NLEN];       /* last raise date */
} names[LISTSIZE];
```

In the example program all fields, including the array size itself, are fixed constant sizes. In a real program, however, these would all be pointers and then would take bits of memory as needed through use of the *malloc()* memory allocation function or similar.

The next global variable defined is "entries", which always contains the number of entries currently active in the database:

```
int entries;      /* number of entries in the database */
```

Finally, the "monthname" array of month abbreviations is defined for use in the various date formatting procedures:

```
char *monthname[12] = { "Jan", "Feb", "Mar", "Apr", "May",
                "Jun", "Jul","Aug", "Sep", "Oct",
                "Nov", "Dec" };
```

This, clearly, will also have to be changed as you internationalize the program.

The structure of the program has it broken down into the following five files; "salary.c" contains the *main()* routine, "sort.c" contains the *sort()* and *compare()* routines, "database.c" contains *open_database()*, *add_entry()* and *add()*, "utils.c" contains all other routines in the program, and "salary.h" contains all the global macro and variable definitions.

8
Compile-Time Internationalization

Now that you have an exemplary program to work with, you can start thinking about what will be required to internationalize, and localize the package. For this chapter you will create a version of the "salary" program that works in Spanish (which will be called "sueldo," since localization refers to everything, including the correct program name).

Let us begin the same way as last chapter, however, with an example of how the program should work. This time, with a difference; it is in Spanish:

Programa del base de datos de sueldo: leer en las entradas por 5

Escoger: añadir, encontrar, registrar, imprimir, estadísticas, dejar:
registrar

Empleados corrientes, con fecha de 25 de diciembre de 1990 a
8.40

Anders, Becky:
    sueldo 950 pesos, alquilado 8 de enero de 1991,
    (no hay registrado aumento)
Bishop, Patrick:
    sueldo 1200 pesos, alquilado 24 de febrero de 1990,
    aumento último: 1 de setiembre de 1990
Davidson, James:
    sueldo 5600 pesos, alquilado 8 de abril de 1989,

aumento último: 1 de diciembre de 1990
Holland, Xaviera:
  sueldo 2200 pesos, alquilado 7 de julio de 1989,
  aumento último: 15 de enero de 1990
Richards, Mary:
  sueldo 4500 pesos, alquilado 5 de octubre de 1988,
  aumento último: 1 de diciembre de 1990

Escoger: añadir, encontrar, registrar, imprimir, estadísticas, dejar:
añadir

Para añadir un empleado. Nombre: **Añejo, Carlos**
Sueldo (en pesos): **9150**
Fecha de empezar (mes/día/año): **12/25/90**
Fecha de aumento último (ENTER=nada):

Escoger: añadir, encontrar, registrar, imprimir, estadísticas, dejar:
registrar

Empleados corrientes, con fecha de 25 de diciembre de 1990 a
8.41

Anders, Becky:
  sueldo 950 pesos, alquilado 8 de enero de 1991,
  (no hay registrado aumento)
Añejo, Carlos:
  sueldo 9150 pesos, alquilado 25 de diciembre de 1990,
  (no hay registrado aumento)
Bishop, Patrick:
  sueldo 1200 pesos, alquilado 24 de febrero de 1990,
  aumento último: 1 de setiembre de 1990
Davidson, James:
  sueldo 5600 pesos, alquilado 8 de abril de 1989,
  aumento último: 1 de diciembre de 1990
Holland, Xaviera:
  sueldo 2200 pesos, alquilado 7 de julio de 1989,
  aumento último: 15 de enero de 1990
Richards, Mary:
  sueldo 4500 pesos, alquilado 5 de octubre de 1988,
  aumento último: 1 de diciembre de 1990

Escoger: añadir, encontrar, registrar, imprimir, estadísticas, dejar:
estadisticas

Hay 6 empleados en el base de datos.
Añejo, Carlos se pague lo más (9150 pesos)
Anders, Becky se pague lo mínimo (950 pesos)
y el aumento promedio está 3933 pesos.

Escoger: añadir, encontrar, registrar, imprimir, estadísticas, dejar:
encontrar

¿Cuál empleado encontrar? **holland**
Nombre: Holland, Xaviera
Fecha de empezar: 7 de julio de 1989
Sueldo: 2200 pesos
Fecha de aumento último: 15 de enero de 1990

Escoger: añadir, encontrar, registrar, imprimir, estadísticas, dejar:
dejar

Notice how far reaching the change in language and culture has
become; not only are the prompts changed, but the monetary notation has changed, and the date format is dramatically different
too. Less obvious, the sorting order has been modified too; Añejo
sorted after Anders but before Bishop, correctly.

Outside of the challenge of correctly translating all prompts and
input parsing to work with Spanish, a more fundamental difficulty
must be dealt with; the Spanish alphabet is different than the English
alphabet. Specifically, Spanish adds "ch," "ll," "rr" and "ñ," oc-
curring after "c," "l," "r," and "n," respectively. As a result, the
alphabet looks similar to:

a b c ch d e f g h i j k l ll m n ñ o p q r rr s t u v w x y z

The greatest difficulty is collation; instead of simply being able to
rely on the ASCII values of different characters to correctly order
words in a list, you now have to understand that "ch" is lexically
lower than "d," but higher than "c." To accomplish this you quite
literally have to create your own table of numeric values for each
of the letters in the alphabet, both upper and lowercase.

The new letters in the alphabet will require ASCII values that are
not found in the standard 7-bit ASCII used with most computers.
Indeed, 7-bit ASCII allows for 128 characters total, of which about
30 are non-printable (end-of-line, form-feed, end-of-file, and so on),
52 are upper and lower case alphabetic, 10 are numeric, and the
remainder (about 36) are punctuation and other printable characters.
Most computers, fortunately, actually consider characters to be 8-

bits of data (a "byte"), so there's a spare "bit," or unit of information that you can exploit for your purposes. Going to 8-bit from 7-bit ASCII gives you 255 possible values, an addition of well over 100 characters.

Sticking with standards, the American National Standards Institute (ANSI) defines five different "ANSI Standards" for 8-bit ASCII definition, which, as you might expect, is not too useful. Standards will be more fully considered in the next few chapters, but at this juncture, source-level internationalization will be easier to accomplish if you simply defined your own 8-bit values for the new characters:

```
#define CH      (int) 130   /* the Spanish "ch" character */
#define LL      (int) 131   /* the Spanish "ll" character */
#define EN      (int) 132   /* the Spanish "ñ" character */
#define RR      (int) 133   /* the Spanish "rr" character */
```

Since you will need to be able to transliterate (translate uppercase characters to lowercase, and vice versa) you will also need definitions for the uppercase equivalent characters:

```
#define CAP_CH    (int) 160   /* Spanish "ch" capitalized */
#define CAP_LL    (int) 161   /* Spanish "ll" capitalized */
#define CAP_EN    (int) 162   /* Spanish "ñ" capitalized */
#define CAP_RR    (int) 163   /* Spanish "rr" capitalized */
```

Now you can go back to the problem of creating an explicit value mapping for each character in the Spanish alphabet, to allow collation and other applications:

```
struct char_order {
    int    key;        /* the character in question */
    int    value;      /* and it is value */
} character_ordering[] = {

    { 'a', 97 }, { 'b', 98 }, { 'c', 99 }, { CH, 100, }, { 'd', 101 },
    { 'e', 102 }, { 'f', 103 }, { 'g', 104 }, { 'h', 105 }, { 'i', 106 },
    { 'j', 107 }, { 'k', 108 }, { 'l', 109 }, { LL, 110 }, { 'm', 111 },
    { 'n', 112 }, { EN, 113 }, { 'o', 114 }, { 'p', 115 }, { 'q', 116 },
    { 'r', 117 }, { RR, 118 }, { 's', 119 }, { 't', 120 }, { 'u', 121 },
    { 'v', 122 }, { 'w', 123 }, { 'x', 124 }, { 'y', 125 }, { 'z', 126 },

    { 'A', 65 }, { 'B', 66 }, { 'C', 67 }, { CAP_CH, 68 }, { 'D', 69 },
    { 'E', 70 }, { 'F', 71 }, { 'G', 72 }, { 'H', 73 }, { 'I', 74 },
    { 'J', 74 }, { 'K', 75 }, { 'L', 76 }, { CAP_LL,77 }, { 'M', 78 },
```

```
{ 'N', 79 }, { CAP_EN,80 }, { 'O', 81 }, { 'P', 82 }, { 'Q', 83 },
{ 'R', 84 }, { CAP_RR,85 }, { 'S', 86 }, { 'T', 87 }, { 'U', 88 },
{ 'V', 89 }, { 'W', 90 }, { 'X', 91 }, { 'Y', 92 }, { 'Z', 93 },

{ STOP, 0 }              /* sentinel value */
};
```

Since you do not want to explicitly keep track of the number of
entries in this, and similar lists, you instead use the common programming technique of having a unique and easily recognized special value as a "stop" value. This STOP value needs to be a character
of some sort, but clearly not alphabetic. To remind you of the importance of the character, "!" is chosen, meaning that at the top of
the routine defining this structure occurs the macro preprocessor
definition "#define STOP '!' ".

In addition to collation, however, you will also want to be able
to reliably transliterate all characters:

```
struct char_map {
    int     lowercase;      /* character in lowercase */
    int     uppercase;      /* character in uppercase */
} transliteration_table[] = {
    { 'a', 'A' }, { 'b', 'B' }, { 'c', 'C' }, { 'd', 'D' }, { 'e', 'E' },
    { 'f', 'F' }, { 'g', 'G' }, { 'h', 'H' }, { 'i', 'I' }, { 'j', 'J' },
    { 'k', 'K' }, { 'l', 'L' }, { 'm', 'M' }, { 'n', 'N' }, { 'o', 'O' },
    { 'p', 'P' }, { 'q', 'Q' }, { 'r', 'R' }, { 's', 'S' }, { 't', 'T' },
    { 'u', 'U' }, { 'v', 'V' }, { 'w', 'W' }, { 'x', 'X' }, { 'y', 'Y' },
    { 'z', 'Z' },

    /* and language specific characters... */

    { EN, CAP_EN },         /* ñ character */
    { CH, CAP_CH },         /* ch character */
    { LL, CAP_LL },         /* ll character */
    { RR, CAP_RR },         /* rr character */

    { STOP, STOP }          /* stopper for list */
};
```

The routines needed to utilize these tables are quite straightforward.
For example, to transliterate:

```
int
tolower(int ch)
{
```

```
/** translates the specified character to lowercase, by
    using transliteration table for the specified language.
    We assume no error will be encountered, because we expect
    isupper() to have been called immediately prior.
**/
int i;


    for (i=0; transliteration_table[i].uppercase != STOP; i++)
        if (transliteration_table[i].uppercase == ch)
            return(transliteration_table[i].lowercase);
}
```

This also shows how the STOP value can be easily used to prevent
looking past the end of the list, without too much confusion. Since
tolower() can be a (faster) macro function when you are working in
ASCII-only characters, the program now actually has the definition:

```
#if ! defined(SPANISH)
# define tolower(ch)          (ch 'A' + 'a')
# define isupper(ch)          (ch >= 'A' && ch <= 'Z')
#endif
```

Clearly, *tolower()* has changed quite a bit to allow support for the
new, foreign language. The structure that is utilized to allow these
modifications to exist in the actual source code is the "#if" statement.
Most typically in the code will be fragments similar to:

```
#if defined(SPANISH)
    printf("Programa del base de datos de sueldo. Leer en las entradas
por ciento %d empleados\n\n",
#else
  printf("Salary database program: read in %d entries\n\n",
#endif
        entries);
```

which offers a number of useful features; the translation between
English and the other language is immediately apparent, both versions can be easily built from the same source code (through a simple
compile-time change), and the conditional statements, since they
are processed before the subroutine calls, can split actual subroutine
calls or other C statements (notice here that the "entries);" line is
shared by both printf statements).

To actually define the variable SPANISH, you need simply use
the "-D" option to the compiler: tcc -DSPANISH will do the trick.

Since you are actually using the make facility and a makefile, things get a bit more complex, however. The makefile ends up written as:

```
# Makefile for SALARY program
#

CC=tcc
RM=rm

salary.exe : salary.obj database.obj sort.obj utils.obj newlib.obj
        $(CC) salary.obj database.obj sort.obj utils.obj newlib.obj

salary.obj: salary.c salary.h
        $(CC) -c -D$(LANG) salary.c

database.obj: database.c salary.h
        $(CC) -c -D$(LANG) database.c

sort.obj: sort.c salary.h
        $(CC) -c -D$(LANG) sort.c

utils.obj: utils.c salary.h
        $(CC) -c -D$(LANG) utils.c

newlib.obj: newlib.c salary.h spanish.h
        $(CC) -c -D$(LANG) newlib.c
```

To change languages, you could easily add "LANG=SPANISH" to the top of the makefile, but even easier is to use the macro definition feature of "make" itself. Using this, the entire salary program could be built by invoking "make -DLANG=SPANISH", which will end up calling "tcc -DSPANISH" for each source file in the program.

The actual organization of the program into separate files will be explained in further detail in the following chapter, on link-time internationalization. Rather than be concerned with the higher level file organization, then, the modifications to each of the routines used in the program will prove more interesting.

8.1 LIST—List the Employees in the Database

This routine has all the prompts conditionally translated into Spanish—the language chosen at compile time based on whether or not the user defined "SPANISH". One subtle note; since the date format

and prompts have become longer, the format of the list output has
lengthened, requiring that you now output three lines of information
per user, rather than two in English. Look for the added "\n\t"
carriage-return and tab characters in the format string.

```
void
list(FILE *outfd)
{
    /** list employees in database **/

    int i;

#if defined(SPANISH)
    fprintf(outfd, "\nEmpleados corrientes, con fecha de %s\n",
            the_date());
#else
    fprintf(outfd, "\nCurrent Employees as of %s\n", the_date());
#endif

    for (i = 0; i < entries; i++) {
#if defined(SPANISH)
        fprintf(outfd, " %s:\n\tsueldo %d pesos, alquilado %s,\n\t",
#else
        fprintf(outfd, " %s:\n\tsalary $%d, hired %s,",
#endif
        names[i].name, names[i].salary, show_date(names[i].sdate));

        if (strlen(names[i].lrdate) > 0)
#if defined(SPANISH)
        fprintf(outfd, " aumento último: %s\n",
                show_date(names[i].lrdate));
#else
        fprintf(outfd, " last raise %s\n", show_date(names[i].lrdate));
#endif
        else
#if defined(SPANISH)
        fprintf(outfd, " (no hay registrado aumento)\n");
#else
        fprintf(outfd, " (no raise recorded)\n");
#endif
    }
    fprintf(outfd, "\n");
}
```

At the same time, a key idea is that we are still able to call the *show_date()* function, as well as all other functions; the changes required for them to work in Spanish are done in each of the routines. This will prove quite handy as the program is changed for other languages.

8.2 STATS—Analyse Data and Output Information

The translation into Spanish of this routine has it as "analizar," or "analyze." This is a more descriptive name, yet outside of this change and the prompts, the routine stays almost untouched:

```
void
stats(void)
{
    /** output some statistics about the current employees **/

    int lowest_id, highest_id, lowest = 32767, highest=0;
    long int sum=0;
    int i;

    for (i=0; i < entries; i++) {
    if (names[i].salary < lowest) {
    lowest = names[i].salary;
    lowest_id = i;
    }
    if (names[i].salary > highest) {
    highest = names[i].salary;
    highest_id = i;
    }
    sum += names[i].salary;
    }

#if defined(SPANISH)
    printf("\nHay %d empleados en el base de datos.\n", entries);
    printf(" %s se pague lo más (%d pesos)\n",
        names[highest_id].name, highest);
    printf(" %s se pague lo mínimo (%d pesos)\n",
        names[lowest_id].name, lowest);
    printf(" y el aumento promedio está %d pesos.\n\n",
        sum / entries);
#else
```

```
    printf("\nThere are %d employees in the database.\n", entries);
    printf(" %s is paid the most ($%d)\n",
          names[highest_id].name, highest);
    printf(" %s is paid the least ($%d)\n",
          names[lowest_id].name, lowest);
      printf(" and the average salary is $%d\n\n", sum / entries);
#endif
}
```

This time the approach to the different languages results in two
different blocks of code, rather than interspersed statements as in
the previous subroutine. Again, notice the change in currency notation.

8.3 THE_DATE—Current Date and Time

Of the different routines that need be modified for another language
and culture, one of the most interesting is that of displaying the date
and time. In Spanish, for example, as with a number of other languages, month names aren't capitalized, for example, so 12 December 1990 (which, to be honest, should probably be written December
12, 1990, a more typical U.S. notation) ends up 12 de diciembre de
1990. A subtle difference is the length of the date too; "12 December
1990" is 16 characters, yet "12 de diciembre de 1990" is 23 characters, an addition of 7 characters. Why should this matter? Because,
just as with the output of the *list()* command having to move to
three lines from two in English, many programs presume certain
spacing being required for information.

```
char *
the_date(void)
{
     /** return the current date and time as a printable string **/
     struct tm *timeptr;
     long     thetime;
     static char buffer[SLEN];

     time(&thetime);
     timeptr = localtime(&thetime);

#if defined(SPANISH)
     sprintf(buffer, "%d de %s de 19%02d a %d.%d\n",
            timeptr->tm_mday, monthname[timeptr->tm_mon],
```

```
            timeptr->tm_year, timeptr->tm_hour,
            timeptr->tm_min);
#else
    sprintf(buffer, "%d %s, 19%02d at %d:%02d\n",
            timeptr->tm_mday, monthname[timeptr->tm_mon],
            timeptr->tm_year, timeptr->tm_hour,
            timeptr->tm_min);
#endif
    return( (char *) buffer);
}
```

The date and time formats clearly change, but we are lucky that in Spanish the actual ordering of data is identical to the format in English (day, month, year, hour, minute). A key difference is with the definition of the monthname[ ] character array, which is now defined as:

```
#if defined(SPANISH)
char *monthname[12] = { "enero", "febrero", "marzo", "abril",
                "mayo", "junio", "julio", "agosto",
                "setiembre", "octubre", "noviembre",
                "diciembre"};
#else
char *monthname[12] = { "Jan", "Feb", "Mar", "Apr", "May",
                Jun", "Jul", "Aug", "Sep", "Oct",
                "Nov", Dec" };
#endif
```

Here you notice yet another difference; the English version of the "salary" program uses abbreviated month names, while the Spanish version will more properly use full month names. This means that the difference in string output length is even more pronounced; "3 Aug, 1991" is only 11 characters, while that same date in Spanish will end up "3 de agosto de 1991", for a total of 19 characters, almost double the length.

8.4 SHOW_DATE—MM/DD/YY to String

Given the change to the previous routine, the modifications required to *show_date()*, which translates numeric month/day/year format into the printable "day monthname, year" format, should be obvious and unsurprising.

```
char *
show_date(char *date)
```

```
{
    /** given MM/DD/YY date, return it as; DD Mon, 19YY **/

    int     mon, day, year;
    static char buffer[SLEN];

    sscanf(date, "%d/%d/%d", &mon, &day, &year);
#if defined(SPANISH)
    sprintf(buffer, "%d de %s de 19%02d", day, monthname[mon-1],
        year);
#else
    sprintf(buffer, "%d %s, 19%02d", day, monthname[mon-1],
        year);
#endif
    return( (char *) buffer);
}
```

One interesting difference in date notation is that while in the English format punctuation is commonly used (the comma), when translated into the Spanish format, punctuation vanishes, replaced by the "de" (of) conjunctions. Indeed, the literal translation of the Spanish date format is "3 of August of 1991".

8.5 LOWERCASE—String into All Lower Case

This routine, surprisingly, requires no modifications to work in the different language because of the modularity of the original design:

```
void lowercase(char *string)
{
    /** translate string, en situ, to all lowercase letters **/

    do {
    if (isupper(*string)) *string =tolower(*string);
    } while (*string++);
}
```

Of course, the definitions of *isupper()* and *tolower()* change quite a bit to accommodate the differences in language and alphabets.

Two other routines that require no modification are *sort()* and *compare()*, which we will skip presenting for that reason. To see why this is true, check back at the code in the previous section.

8.6 LOAD_DATABASE—Read Database Off Disk

Earlier it was suggested that using spaces as field delimiters would pose a problem with more complex names. As part of the internationalization and localization of "salary" to "sueldo," you have now sidestepped that problem, changing the format of the data file to use colons as separators instead ("name:start-date:wage:raise-date"). The actual parsing of the fields is done in a new routine called "breakdown", which will be presented immediately following load_database().

```
int
load_database(void)
{
    FILE *fd;
    char buffer[SLEN];
    int index = 0, i;

    if ((fd = fopen(DATAFILE, "r")) == NULL) {
#if defined(SPANISH)
    fprintf(stderr, "No se podria abrir el base de datos %s\n",
    DATAFILE);
#else
    fprintf(stderr, "Couldn't open database %s\n", DATAFILE);
#endif
    exit(1);
    }

    while (fgets(buffer, SLEN, fd) != NULL) {
    if (buffer[0] == COMMENT) continue; /* skip comments */

    remove_return(buffer);

    breakdown(buffer, names[index].name, names[index].sdate,
        &(names[index].salary), names[index].lrdate);

    index++;
    }
    entries = index;

    fclose(fd);
}
```

The differences between the two versions of this routine are the obvious addition of the Spanish error message and the replacement of the original *sscanf()* routine with the *breakdown()* routine.

Additionally, we have added a macro function "remove_return", which ensures that there are no spurious carriage-return or linefeed characters at the end of the input buffer. This is defined as:

```
#define remove_return(s)    { int i = strlen(s)-1;            \
                              if (s[i] == '\n' || s[i] == '\r')   \
                              s[i] = '\0';                     \
                            }
```

The "\" characters at the end of each line indicate to the preprocessor that the macro definition continues on multiple lines. Notice also that macro functions can have their own local variables for performance (which, then again, was shown last chapter with the *swap()* routine used within *sort()*).

8.7 BREAKDOWN—Parse Colon Delimited Line

Replacing the *sscanf()* call requires a fair amount of sophistication, since the different fields are represented in different formats, and, for even more difficulty, the *scanf()* family does not allow spaces as part of a string (if they did, then a possible solution would be to have scanf("%s:%s:%d:%s\n", . . .) replace the original call to the *scanf()* function).

On the positive side, however, you can write a much faster routine because instead of having to parse a format string each time the routine is invoked, you can build into the routine explicit knowledge of the formats involved.

```
void
breakdown(char *buffer, *name, *sdate; int *salary; char *lrdate)
{
    /** given buffer as a set of fields separated by colons, break
       it down, putting each field in it is appropriate variable **/

    char number[NLEN];
    int i = 0;

    copy_up_to(COLON, buffer, name, &i);
    copy_up_to(COLON, buffer, sdate, &i);
```

```
copy_up_to(COLON, buffer, number, &i);  /* get as string */
*salary = atoi(number);                 /* convert to int */

if (i+2 < strlen(buffer))               /* last raise date? */
strcpy(lrdate, (char *) buffer + i);    /* get if there */
else
lrdate[0] = '\0';                       /* default if not */
}
```

Allowing for the final field to be optional, with a meaningful default if nothing is found, proves to be the only tricky part of this routine, as can be seen. This is really an unfortunate side-effect of the design of C; many programming languages, including notably Pascal, guarantee that all uninitialized variables will have zero as their value. C, on the other hand, promises nothing at all, and consequently it is exceptionally rare for an uninitialized variable to have a meaningful value at all, let alone one that can be used to check whether the field has been initialized or not.

8.8 COPY_UP_TO—Copy String thru Delimiter

The companion routine to *breakdown()*, *copy_up_to()* simply copies from the source buffer into the target buffer, starting at the specified character in the source buffer, until either the end of line is encountered, or the specified field delimiter is encountered (the field delimiter in this case being the colon character).

```
void
copy_up_to(char field_separator, *source, *target; int *index)
{
    /** copy characters from source, starting at character #index
        up to field_separator or end of line into target.
    **/

    int i=0;

    while (source[(*index)] != field_separator && source[(*index)])
    target[i++] = source[(*index)++];
    target[i] = '\0';

    if (source[*index] == field_separator) (*index)++;
}
```

There is a bit of C shorthand that shows up here, as well as elsewhere in the programming examples; the "&& source[(*index)])" clause ending the *while()* statement. In essence, the idea is that in C all tests that return non-zero are considered true, while all zero-returns are false. Therefore, as the shorthand logic has it, a test such as "while (*string)" is identical in function to the longer "while (*string != 0)", or even more correctly (and in a more longwinded fashion), "while (*string != '\0')". The latter change is another notational convenience common in C programming; since all characters are actually translated into integer values by the compiler, the two statements "a = 0" and "a = '\0' " are identical, as are "string[2] = 'A' " and "string[2] = 97".

8.9 ADD_ENTRY—Add New User to Database

The modifications required for this routine are perhaps the most common and traditional changes encountered with internationalization of a program. In this example, the change required is to an error message.

```
void
add_entry(char *name, *start_date; int salary; char *last_raise)
{
    /** append this entry to our database. **/

    FILE *fd;

    if ((fd = fopen(DATAFILE, "a")) == NULL) {
#if defined(SPANISH)
    fprintf(stderr,
        "No se puede anexar '%s' al base de datos %s\n",
#else
    fprintf(stderr, "Cannot append '%s' to database %s\n",
#endif
            name, DATAFILE);
    exit(1);
    }

    fprintf(fd, "%s:%s:%d:%s\n", name, start_date, salary,
        last_raise);
```

```
        fclose(fd);
}
```

Eagle-eyed readers will notice a second modification to this routine when compared with the last version, in the previous chapter. Since you changed the on-disk database file format to having colons as separators, the output format from this routine needed to change too, and so the format string in the *fprintf()* routine has been altered appropriately.

8.10 ADD—Prompt for New Employee

This is another routine that requires simple modifications to allow it to work in the new language.

```
void
add(void)
{
        /** add a new employee! **/
        char buffer[SLEN];

#if defined(SPANISH)
        output("\nPara añadir un empleado. Nombre: ");
        gets(names[entries].name);

        output("Sueldo (en pesos): ");
        gets(buffer);
        sscanf(buffer, "%d\n", &(names[entries].salary));

        output("Fecha de empezar (mes/día/año): ");
        gets(names[entries].sdate);

        output("Fecha de aumento último (ENTER=nada): ");
#else
        output("\nAdding an employee. Name: ");
        gets(names[entries].name);

        output("Salary: $");
        gets(buffer);
        sscanf(buffer, "%d\n", &(names[entries].salary));

        output("Start date MM/DD/YY: ");
        gets(names[entries].sdate);
```

```
    output("Date of last raise (ENTER=none): ");
#endif
    gets(names[entries].lrdate);
    printf("\n");

    add_entry(names[entries].name, names[entries].sdate,
        names[entries].salary, names[entries].lrdate);
    entries++;
    sort();
}
```

Certain traits of programming interfaces can change as programs are localized for different cultures. An obvious one is that some languages will require prompts to be commanding (enter your name) while others will be better accepted as polite options (please enter your name).

8.11 FIND—Find Specific Person in Database

The *find()* routine introduces an interesting change to the program because of a notational difference in Spanish. Namely, interrogative and exclamatory statements are prefaced with an upside down punctuation mark. A question, for example, does not just have the question mark at the end, similar to English, but also has an upside down one before the question too. "What is it?" in Spanish is correctly printed as: "¿Qué es esto?". The *find()* routine has a prompt in the form of a question ("Find whom?") which will prove an interesting localization challenge:

```
void
find(void)
{
    /** look for a specific person in the database **/

    char buffer[SLEN];   /* a working character buffer */
    int i;            /* and a int for looping */

#if defined(SPANISH)
    output("\n¿Cuál empleado encontrar? ");
#else
    output("\nFind which employee? ");
#endif
```

```
    gets(buffer);

    for (i=0; i < entries; i++) {

    if (compare(names[i].name, buffer, strlen(buffer), TRUE) == 0) {
#if defined(SPANISH)
    printf("\nNombre: %s\nFecha de empezar: %s\n",
            names[i].name, show_date(names[i].sdate));
    printf("Sueldo: %d pesos\n", names[i].salary);
#else
    printf("\nName: %s\nStarting Date: %s\n",
            names[i].name, show_date(names[i].sdate));
    printf("Salary: $%d\n", names[i].salary);
#endif

#if defined(SPANISH)
    if (strlen(names[i].lrdate))
     printf("Fecha de aumento último: %s\n\n",
            show_date(names[i].lrdate));
    else
     printf("(no hay registrado fechas de aumento)\n\n");
#else
    if (strlen(names[i].lrdate))
     printf("Last Raise Date: %s\n\n",
            show_date(names[i].lrdate));
    else
     printf("(no raise dates recorded)\n\n");
#endif

    return;
    }
    }

#if defined(SPANISH)
    printf(
     "No encontré el empleado '%s' en el base de datos.\n\n",
       buffer);
#else
    printf("I couldn't find that employee in the database.\n\n");
#endif
}
```

Also note that we have taken a liberty with the error message at the end of this routine; in the original English version the error simply refers to "that employee," whereas in the new Spanish error message, it states "no employee with the name %s". This, and the change in datafile format to using colons as field separators, are examples of how a program can be improved as it is internationalized and subsequently localized.

8.12 OUR_STRNCMP—Compare Lexically

As alluded to earlier, one of the subtle, through difficult, changes required by localization is replacing many of the built-in string functions. We have already seen that the character classification routines must be replaced, including *tolower()* and *isupper()*, but a more challenging library call is the string-comparison routine *strncmp()*. The standard routine compares two strings up to the end of either string or for the specified number of characters, returning less than zero if the first string is lexically less than the second, zero if they're equal, or greater than zero if the first is lexically greater:

```
int
our_strncmp(char *str1, *str2; int len)
{
    /** Given two strings, compare them (for a maximum of len
       chars, if specified) and return <0 if str1 < str2, =0 str1 = str2,
       or >0 if str1 > str2
    **/

    int diff;

    if (len < 0) len = maximum(strlen(str1), strlen(str2));

    while (−len && *str1 && *str2) {
     if ((diff = (valueof(*str1) − valueof(*str2))) != 0)
      return(diff);
     str1++; str2++;
    }

    return(valueof(*str1) − valueof(*str2));
}
```

One trick we have used in this routine that is worth noting is that we have expanded the algorithm to include the functionality of the companion routine *strcmp()* too. *strcmp()* compares two strings until one of them ends, or they differ, and *our_strncmp()* with a length parameter of -1 will perform an identical comparison.

The routine *maximum()*, again, is a macro function:

#define maximum(a,b)   (a > b ? a : b)

and helps keep the source easier to read and understand.

Notice the calls to *valueof()* to ascertain the numeric value of each character in the two strings. This, really, is the key to the now-internationalized *strcmp()* routine, as these values can be computed based on lookup tables, ASCII values, or just about any other computation desired, all without affecting the speed and accuracy of the *strcmp()* routine itself.

8.13 VALUEOF—Return Value of Character

With the addition of the character_ordering table for Spanish, the "salary" program has been extended to work with multiple languages. To access the character-ordering information easily, however, requires a simple routine:

```
int
valueof(char ch)
{
    /** return the value of the specified character from the
       lookup table, or, if not therein, the ASCII value.
    **/

    int i;

    for (i=0; character_ordering[i].key != STOP; i++)
      if (character_ordering[i].key == ch) {
       return(character_ordering[i].value);
      }

    return( (int) ch);
}
```

This has been left as a linear search algorithm for convenience, and if this were production code, since the table is static, a better choice would be something similar to a hash table or other search choice that would optimize lookup speed.

The default return value, if a character is not in the language alphabet table, is to return the ASCII value of that character. This is not necessarily correct behaviour across all languages, however, since, for example, if we are working in Turkish, the letters "q" and "w" do not appear at all. If we are given a word that contains a "q" how should it be collated? Does it occur before all the valid letters in the Turkish alphabet? Or after?

This sort of question poses a thorny dilemma for the group localizing a package, and in deference to the ubiquity of common ASCII characters ("a" through "z"), almost all software will accept these letters as if they were part of the actual language. Indeed, if using an explicit table-of-values approach to collation data, the best approach is to simply include all common English letters, noting perhaps the nature of the exceptions, such as the "q" and "w" in Turkish.

Indeed, there is another subtle problem with this approach that we will opt to accept rather than deal with the extremely difficult workaround. The problem is that if you rely on ASCII values at all for any characters in the alphabet, then there is likely to be conflict between ASCII and non-ASCII localized values. To illustrate, in the Spanish character_ordering table, "z" ends up with the value of 126, versus its ASCII value of 122. The problem becomes obvious if you imagine what happens if *our_strncmp()* is given the following two strings to compare: "the zebra" and "the {cat dog}". With pure ASCII values, the ordering would be as shown, since "z" is numerically lower than "{" ("z" = 122 ASCII, and "{" = 123 ASCII). With the new lookup table, however, "z" is 126, meaning that these two would now sort to "the {cat dog}" before "the zebra."

The saving grace here is that almost all collation tasks required of a program are lexographic, and lexographic collation doesn't define values for non-alphabetic characters, especially punctuation.

8.14 FIRST_WORD—Return First Word of String

A much more simple routine is *first_word()*, which is required for the new command parsing algorithm required to support foreign language commands. Simply put, it is given a line of text and returns the first word.

```
first_word(char *string, *word)
{
    /** given the string, return the first word as 'word'. **/
```

```
    while (! whitespace(*string))
    *word++ = *string++;


    *word='\0';
}
```

Words are defined as being separated by whitespace, which in this case is a macro preprocessor function:

```
#define whitespace(c)        (c == ' ' || c == '\t' || c == '\0')
```

The "\t" is a tab character, and the "\0" is the NULL character, which delimits then end of character arrays and strings in the C programming language.

8.15 ISUPPER—True if Character is Uppercase

Replacing the earlier macro function definition, the new version of the character classification routine *isupper* now must use the transliteration-table to ascertain whether the given character is actually uppercase, returning true if so.

```
int
isupper(int ch)
{
    /** returns TRUE if character ch is uppercase. We note this
        when in a foreign language by checking the translation table
        for the presence of the character; if it is there, then return
        TRUE.
    **/
    int i;


    for (i=0; transliteration_table[i].uppercase != STOP; i++) {
    if (transliteration_table[i].uppercase == ch)
      return(TRUE);
    }
    return(FALSE);
}
```

Compare this routine to the "tolower()" routine below . . .

8.16 TOLOWER—Return Character as Lowercase

Similar to *isupper()*, this routine uses the transliteration_table data to map the given uppercase character to a lowercase character.

```
int
tolower(int ch)
{
    /** translates the specified character to lowercase, by
        using the transliteration table for the specified language.
        We assume no error will be encountered, because we expect
        isupper() to have been called immediately prior.
    **/

    int i;

    for (i=0; transliteration_table[i].uppercase != STOP; i++)
    if (transliteration_table[i].uppercase == ch)
    return(transliteration_table[i].lowercase);
}
```

This time, however, the routine returns the second part of the table entry, rather than simple verification that the character given is present in the table.

8.17 MAIN—The Main Program

Finally, then, the main program itself, including the completely redesigned input parsing section:

```
void
main(void)
{
    char command[SLEN];    /* space for user command input */
#if defined(SPANISH)
    char word[SLEN];       /* space for parsing */
#endif

    load_database();       /* initialize ... */
    sort();                /* ... and sort the database */

#if defined(SPANISH)
    printf("Programa del base de datos de sueldo:");
```

```
     printf(" Leer en las entrados %d empleados\n\n",
#else
     printf("Salary database program: read in %d entries\n\n",
#endif
          entries);


     do {
#if defined(SPANISH)
     output(
"Escoger: añadir, encontrar, registrar, imprimir, estadísticas, dejar:");
#else
     output("Please select: Add, Find, List, Print, Stats, Quit: ");
#endif
     gets(command);

#if defined(SPANISH)
     first_word(command, word);

        if (matches_word("añadir"))          add();
     else if (matches_word("encontrar"))         find();
     else if (matches_word("registrar"))         list(stdout);
     else if (matches_word("imprimir"))       list(stdprn);
     else if (matches_word("estadísticas"))   stats();
     else if (matches_word("dejar"))          exit(0);
     else
        printf("No lo entiendo. Trátele otra vez.\n");
#else
     switch ( isupper(command[0]) ?
             tolower(command[0]) : command[0] ) {
     case 'a' : add();                break;
     case 'f' : find();               break;
     case 'l' : list(stdout);         break;
     case 'p' : list(stdprn);         break;
     case 'q' : exit(0);          break;
     case 's' : stats();          break;
     default : printf("I do not understand. Try again.\n");
     }
#endif
     } while (1);          /* infinite loop: exit by "quit" command */
}
```

As predicted, when translated into another language, the user commands did not remain unique by first character. In fact, of the six commands, two of them now start with the letter "e". Also, take note of the variable definition for "word_buffer"; it is only declared (and used) if the compilation option includes SPANISH, otherwise the space is saved. Finally, *matches_word()* is yet another type of macro function definition, this time exercising as a shorthand:

```
#if defined(SPANISH)
# define matches_word(m)     (compare(word,m,-1,TRUE) == 0)
#endif
```

Using matches_word() allows the program to be neater and clearer, and each conditional actually expands from:

```
if (matches_word("añada"))
```

to:

```
if ((compare(word,"añada",-1,TRUE) == 0))
```

which is considerably more confusing to read.

8.18 Thoughts on Compile-Time Internationalization

We have now gone through the sample program and modified and extended the algorithms to allow two versions of the "salary" program to be created, one working in Spanish and the other in English, based on a simple compile-time switch.

While working on the program to internationalize and then localize it, a number of improvements have been added, including a better command parsing algorithm and an improved format for the datafile. These types of incremental improvements are typical of internationalization efforts, and indeed simply reflect the evolutionary lifecycle of good software design. Rather than shy away from them, good designers will continually re-evaluate the existing design, trying to ascertain if improvements can be made to the overall software.

On the down side, the reason that these improvements to the program could be made was because the person localizing the program absolutely had to be able to modify—in some cases substantially—the actual program source code. The few routines that were not modified at all were generically written utility routines. Because of this, the localization person had to be a competent programmer, well versed in not only the programming language and target language and culture, but also savvy of the algorithms used by the program itself.

Also, the final program executable works in one language. To have both versions available, you have to explicitly put one version aside and rebuild the program for the second version too. The end result might well be "salary.exe" and "sueldo.exe" (allowing English speaking users to type "salary" and Spanish speaking users to type "sueldo", but the disk space and other resources used are expensive.

The final thought about this approach is; imagine how this code would appear if you wanted to support French, Italian and German, as well as Spanish and English. Or even more confusingly, Arabic.

9
Link-Time Internationalization

While the goal of compile time internationalization is to incorporate all the changes into the files that contain the actual code and algorithms, the goal of link-time internationalization is to extract all culture and language dependent information. In fact, this version of the program will be the first that is truly internationalized, then, as a separate step, localized.

There are two classes of information to be extracted from the program at this point; textual strings and more language and culturally dependent algorithms. While the first has not been done previously in the evolution of the "salary" program, the new subroutines added in the previous chapter begin the process of internationalizing the algorithms.

This time, in addition, we will need to understand how the subroutines are split into separate files, because the goal here will be to have a set of ".obj" object files and the source to a set of language dependent external files, containing the strings, the collation and transliteration information, and the internationalized library subroutines. Putting it all together is the "make" facility, which we will exploit to offer an easy switch between versions of the program.

First off, let us look at the file that contains all the string constants, in English, "english.h".

```
static char *welcome_msg =
    "Salary database program: read in %d entries\n\n";
static char *prompt_msg =
    "Please select: Add, Find, List, Print, Stats, Quit: ";
```

```
static char *add1_msg = "\nAdding an employee. Name: ";
static char *add2_msg = "Salary: $";
static char *add3_msg = "Starting date (MM/DD/YY): ";
static char *add4_msg = "Date of last raise (ENTER=none): ";
static char *add_msg = "add";
static char *find_msg = "find";
static char *list_msg = "list";
static char *print_msg = "print";
static char *stats_msg = "stats";
static char *quit_msg = "quit";
static char *try_again_msg = "I do not understand. Try again.\n";
static char *error1_msg = "Couldn't open database %s\n";
static char *error2_msg = "Cannot append '%s' to database %s\n";

static char *find_msg1 = "\nFind which employee? ";
static char *find_msg2 = "\nName: %s\nStarting Date: %s\n";
static char *find_msg3 = "Salary: $%d\n";
static char *find_msg4 = "Last Raise Date: %s\n\n";
static char *find_msg5 = "(no raise dates recorded)\n\n";
static char *find_msg6 =
    "I couldn't find employee '%s' in the database.\n\n";
static char *list_msg1 = "\nCurrent Employees as of %s\n";
static char *list_msg2 = " %s:\n\tsalary $%d, hired %s,";
static char *list_msg3 = " last raise %s\n";
static char *list_msg4 = " (no raise recorded)\n";
static char *stats_msg1 =
    "\nThere are %d employees in the database.\n";
static char *stats_msg2 = " %s is paid the most ($%d)\n";
static char *stats_msg3 = " %s is paid the least ($%d)\n";
static char *stats_msg4 = " and the average salary is $%d\n\n";
static char *the_date_msg = "%d %s, 19%02d at %d:%02d\n";
static char *show_date_msg = "%d %s, 19%02d";
```

These are, of course, all the prompts and character values checked
in the program itself. There are a few more that you need to add,
but rather than the memory-efficient static character arrays used so
far in this process, these must be macro preprocessor defines:

```
#define mon1        "Jan"
#define mon2        "Feb"
#define mon3        "Mar"
#define mon4        "Apr"
#define mon5        "May"
#define mon6        "Jun"
```

```
#define mon7        "Jul"
#define mon8        "Aug"
#define mon9        "Sep"
#define mon10       "Oct"
#define mon11       "Nov"
#define mon12       "Dec"
```

Why not static character buffers? Because they appear within the context of a static character buffer array:

```
char *monthname[12] = { mon1, mon2, mon3, mon4, mon5, mon6,
                        mon7, mon8, mon9, mon10, mon11,
                        mon12 };
```

and static buffers with elements being separate static buffers is a bit too confusing, even for sophisticated compilers and linkers, and is also outside of the scope of this feature in the language.

What this extraction of strings gains, immediately, is the ability to substitute another set of definitions for the English phrases already presented. For example, the Spanish version:

```
static char *welcome_msg =
   "Programa del base de datos de sueldo: Leer en las entradas %d
   empleados.\n\n";
static char *prompt_msg =
   "Escoger: añadir, encontrar, registrar, imprimir, estadísticas,
    dejar: ";

static char *add1_msg = "\nPara añadir un empleado. Nombre: ";
static char *add2_msg = "Sueldo (en pesos): ";
static char *add3_msg = "Fecha de empezar (mes/día/año): ";
static char *add4_msg = "Fecha de aumento último (ENTER=nada):
                        ";
static char *add_msg = "añadir";
static char *find_msg = "encontrar";
static char *list_msg = "registrar";
static char *print_msg = "imprimir";
static char *stats_msg = "estadísticas";
static char *quit_msg = "dejar";
static char *try_again_msg =
      "No lo entiendo. Trátele otra vez.\n";
static char *error1_msg = "No se podria abrir el base de datos
                          %s\n";
static char *error2_msg =
      "No se puede anexar '%s' al base de datos %s\n";
```

```
static char *find_msg1 = "\n¿Cuál empleado encontrar? ";
static char *find_msg2 = "\nNombre: %s\nFecha de empezar:
                          %s\n";
static char *find_msg3 = "Sueldo: %d pesos\n";
static char *find_msg4 = "Fecha de aumento último: %s\n\n";
static char *find_msg5 =
    "(no hay registrado fechas de aumento)\n\n";
static char *find_msg6 =
    "No encontré el empleado '%s' en el base de datos\n\n";
static char *list_msg1 = "\nEmpleados corrientes, con fecha de
                          %s\n";
static char *list_msg2 =
    " %s:\n\tsueldo %d pesos, alquilado %s,\n\t";
static char *list_msg3 = " fecha de aumento último: %s\n";
static char *list_msg4 =
    " (no hay registrado aumentoo)\n";
static char *stats_msg1 =
    "\nHay %d empleados en el base de datos.\n";
static char *stats_msg2 = " %s se pague lo más (%d pesos)\n";
static char *stats_msg3 = " %s se pague lo mínimo (%d pesos)\n";
static char *stats_msg4 =
    " y el aumento promedia está %d pesos.\n\n";

static char *the_date_msg = "%d de %s de 19%02d a %d.%d\n";
static char *show_date_msg = "%d de %s de 19%02d";

/* the next set are done as #define's because C will not allow you
   to define a static array of characters, each element of which
   is itself a static character buffer.
*/

#define mon1      "enero"
#define mon2      "febraro"
#define mon3      "marzo"
#define mon4      "abril"
#define mon5      "mayo"
#define mon6      "junio"
#define mon7      "julio"
#define mon8      "agosto"
#define mon9      "setiembre"
#define mon10     "octubre"
#define mon11     "noviembre"
#define mon12     "diciembre"
```

This information is contained in a file called "spanish1.h". The second language-specific include file is "spanish2.h", which contains the collation and transliteration data structures previously presented in the last chapter (namely the two tables "character_ordering" and "transliteration_table").

The third localized file is "local_lib.c", which contains a number of routines already presented, but rewritten to serve as more generic functions. An interesting header appears in this file too, one that allows an externally specified file (from "make") to be included, or, if not defined, the default comparisons, ASCII, to be used instead:

```
#ifdef INCLUDE2
# include INCLUDE2      /* explicit character relationships */
#else                   /*         or        */
# define ASCII          /* using ASCII character relationships */
#endif
```

This takes advantage of the compiler being invoked as:

'cc -DINCLUDE2="filename" sample.c'

which is done within the makefile.

The following routines all appear in the file "local_lib.c".

9.1 OUR_STRNCMP—Compare Lexographically

Yet another version of the string comparison function, this time it will either directly invoke the built-in string comparison functions, if "ASCII" is true, or will use the language-specific algorithms using data as defined in the character_values data file.

```
int
our_strncmp(char *str1, *str2; int len)
{
    /** Given two strings, compare them (for a maximum of len
        chars, if specified) and return <0 if str1 < str2, =0 str1 = str2,
        or >0 if str1 > str2
    **/
#ifdef ASCII
    return ( len < 0 ? strcmp(str1, str2) : strncmp(str1, str2, len) );
#else
    int diff;

    if (len < 0) len = maximum(strlen(str1), strlen(str2));
```

```
    while ( len && *str1 && *str2) {
    if ((diff = (valueof(*str1) valueof(*str2))) != 0)
      return(diff);
    str1++; str2++;
    }
    return(valueof(*str1) valueof(*str2));
#endif
}
```

This time the relationship between the value of "len" and whether
the program should use a regular string comparison or limited string
comparison is more obvious as well.

9.2 VALUEOF—Value of a Character

This routine is only needed if a specific language other than English
(ASCII) is being used, and in fact is only included in that circum-
stance:

```
#ifndef ASCII
int
valueof(char ch)
{
    /** return the value of the specified character from the
     lookup table, or, if not therein, the ASCII value.
    **/
    int i;
    for (i=0; character_ordering[i].key != STOP; i++)
     if (character_ordering[i].key == ch)
      return(character_ordering[i].value);
    return( (int) ch);
}
#endif
```

If ASCII is defined, *our_strncmp()* uses the built in comparison functions, and therefore does not need *valueof()* at all.

9.3 ISUPPER—TRUE if Character is Uppercase

Again, this can either return a simple ASCII based value, or if a
specific language is being used other than English, it will need to
step through the possible uppercase letters to see if any match.

```
int
isupper(int ch)
{
     /** returns TRUE if character ch is uppercase. We note this
         when in a foreign language by checking the translation table
         for the presence of the character; if it is there, then return
         TRUE.
     **/
#ifdef ASCII
     return( ch >= 'A' && ch <= 'Z' );
#else
     int i;
     for (i=0; transliteration_table[i].uppercase != STOP; i++)
     if (transliteration_table[i].uppercase == ch)
       return(TRUE);
     return(FALSE);
#endif
}
```

This represents an amalgamation of information presented earlier
in this book. Recall that we have seen the "#define" macro for the
regular version of *isupper()*, as well as the latter block, which is
identical to the version shown in the source-level internationalization routine.

9.4 TOLOWER—Translate Character to Lowercase

The final language dependent routine.

```
int
tolower(int ch)
{
     /** translates the specified character to lowercase, by
         using the transliteration table for the specified language.
         We assume no error will be encountered, because we expect
         isupper() to have been called immediately prior.
     **/
#ifdef ASCII
     return( ch 'A' + 'a' );
#else
     int i;
     for (i=0; transliteration_table[i].uppercase != STOP; i++)
```

```
    if (transliteration_table[i].uppercase == ch)
        return(transliteration_table[i].lowercase);
#endif
}
```

By modification of the two included files, "spanish1.h" and
"spanish2.h", and indication of the appropriate flags to the third,
"local_lib.c", the program can now change languages and cultures
without too much fuss.

How do the routines appear, gutted of their strings and cultural
context information? Rather curiously generic, really.

9.5 LOAD_DATABASE—Read in Database File

Originally the spot of a simple modification to change an error message for the appropriate language, *load_database()* now appears much
more generic:

```
int
load_database(void)
{
    FILE *fd;
    char buffer[SLEN];
    int index = 0, i;
    if ((fd = fopen(DATAFILE, "r")) == NULL) {
    fprintf(stderr, error1_msg, DATAFILE);
    exit(1);
    }
    while (fgets(buffer, SLEN, fd) != NULL) {
    if (buffer[0] == COMMENT) continue; /* skip */
    remove_return(buffer);
    breakdown(buffer, names[index].name, names[index].sdate,
            names[index].lrdate, &(names[index].salary));
    index++;
    }
    entries = index;
    fclose(fd);
}
```

Notice the "error1_msg" reference. If you go back to the beginning
of this chapter, where the static character strings are defined, you
will find that this string is defined as:

static char *error1_msg = "Couldn't open database %s\n"

Unfortunately, by choosing this reference by mnemonic rather than having the actual string present, it is difficult to track changes in the code with changes in the message file. For example, a designer reading through the source code might encounter "printf(error1_msg)" and, not surprisingly, have no idea what it means and what error is being flagged, if any, to the user. This problem will arise again, and worse, in the next section when considering run-time internationalization.

9.6 ADD_ENTRY—Add Entry to Database File

Another routine with subtle changes because of error messages.

```
void add_entry(char *name, *start_date; int salary; char *last_raise)
{
    /** append this entry to our database. **/
    FILE *fd;
    if ((fd = fopen(DATAFILE, "a")) == NULL) {
    fprintf(stderr, error2_msg, name, DATAFILE);
    exit(1);
    }
    fprintf(fd, "%s:%s:%d:%s\n", name, start_date,
            salary, last_raise);
    fclose(fd);
}
```

Note the retention of the colon separation: this will change as the program evolves and becomes completely internationalized.

9.7 ADD—Prompt User for New Employee

This routine becomes a bit more interesting because of the prompts and output related to user input.

```
void add(void)
{
    /** add a new employee! **/
    char buffer[SLEN];

    output(add1_msg);
    gets(names[entries].name);
```

```
output(add2_msg); gets(buffer);
sscanf(buffer, "%d\n", &(names[entries].salary));
output(add3_msg);
gets(names[entries].sdate);
output(add4_msg);
gets(names[entries].lrdate);
printf("\n");

add_entry(names[entries].name, names[entries].sdate,
        names[entries].salary, names[entries].lrdate);
entries++;
sort();
}
```

This new, generic, version is much easier to read than the previous version, which had a number of if-then-else defines. Among the benefits of this separation of source code is that programmers are less likely to forget to modify all versions of a program (such as instructions repeated within multiple conditional compilation blocks).

9.8 LIST—List Employees in Database

This routine, and those following, have been rewritten to reference the extracted strings, but otherwise are identical to those presented in the previous chapter.

```
list(outfd)
FILE *outfd;
{
    /** list employees in database **/
    int i;
    fprintf(outfd, list_msg1, the_date());

    for (i = 0; i < entries; i++) {
    fprintf(outfd, list_msg2, names[i].name, names[i].salary,
            show_date(names[i].sdate));
    if (strlen(names[i].lrdate) > 0)
    fprintf(outfd, list_msg3, show_date(names[i].lrdate));
    else
    fprintf(outfd, list_msg4);
    }
    fprintf(outfd, "\n");
}
```

9.9 STATS—Display Statistics About Employee List

```
void stats(void)
{
    /** output some statistics about the current employees **/
    int lowest_id, highest_id, lowest = 32767, highest=0;
    long int sum=0;
    int i;
    for (i=0; i < entries; i++) {
     if (names[i].salary < lowest) {
      lowest = names[i].salary;
      lowest_id = i;
     }
     if (names[i].salary > highest) {
      highest = names[i].salary;
      highest_id = i;
     }
     sum += names[i].salary;
    }
    printf(stats_msg1, entries);
    printf(stats_msg2, names[highest_id].name, highest);
    printf(stats_msg3, names[lowest_id].name, lowest);
    printf(stats_msg4, sum / entries);
}
```

9.10 THE_DATE—Current Date and Time

```
char *
the_date(void)
{
    /** return the current date and time as a printable string **/
    struct tm *timeptr;
    long     thetime;
    static char buffer[SLEN];
    time(&thetime);
    timeptr = localtime(&thetime);
    sprintf(buffer, the_date_msg,
                  timeptr->tm_mday,
                  monthname[timeptr->tm_mon],
                  timeptr->tm_year, timeptr->tm_hour,
                  timeptr->tm_min);
```

```
        return( (char *) buffer);
}
```

9.11 SHOW_DATE—MM/DD/YY to DD Mon, YY

```
char *
show_date(char *date)
{
        /** given MM/DD/YY date, return it as; DD Mon, 19YY **/

        int     mon, day, year;
        static char buffer[SLEN];

        sscanf(date, "%d/%d/%d", &mon, &day, &year);
        sprintf(buffer, show_date_msg, day, monthname[mon-1], year);

        return( (char *) buffer);
}
```

9.12 FIND—Find Employee in Database

```
void find(void)
{
        /** look for a specific person in the database **/

        char buffer[SLEN];   /* a working character buffer */
        int i;               /* and a int for looping */

        output(find_msg1);
        gets(buffer);

        for (i=0; i < entries; i++) {
        if (compare(names[i].name, buffer, strlen(buffer), TRUE) ==0) {
         printf(find_msg2, names[i].name, show_date(names[i].sdate));
         printf(find_msg3, names[i].salary);
         if (strlen(names[i].lrdate))
          printf(find_msg4, show_date(names[i].lrdate));
         else
          printf(find_msg5);
         return;
         }
```

```
    }
    printf(find_msg6, buffer);
}
```

9.13 MAIN—The Main Program

```
void main(void)
{
    char command[SLEN];      /* space for user command input */
    char word[SLEN];         /* space for parsing */
    load_database();         /* initialize ...              */
    sort();                  /* ... and sort the database */
    printf(welcome_msg, entries);

    do {
    output(prompt_msg);
    gets(command);
    first_word(command, word);
      if (matches_word(add_msg))        add();
    else if (matches_word(find_msg))    find();
    else if (matches_word(list_msg))    list(stdout);
    else if (matches_word(print_msg))       list(stdprn);
    else if (matches_word(stats_msg))      stats();
    else if (matches_word(quit_msg))    exit(0);
    else                                printf(try_again_msg);
    } while (1); /* infinite loop: exit by "quit" command */
}
```

9.14 Organization of Files

The subroutines are organized by function, and show up in files as indicated in Table 9.1.

The "make" facility is utilized to help build the final executable, keeping track of each of the individual modules, compiling them as needed, and linking the final object files with the language-specific version of "int_lib". The relationship between the files is specified in the Makefile file, as follows:

```
CC=tcc
RM=rm


# a couple of include files for link-based international support
# INCLUDE1="english.h"
```

Table 9.1. Contents of Project Specific Files.

database.c	*load_database()* *add_entry()*
sort.c	*sort()* *compare()*
cmds.c	*add()* *find()* *list()* *stats()*
utils.c	*the_date()* *show_date(date) lowercase(string)* *breakdown()* *copy_up_to()* *first_word()*
salary.c	*main()*
local_lib.c	*our_strncmp()* *valueof()* *isupper()* *tolower()*

```
# INCLUDE2=
# or, for a different language:
INCLUDE1="spanish1.h"
INCLUDE2='INCLUDE2="spanish2.h"'


salary.exe : cmds.obj database.obj salary.obj sort.obj utils.obj
int_lib.obj
    $(CC) cmds.obj database.obj salary.obj sort.obj \
        utils.obj int_lib.obj
cmds.obj: cmds.c salary.h
    $(CC) -c -DINCLUDE1=$(INCLUDE1) cmds.c
salary.obj: salary.c salary.h
    $(CC) -c -DINCLUDE1=$(INCLUDE1) salary.c
database.obj: database.c salary.h
    $(CC) -c -DINCLUDE1=$(INCLUDE1) database.c
sort.obj: sort.c salary.h
    $(CC) -c -DINCLUDE1=$(INCLUDE1) sort.c
utils.obj: utils.c salary.h
    $(CC) -c -DINCLUDE1=$(INCLUDE1) utils.c
int_lib.obj: int_lib.c salary.h
    $(CC) -c -DINCLUDE1=$(INCLUDE1) \
        -D$(INCLUDE2) int_lib.c
```

As can be seen in the Makefile, a change in language can be accomplished by simply modifying the two INCLUDE lines at the top of the file and recompiling the program.

9.15 Link-Time Internationalization Thoughts

The desire to ship to a foreign localization team the object files instead of the source can now be realized, since you merely need to have the source to int_lib.c and the include files that contain the definition for the static strings and the collation and transliteration data tables. For example, creating a French version of the program might now be accomplished by sending the localization team the routines that require localization, the header files associated with them and specifications of which routine does what. Because the sample code is so simple, most of the routines actually end up directly referencing localized information, but you can imagine a program considerably more complex where only a few basic input/output routines, and some basic sorting and utility functions need be localized, and all the other parts of the package can be shipped in pre-compiled binary (object file) format.

10
Run-Time
Internationalization

Extracting the data from the program to allow link-time alteration of the language and culture is a significant step in the direction in which we are headed, as was shown in the last chapter. The ideal, however, would be a system whereby the program can simply get all the language and culture dependent information on the fly, each time it is needed. Further, messages that the program requires (such as prompts and command words to check against) should also be obtained at run time, to allow the maximum flexibility possible.

To accomplish this, however, considerably more software must be available. Instead of being able to modify the *show_date()* routine, for example, programmatically, to choose between month-day-year and day-month-year notational formats, this information instead must be available and acted upon during run time.

The key to run time internationalization is that the internationalized information program must be split into two different portions, unlike the previous versions. Constant language and cultural information can be centrally placed in a cultural database, accessed at run time by previously supplied libraries of subroutines.

Messages, prompts, and other program specific information is then placed in a separate data file which is accessed by supplied run-time library routines. The data file will have a format vaguely similar to the "spanish1.h" file in the link-time internationalization chapter, in which each message in the program was denoted by a unique integer "index number."

Rather than have a single chunk of messages, however, the message "catalog" is partitioned into "sets" of messages, resulting in a format similar to:

set 1
1   set 1, message 1
2   set 1, message 2
set 2
1   set 2, message 1

These messages can then be referenced uniquely by "set 1, message 1", or more succinctly "1,1", "1,2", and so on. If a library routine, given the set and message information, can return the actual message string, then programs can now transform from:

printf("this is a test");

(source level internationalization) to:

char *test_message = "this is a test";
printf(test_message);

(link level internationalization) to, finally:

printf(get_msg(1,1));

This allows the information to be extracted as needed during execution by the program. This approach is so useful because programs can now be easily modified without any compilation or alteration whatsoever.

Imagine, we are running the program with the *printf()* statement above, and the output is:

this is a tste

which is clearly wrong. With other forms of internationalization, we would have to actually go into source code somewhere, find the message, modify it, and rebuild the entire executable. With run time internationalization, however, you open the message catalog and find an entry such as:

set 0
1   this is a tste

Once the typographic mistake is corrected, you are done. No other modification is required to the program or data files.

Further, switching languages becomes easy too; if the message catalog referenced contained:

set 0
1   esa es una prueba

instead, then the program, upon referencing that particular catalog, would output a prompt in Spanish rather than English. No fuss, and no recompilation or relinking.

With this approach in mind, let us look at how the "salary" program would be modified to work with run time internationalization.

10.1 Run-Time Internationalization

10.1.1 The Message Catalog

The first item to consider is the message catalog. Not surprisingly, it ends up looking quite similar to the "english.h" file from the previous chapter:

```
# Message catalog for the salary program
#
# LANGUAGE = english


$set 0     WORDS
1     Salary database program: read in %d entries\n\n
2     Please select: Add, Find, List, Print, Stats, Quit:
3     add
4     find
5     list
6     print
7     stats
8     quit
9     I do not understand. Try again.\n


$set 1 FIND
1     \nFind which employee?
2     \nName: %s\nStarting Date: %s\n
3     Salary: $%d\n
4     Last Raise Date: %s\n\n
5     (no raise dates recorded)\n\n
6     I couldn't find employee '%s' in the database.\n\n


$set 2 FADD
1     \nAdding an employee. Name:
2     Salary: $
3     Starting date (MM/DD/YY):
4     Date of last raise (ENTER=none):
```

$set 3 FLIST

1   \nCurrent Employees as of %s\n\n
2   %s:\n\tsalary $%d, hired %s,
3   last raise %s\n
4   (no raise recorded)\n

$set 4 FSTATS
1   \nThere are %d employees in the database.\n
2   %s is paid the most ($%d)\n
3   %s is paid the least ($%d)\n
4   and the average salary is $%d\n\n

$set 5 FERROR
1   Couldn't open database %s\n
2   Cannot append '%s' to database %s\n

Notice how we have neatly broken the messages up into six different sections, divided approximately by subroutines. The notation used in this message catalog is based on standard message catalog notation, as will be shown in later chapters; "$set" denotes sets, <digit><tab><message> indicates each message in the set, and lines beginning with a "#" are comments. (Actually, in the X/Open Native Language System and similar standard notations, lines prefaced with a "$" and the second letter being either a space or a tab are considered comments, confusingly enough. We will stick with "#" to be consistent.)

As important as what is in this catalog file is what is not. The most notable removals are the month and day name information, the collation and transliteration data, and the formats for date, time, currency, and so on. These are, instead, stored in a central language and culture database, since they are common across all applications that work in that particular language and culture. The central data store, as well as the library routines themselves, will be the subject of the next chapter.

This time, the program will be almost completely rewritten to take advantage not only of the external locale-knowledgeable library of utility routines, but of the required message catalog access too. Let us look at the code starting with the few utilities that remain in the actual user program.

10.1.2 LOWERCASE—String into Lowercase

As with the previous presentation of this routine, the internationalized version of *lowercase()* relies on other library calls to ascertain what is an uppercase character and then on how to translate it—or transliterate it—into lower case:

```
void lowercase(char *string)
{
    /** translate string, en situ, to all lowercase letters **/
    do {
     if (isupper(*string)) *string = tolower(*string);
    } while (*string++);
}
```

The other basic utility routines, *first_word( )*, *breakdown( )*, and *copy_up_to()*, are all identical to the previous versions of the program (demonstrating the value of modular code design). Similarly, the *sort()* and *compare()* routines are also untouched from the original design.

Routines that output messages of any nature, or process text of any type, require changes to ensure that they reference the catalog of messages for the specific language chosen, and the following routines demonstrate the type of changes required.

10.1.3 LOAD-DATABASE—Read in Database

Earlier in the evolution of the "salary" program, you changed the field delimiter in the salary database from a space to a colon, and that change holds true for the final version of the program too. Note especially the use of *get_msg()* for the *cannot open database* error message.

```
void load_database(void)
{
    FILE *fd;
    char buffer[SLEN];
    int index = 0;
    if ((fd = fopen(DATAFILE, "r")) == NULL) {
     fprintf(stderr, get_msg(FERROR,1,NULL), DATAFILE);
     exit(1);
    }

    while (fgets(buffer, SLEN, fd) != NULL) {
     if (buffer[0] == COMMENT) continue;  /* skip comments */
```

```
    remove_return(buffer);
    breakdown(buffer, names[index].name, names[index].sdate,
         names[index].lrdate, &(names[index].salary));
    index++;
    }
    entries = index;

    fclose(fd);
}
```

One modification that is required for this to work is that you change
the size of some of the buffers to ensure that as fields expand due
to changes in language the data space is not overwritten. In particular, translation from English to Spanish often requires about 50%
more space, a particular challenge on annotated illustrations in design packages and documentation.

The *get_msg()* routine will be further explained in the following
chapter, but note here that we are again taking advantage of the
mnemonic constants allowed by the C preprocessor, with a *get_msg()*
of "FERROR,1" (the first message in the FERROR message set). Note
the similarity in *get_msg()* in the following routine too.

10.1.4 ADD_ENTRY—Add a New Employee

Reflecting a minor change from the previous version of this routine,
add_entry() simply invokes *get_msg()* for the appropriate error message:

```
void add_entry(char *name, char *start_date, int salary, char
*last_raise)
{
    /** append this entry to our database. **/
    FILE *fd;
    if ((fd = fopen(DATAFILE, "a")) == NULL) {
    fprintf(stderr, get_msg(FERROR,2,NULL), name, DATAFILE);
    exit(1);
    }
    fprintf(fd, "%s:%s:%d:%s\n", name, start_date,
         salary, last_raise);
    fclose(fd);
}
```

Notice that the message returned from *get_msg()* is expected to have
space for two arguments ("name" and "DATAFILE"). Most imple-

mentations of the *printf()* routine work correctly if more arguments
are given than are specified in the format string (for example;
printf("hi\n", name), which would output "hi" and ignore the parameter "name" given to the routine). On the other hand, the routine
cannot ascertain when a required number of parameters have not
been given, leading to potentially dangerous situations such as
"printf("hi %s\n")" which will use the next address in the stack as
the beginning address of the undefined string variable. This is a
common cause of unexpected program termination in C programs,
and is a danger to which you will have to pay particular attention,
by keeping the *printf* format strings in a different file from the invocations.

10.1.5 FIND—Find Specific Person in Database

The modifications to this routine demonstrate the type of changes
required to allow for run-time internationalization. Note, unfortunately, that the routine has become quite difficult to follow, considerably more so than the original version presented.

```
void find(void)
{
    /** look for a specific person in the database **/

    unsigned char buffer[SLEN]; /* a working character buffer */
    int i;        /* and a int for looping */
    output(get_msg(FFIND,1,NULL));
    gets(buffer);
    for (i=0; i < entries; i++) {
     if (compare(names[i].name, buffer, strlen(buffer), TRUE) ==0) {
      printf(get_msg(FFIND,2,NULL), names[i].name,
           translate_date(names[i].sdate));
      printf(get_msg(FFIND,3,NULL), names[i].salary);
      if (strlen(names[i].lrdate))
       printf(get_msg(FFIND,4,NULL),
            translate_date(names[i].lrdate));
      else
       printf(get_msg(FFIND,5,NULL));
      return;
      }
     }
    printf(get_msg(FFIND,6,NULL), buffer);
}
```

This gradual obfuscation of the algorithms is a difficult challenge to overcome, and is one of the reasons that mnemonic parameters to the *get_msg()* routine are of utmost importance. In fact, for true production code, the mnemonics might be even more heavily used, with calls such as "printf(get_msg(FFIND_NOT_FOUND . . .", that mnemonic expanding to both the specified set ("FFIND") and message within the set. Ideally, alphanumeric mnemonics should be usable as actual indices into the message catalog (and used within the message catalog to denote specific messages also), but there are some significant problems with that, notably in the areas of performance and storage space.

10.1.6 ADD—Add a New Employee

In the original version of this routine, each of the calls to the routine *output()* were prompts for user input. For example, the very first statement was:

output("\nAdding an employee. Name: ");

With the format string extracted and placed into a message catalog, you can see that the new routine, similar to *find()*, is harder to read and understand, making well designed and commented code even more imperative:

```
void add(void)
{
    /** add a new employee **/
    unsigned char buffer[SLEN];

    output(get_msg(FADD,1,NULL));
    gets(names[entries].name);
    output(get_msg(FADD,2,NULL));
    gets(buffer);
    sscanf(buffer, "%d\n", &(names[entries].salary));
    output(get_msg(FADD,3,NULL));
    gets(names[entries].sdate);
    output(get_msg(FADD,4,NULL));
    gets(names[entries].lrdate);
    printf("\n");
    add_entry(names[entries].name, names[entries].sdate,
            names[entries].salary, names[entries].lrdate);
    entries++;
    sort();
}
```

Notice that not all output statements have been moved into the message catalog. In particular, we have left the "output blank line" statement intact: printf("\n"); This decision is an excellent example of some of the trade-offs involved with run-time internationalization, and the more general strategy of extracting important information into an external catalog. The problem is; should all input or output statements be pulled into the message catalog, even where there is no gain for the performance degradation, or should certain simple statements be left in the code, thereby possibly causing confusion for later code reading ("I don't see where that blank line is coming from"). No definite answer here, just another in the many trade-offs involved in programming. Nonetheless, adopting a standard convention is clearly worthwhile for both the developer and later localization efforts.

10.1.7 LIST—List All Employees

This routine demonstrates that some of the entries in the message catalog can be quite complex. In particular, message FLIST, 2 is:

2   %s:\n\tsalary $%d, hired %s,

note again the importance and difficulty of matching not only the number of parameters, but the type of parameters in format statements where the actual format string is stored externally.

```
void list(FILE *outfd)
{
    /** list employees in database **/
    int i;
    fprintf(outfd, get_msg(FLIST,1,NULL), the_date());
    for (i = 0; i < entries; i++) {
    fprintf(outfd, get_msg(FLIST,2,NULL), names[i].name,
            names[i].salary,
            translate_date(names[i].sdate));
    if (strlen(names[i].lrdate) > 0)
     fprintf(outfd, get_msg(FLIST,3,NULL),
            translate_date(names[i].lrdate));
    else
     fprintf(outfd, get_msg(FLIST,4,NULL));
    }
    fprintf(outfd, "\n");
}
```

Again, we have opted to leave the simple "add blank line" formatting statement intact, as seen in the last *fprintf()* call in the routine.

10.1.8 STATS—Compute and Show Statistics

This routine has a significant internationalization error. Can you spot it?

```
void stats(void)
{
    /** output some statistics about the current employees **/
    int lowest_id, highest_id, lowest = 32767, highest=0;
    long int sum=0;
    int i;

    for (i=0; i < entries; i++) {
    if (names[i].salary < lowest) {
     lowest = names[i].salary;
     lowest_id = i;
    }
    if (names[i].salary > highest) {
     highest = names[i].salary;
     highest_id = i;
    }
    sum += names[i].salary;
    }
    printf(get_msg(FSTATS,1,NULL), entries);
    printf(get_msg(FSTATS,2,NULL), names[highest_id].name,
            highest);
    printf(get_msg(FSTATS,3,NULL), names[lowest_id].name,
            lowest);
    printf(get_msg(FSTATS,4,NULL), sum / entries);
}
```

The error is a subtle one, and is a classic mistake made with international code: monetary values are being viewed as integer values. Integers, at least 16-bit integers, are constrained to be no greater than 2^{15}, or 32767. The error is in the code relying on the user never choosing to enter larger numbers. This error has actually been in the code all along; what if the programmer had chosen to have yearly salary stored, rather than monthly? Testing for clerical employees might have never revealed that those earning more than $33,000/year will cause the program to fail, and when foreign currencies are used, this arbitrary constraint will become even more unacceptable.

Among other things, it might well be the case that the culture of the target country for the application simply does not consider monthly salary a significant number, using quarterly or annual pay as the appropriate gauge.

10.1.9 SALARY—The Main Program

Reflecting the greatest change, the main routine now must perform the required initialization of the run-time library. This consists of ascertaining which language is being used through checking the environment variable "LANG", ensuring that there is support for the designated language, then opening the program-specific message catalog for the specified language.

For hopefully obvious reasons, the error messages associated with the initialization will always be hard-coded into the program, in English (or whatever compile-time language is used).

```
void main(void)
{
    char command[SLEN];    /* space for user command input */
    char word[SLEN];       /* space for language-based parsing */
    char *language;

    if ((language = getenv("LANG")) == NULL)
     language = DEFAULT_LANG;
    if (! international_support(language)) exit(1);
    if (! open_message_catalog(PROGNAME, language)) {
     printf("%s: cannot find '%s' message catalog\n",
         PROGNAME, language);
     exit(1);
    }

    load_database(); /* initialize ... */
    sort(); /* ... and sort the database */
    printf(get_msg(FWORDS, WELCOME,NULL), entries);
    do {
     output(get_msg(FWORDS, PROMPT,NULL));
     gets(command);
     first_word(command, word);
       if (matches_word(get_msg(FWORDS,WADD,NULL)))
           add();
```

```
      else if (matches_word(get_msg(FWORDS,WFIND,NULL)))
            find();
      else if (matches_word(get_msg(FWORDS,WLIST,NULL)))
            list(stdout);
      else if (matches_word(get_msg(FWORDS,WPRINT,NULL)))
            list(stdprn);
      else if (matches_word(get_msg(FWORDS,WSTATS,NULL)))
            stats();
      else if (matches_word(get_msg(FWORDS,WQUIT,NULL)))
            exit(0);
      else
            printf(get_msg(FWORDS,TRY_AGAIN, NULL));


   } while (1);        /* infinite loop: exit by "quit" command */
}
```

This routine also demonstrates the use of more explicit mnemonics
for accessing entries in the message catalog. In particular, the welcome message is now displayed through the call:

printf(get_msg(FWORDS, WELCOME,NULL), entries);

Where "FWORDS" is defined to be set 1, and "WELCOME" is entry
1. Just as using 16-bit integers can return and haunt the incautious
programmer, the use of *gets()* here and in other places to read user
input can cause strange problems on some machines. What if, for
example, the system expects to be able to work with 7-bit ASCII
and automatically masks the high bit on all characters input? The
result would be that while the user responds to the prompts with
the appropriate locale-specific information, the characters actually
returned to the program by the *gets()* program might be considerably
different.

   While this masking of the eighth-bit may seem unlikely, it is rather
startling to find out how much software actually utilizes the high
bit for other purposes. Indeed, the original versions of such popular
and well-used Unix utilities as *vi* (a screen-based text editor) and
awk (a sophisticated interpreted programming language) strip the
top bit for their own use.

   With the addition of the mnemonics for accessing the run-time
library also comes the addition of some different header and include
files, as well as a completely redesigned Makefile to aid in compilation and modification.

10.1.10 SALARY.H—Include File for Program

Allowing a single, central location for all defines, structure definitions, and global variables, the file "salary.h" is included by all the
different pieces of the run-time internationalized salary program. To
avoid having two separate include files, one for the main program
and another for all the other routines, the program utilizes a simple
feature of the C pre-processor; the main file defines a macro
"_MAIN_" before including the file, therefore giving it slightly different information than the other files (the main program gets variable declarations such as "int entries", while all other files receive
"extern int entries")

```
/**                        salary.h                        **/

#include <stdio.h>              /* standard I/O utils library */
#include <time.h>               /* clock manipulation library */
#include <string.h>            /* string function prototypes */
#include "intl_lib/intl_lib.h"  /* international library */

#include "proto.h"             /* our function prototypes */
#include "int_salary.h"        /* localized defines for program */

#ifndef TRUE
# define TRUE       1          /* not FALSE */
# define FALSE      0          /* not TRUE */
#endif

#define LISTSIZE    20         /* maximum database size */
#define SLEN        80         /* string length */
#define NLEN        20         /* short string length */

#define output(s) printf(s); fflush(stdout)

#define remove_return(s) { int i = strlen(s)-1;             \
                           if (s[i] == '\n' || s[i] == '\r')  \
                              s[i] = '\0';                   \
                         }
#ifndef _MAIN_
 extern
#endif

struct namelist {
    unsigned char      name[SLEN];      /* persons name */
```

```
        unsigned char      sdate[NLEN];      /* starting date */
        int    salary;                        /* salary */
        unsigned char      lrdate[NLEN];     /* last raise date */
    } names[LISTSIZE];

#ifndef _MAIN_
 extern
#endif

int entries;        /* number of entries in the database */

void exit(int);

#define FWORDS   0
#define FFIND          1
#define FADD           2
#define FLIST          3
#define FSTATS         4
#define FERROR    5

/** and within the FWORDS set **/

#define WELCOME        1
#define PROMPT    2
#define WADD           3
#define WFIND          4
#define WLIST          5
#define WPRINT    6
#define WSTATS    7
#define WQUIT          8
#define TRY_AGAIN      9
```

Two other files are included that are of interest here; "proto.h", which contains all the ANSI C style function prototypes for all subroutines used in the program, and "intl_lib.h", which contains definitions and function prototypes allowing the program to access the separately compiled internationalization library.

10.1.11 INT_SALARY.H—Localized Definitions for Salary Program

While the internationalization library has its own include file, there are also still a few elements of the salary program that can be localized if necessary, and these are included in a separate file "int_salary.h":

```
/*                        int_salary.h                        **/
```

```
#define DATAFILE      "salary.dat"
#define PRINTER       "PRN:"
```

```
#define COMMENT       '#'''   /* comment lines in datafile */
#define COLON         ':'    /* field separator in datafile */
#define STOP          '!'    /* stopper value for lists */
```

Note that extracting these items in this manner improves the portability of the program, but violates the goal of being able to ship just binaries, rather than any source code. That is, if one of these entries is modified, the program must be recompiled for it to take effect. In fact a much better solution to the problem is to include the definition of these various fields within the message catalog, with these compiled-in values as the default if they are not defined at all. This allows countries that might use the colon as a date format, for example, to redefine "COLON" to another character that will avoid any conflict.

10.1.12 PROTO.H—Function Prototypes

Straightforward ANSI C function prototypes, most of these have remained constant for the entire evolution of the program:

```
/**                        proto.h                        **/
```

```c
int compare(char *word1, char *word2, int minlen, int sensitive);

void add(void);
void add_entry(char *name, char *start_date, int salary,
    char *last_raise);
void breakdown(char *buffer, char *name, char *sdate, char *lrdate,
    int *salary);
void copy_up_to(char field_separator, char *source, char *target,
    int *index);
void find(void);
void first_word(char *string, char *word);
void list(FILE *outfd);
void load_database(void);
void lowercase(char *string);
void main(void);
void sort(void);
void stats(void);
```

Note the programming form of using "void" as the return type for a function that does not actually return a type. This is to ensure that subtle type errors will not creep up later in the development.

10.1.13 INTL_LIB.H—Include file for Internationalization Library

This contains not only the definition of the default language (in this case "English") but function prototypes for all the routines used in the internationalization library.

```
/**                          intl_lib.h                          **/

/** include library for programs using the international library **/

#define DEFAULT_LANG "english"

/** Plus ANSI C style function prototypes for all C source files **/

char *get_msg(int msg_set, int msg_index, char *buffer);
char *is_a_macro(char *word);
char *short_date(void);
char *the_date(void);
char *translate_date(char *date);

int get_next_line(char *buffer, FILE *fd);
int international_support(char *language);
int islower(unsigned char ch);
int isupper(unsigned char ch);
int open_message_catalog(char *program, char *language);
int our_strncmp(char *str1, char *str2, int len);
int read_in_data(FILE *fd);
int valueof(unsigned char ch);

unsigned char tolower(unsigned char ch);
unsigned char toupper(unsigned char ch);

void close_message_catalog(void);
void currency(FILE *fd);
void date_format(FILE *fd);
void error(int num, char *arg);
void expand_macros(char *buffer);
void fulldaynames(FILE *fd);
```

```
void get_macro(char *buffer);
void months(FILE *fd);
void numbers(FILE *fd);
void sorting_data(FILE *fd);
void time_data(FILE *fd);
void translate_slash_cmds(char *target, char *source);
void upper_lower_data(FILE *fd);
```

The default language here is "English", not "n-computer" or "C", as per existing standards which will be examined more closely in the following section of the book. The reason for this is because the target user speaks English, not some obscure computer-type language, so to avoid needless jargon . . .

10.1.14 MAKEFILE—For Run-Time Internationalized Program

This makefile is quite similar to the previous makefile shown for the original non-internationalized program, because at this juncture we have been able to shift all language/locale specific changes into the source code and external message catalogs. The only interesting modification is that you are now including your own library "int_lib.lib", as explained in the next chapter.

Note the various compile-time flags required for the C compiler on the PC too.

```
# Makefile for SALARY program

CC=tcc -A -N -w -ms -K
PROG=-DPROGNAME="salary"
RM=rm

salary.exe : cmds.obj database.obj salary.obj sort.obj utils.obj
int_lib.lib
    $(CC) -e salary cmds.obj database.obj salary.obj sort.obj \
      utils.obj int_lib.lib

cmds.obj: cmds.c salary.h
    $(CC) -c cmds.c

salary.obj: salary.c salary.h
    $(CC) -c $(PROG) salary.c

database.obj: database.c salary.h
```

```
        $(CC) -c database.c

sort.obj: sort.c salary.h
        $(CC) -c sort.c

utils.obj: utils.c salary.h
        $(CC) -c utils.c

int_lib.lib: intl_lib/int_lib.lib
        cp intl_lib/int_lib.lib int_lib.lib

clean:
        rm -f *.obj
```

The target "int_lib.lib" is a bit confusing; what it says is that the
file "int_lib.lib" depends on a file of the same name in the subdi-
rectory "intl_lib". If that file is newer than the one in this directory,
then the solution is to copy the newer one into this directory.

Finally, the "clean" target is a typical entry in a Makefile and
allows the programmer to easily save space by removing all intermediate files with a single command ("make clean"). Note that the
sequence of "make clean" and "make" will ensure that all files are
recompiled and up-to-date.

10.2 Other Languages

With all this, let us see how catalogs for other languages might look,
as well as how easily you can now switch between languages.

10.2.1 Spanish

```
## Message catalog for the salary program
##
## LANGUAGE=spanish

$set 0
1       Programa del base de datos de sueldo: Leer en las entradas \
        por %d empleados.\n\n
2       Escoger por favor: añadir, encontrar, registrar, imprimir, \
        estadísticas, dejar:
3       añadir
4       encontrar
5       registrar
```

6   imprimir
7   estadísticas
8   dejar
9   No lo entiendo. Trátele otra vez.\n

$set 1   FIND
1   \n¿Cuál empleado encontrar?
2   \nNombre: %s\nfecha de empezar: %s\n
3   Sueldo: %d pesos\n
4   Fecha de aumento último: %s\n\n
5   (no hay registrado fechas de aumento)\n\n
6   No encontré el empleado '%s' en el base de datos\n\n

$set 2   ADD
1   \nPara añadir un empleado. Nombre:
2   Sueldo (en pesos):
3   Fecha de empezar (mes/día/año):
4   Fecha de aumento último (ENTER=nada):

$set 3   LIST
1   \nEmpleados corrientes, con fecha de %s\n
2   %s:\n\tsueldo %d pesos, alquilado %s,\n\t
3   aumento último: %s\n
4   (no hay registrado aumento)\n

$set 4   STATS
1   \nHay %d empleados en el base de datos.\n
2   %se pague lo más (%d pesos)\n
3   %s se pague lo mínimo (%d pesos)\n
4   y el aumento promedia está %d pesos.\n\n

$set 5   ERRORS
1   No se podria abrir el base de datos %s\n
2   No se puede anexar '%s' al base de datos %s\n

That's it. So long as the language itself is supported by the internationalization library—something we will look at closer in the next
section—you now need merely define a new language catalog to add
another language to the program, a language that might not ever
have been anticipated by the programmer.

10.2.2 German

For example, here is a German message catalog:

Message catalog for the salary program
#
LANGUAGE = German

$set 0   WORDS—the top level message set
1   Gehalts Datenbank Programm: einlesen in %d
      Eintragungen\n\n
2   Bitte waehlen Sie: \n\tAddiere, Finde, Aufliste,\n\tDrucke,
      Statistik, Beende:
3   addiere
4   finde
5   aufliste
6   drucke
7   statistik
8   beende
9   Ich verstehe Sie Nicht. Bitte wiederholen Sie.\n

$set 1   FIND
1   \nWelcher Angestellte wird gesucht?
2   \nName: %s\nAnfangsdatum: %s\n
3   Gehalt: %d DM\n
4   Letzte Gehaltserhoehung: %s\n\n
5   (keine Gehaltserhoehung festgehalten in der Datenbank)\n\n
6   Angestellter nicht gefunden '%s' in der Datenbank.\n\n

$set 2   FADD
1   \nAngestellten hinzufuegen. Name:
2   Gehalt: DM
3   Eintrittsdatum (DD/MM/YY):
4   Datum der letzten Ghaltserhoehung (ENTER=none):

$set 3   FLIST
1   \nLaufende Angestelltenliste am %s\n\n
2   %s:\n\tGehalt DM %d, Eintrittsdatum %s,
3   \n\tLetzte Gehaltserhoehung %s\n
4   \n\t(Keine Gehaltserhoehung eingetragen)\n

$set 4   FSTATS
1   \nEs befinden sich %d Angestellte in der Datenbank.\n
2   %s Hat hoechstes Gehalt (%d DM)\n
3   %s Hat niedrigstes Gehalt (%d DM)\n
4   und das Durchschnitssgehalt ist %d DM\n\n

$set 5   FERROR
1   Kann die Datenbank nicht oeffnen %s\n
2   Kann nicht zufuegen '%s' zur Datenbank %s\n

This could be used by putting it in the correct place in the file heirarchy, then setting the user LANG environment variable to the new language:

LANG=german
salary
Gehalts Datenbank Programm: einlesen in 9 Eintragungen
Bitte waehlen Sie:
          Addiere, Finde, Aufliste,
          Drucke, Statistik, Beende: **aufliste**
Laufende Angestelltenliste am 25 März 1991, 20.59

Anders, Becky:
     Gehalt DM 950, Eintrittsdatum 8. Januar 1991,
     (Keine Gehaltserhoehung eingetragen)
Bishop, Patrick:
     Gehalt DM 1200, Eintrittsdatum 24. Februar 1990,
     Letzte Gehaltserhoehung 1. September 1990
Davidson, James:
     Gehalt DM 5600, Eintrittsdatum 8. April 1989,
     Letzte Gehaltserhoehung 1. Dezember 1990
Eñerson, Raul:
     Gehalt DM 3300, Eintrittsdatum 15. Dezember 1990,
     (Keine Gehaltserhoehung eingetragen)
Epleänâda, François:
     Gehalt DM 1200, Eintrittsdatum 4. Merz 1988,
     (Keine Gehaltserhoehung eingetragen)
Holland, Xaviera:
     Gehalt DM 2200, Eintrittsdatum 7. Juli 1989,
     Letzte Gehaltserhoehung 15. Januar 1990
Richards, Mary:
     Gehalt DM 4500, Eintrittsdatum 5. Oktober 1988,
     Letzte Gehaltserhoehung 1. Dezember 1990

Bitte waehlen Sie:
     Addiere, Finde, Aufliste,
     Drucke, Statistik, Beende: **statistik**
Es befinden sich 9 Angestellte in der Datenbank.
 Davidson, James Hat hoechstes Gehalt (5600 DM)
 Anders, Becky Hat niedrigstes Gehalt (950 DM)

und das Durchschnitssgehalt ist 2874 DM
Bitte waehlen Sie:
   Addiere, Finde, Aufliste,
   Drucke, Statistik, Beende: **beende**

Quite a step from the original English-only version!

10.3 Thoughts on Run-Time Internationalization

At this point, you have accomplished your goal on this evolutionary set of modifications, and have reached a point where the program can work in any 8-bit language, with new languages added as easily as translating the message catalog into the target language. The constraints on internationalization are now those of the low level hardware (such as, can it display Arabic? Can the user input Chinese?) and the ingenuity of the software developer.

There are some tradeoffs that are more obvious now, especially the performance degradation due to having to externally reference a separate message catalog for each prompt or output the program uses. In real life, however, this penalty seems quite minimal, and even on a small notebook computer there is no perceptible difference between the original program and the run-time internationalized version.

The Run-Time
Internationalization Library

In the previous chapters, we have seen that isolating the language-specific elements, and ultimately moving them into a separate library, considerably aids in the internationalization, and subsequent localization, of a program. As the information has been extracted, however, it has ended up in a separate library to support run-time internationalization. In this chapter we will look at just how that database looks, and the routines required to not only access it, but build a programmer-accessible library to aid internationalization.

The culture and language-specific information database is quite straightforward, containing information on the character set (both for sorting and transliteration), currency notation, various date notations, full month and day names, numeric formats, and formats for the display of time.

The default language, English, avoids having to specify any formats for the library. Rather than skipping the default, however, we will ensure that a file called "english" exists in the appropriate directory so that users can specify English as easily as any other format, through the use of the "LANG" environment variable.

```
## File = "/usr/int_lib/library/english.db"
##
## No information : use all default values.
##
## The existence of this file will allow users to specify
## LANG=english without problems.
```

Notice that we are placing all of the language and culture database

information files in a common location: "/usr/int_lib". Within that
directory we will create a directory for each of the internationalized
programs (for example, for the "salary" program, we have a directory "/usr/int_lib/salary" with each message catalog file stored
within that directory: "english.cat", "spanish.cat", and so on).

While the defaults are correct for U.S. English, a few items must
be changed to allow those in the United Kingdom to comfortably
use the software:

```
## File = "/usr/int_lib/library/uk-english.db"
##
## Language and culture database for UK ENGLISH

$currency
£%d
%d pounds

$date
## notation: D=day M=Mon Y=Year,
## uppercase=digit, lowercase=word

DmY %d %s, 19%02d
DmY %d %s, 19%02d, at %d:%02d\n
MDY %d/%d/19%02d

$time
%d:%02d
```

With this available (notice the change in information ordering in the
third date format: MDY rather than DMY as is common in the United
States), and with a suitable set of phrases in a message catalog, users
in the United Kingdom can easily now use a version of the salary
program (or any other program, for that matter) with their own local
variation on various notational conventions.

For many languages, however, the database is considerably more
extensive, as it includes transliteration information, as well as collation information and other language and cultural information.
Consider this language database for French:

```
## File = "/usr/int_lib/library/french.db"
##
## Language and culture database for FRENCH

#define STOP
```

integer values here are from the Latin-1 ISO 8859-1 charset

#define A_GRAVE	200
#define A_CIRCUMFLEX	192
#define C_CEDILLA	181
#define E_GRAVE	201
#define E_CIRCUMFLEX	193
#define E_ACUTE	197
#define E_DIERESIS	205
#define I_CIRCUMFLEX	209
#define I_DIERESIS	221
#define O_CIRCUMFLEX	194
#define U_CIRCUMFLEX	195
#define U_DIERESIS	207
#define CAP_C_CEDILLA	180
#define CAP_E_GRAVE	163
#define CAP_E_CIRCUMFLEX	164
#define CAP_E_ACUTE	220
#define CAP_E_DIERESIS	165
#define CAP_I_CIRCUMFLEX	166
#define CAP_I_DIERESIS	167
#define CAP_O_CIRCUMFLEX	223
#define CAP_U_CIRCUMFLEX	174
#define CAP_U_DIERESIS	219

$sorting-data

A	65
B	66
C	67
CAP_C_CEDILLA	68
D	69
E	70
CAP_E_GRAVE	71
CAP_E_CIRCUMFLEX	72
CAP_E_ACUTE	73
CAP_E_DIERESIS	74
F	75
G	76
H	77
I	78
CAP_I_CIRCUMFLEX	79

CAP_I_DIERESIS	80
J	81
K	82
L	83
M	84
N	85
O	86
CAP_O_CIRCUMFLEX	87
P	88
Q	89
R	90
S	91
T	92
U	93
CAP_U_CIRCUMFLEX	94
CAP_U_DIERESIS	95
V	96
W	97
X	98
Y	99
Z	100
a	101
A_GRAVE	102
A_CIRCUMFLEX	103
b	104
c	105
C_CEDILLA	106
d	107
e	108
E_GRAVE	109
E_CIRCUMFLEX	110
E_ACUTE	111
E_DIERESIS	112
f	113
g	114
h	115
i	116
I_CIRCUMFLEX	117
I_DIERESIS	118
j	119
k	120
l	121

m	122
n	123
o	124
O_CIRCUMFLEX	125
p	126
q	127
r	128
s	129
t	130
u	131
U_CIRCUMFLEX	132
U_DIERESIS	133
v	134
w	135
x	136
y	137
z	138

STOP   0

$upper-lower-data

a	A
b	B
c	C
d	D
e	E
f	F
g	G
h	H
i	I
j	J
k	K
l	L
m	M
n	N
o	O
p	P
q	Q
r	R
s	S
t	T
u	U

v   V
w   W
x   X
y   Y
z   Z

A_GRAVE   A
A_CIRCUMFLEX   A
C_CEDILLA   CAP_C_CEDILLA
E_GRAVE   CAP_E_GRAVE
E_CIRCUMFLEX   CAP_E_CIRCUMFLEX
E_ACUTE   CAP_E_ACUTE
E_DIERESIS   CAP_E_DIERESIS
I_CIRCUMFLEX   CAP_I_CIRCUMFLEX
I_DIERESIS   CAP_I_DIERESIS
O_CIRCUMFLEX   CAP_O_CIRCUMFLEX
U_CIRCUMFLEX   CAP_U_CIRCUMFLEX
U_DIERESIS   CAP_U_DIERESIS

STOP   STOP   /* stopper for list */

$currency
%dFF*
%d francs

$date
notation: D=day M=Mon Y=Year,
uppercase=digit, lowercase=word
DmY %d %s 19%02d
DmY %d %s 19%02d à %dh%02d\n
DMY %d.%d.19%02d

$full day names
dimanche
lundi
mardi
mercredi
jeudi
vendredi

---

*Note that the only difference between France, Belgium, Switzerland, Canada, Senegal, and other French-speaking countries is the currency notation, as specified here.

samedi

$months
janvier
février
mars
avril
mai
juin
juillet
août
septembre
octobre
novembre
décembre

$numbers
radix
,
separator
.

$time
%d.%02d

With the pressure to internationalize software, a number of different companies and industry organizations have devised various schemes to allow easy interchange of data. In particular, the International Organization for Standardization (ISO) has produced a number of different standards and specifications to aid in the internationalization of computer software and hardware. Of interest here is the reference to the ISO 8859-1 character set. Commonly known as "Latin-1", this character set defines a particular 8-bit (i.e. 255 value) character value table, allowing diacriticals and other non-U.S. ASCII values to be identical from system to system.

The down side of this, however, is that since these character values are at the "top" of the table, numerically, the challenge of correctly sorting words can become exceptionally difficult. In particular, when a German ß is supposed to sort after the "s" but before the "t," numerically-based sorting algorithms can no longer be used: "s" = 101, "ß" = 215, and "t" = 102, so clearly by simple numeric comparisons these relationships are not correct. Instead, the approach we are taking here is to simply remap all alphabetic characters to have new values, so "s" = 101, "ß" = 102 and "t" = 103, allowing speedy comparison and sorting.

Since we are not remapping all printable ASCII characters, however, there are some shortcomings. In particular, non-alphanumeric characters can sort to rather peculiar places; if the newly mapped "z" is 165 and the regular ASCII value for "{" is 164, then the two entries "zebra" and "{cat}" will sort differently than expected; "zebra" will come *after* "{cat}", not before. For illustrative purposes, the smaller set of character definitions allows quick and understandable language-sensitive collation, but actual production versions of the internationalization database information would need to take this subtlety into account.

To aid in writing and maintaining the language information database files, a simple macro preprocessor feature has been included, which allows mnemonic definitions for various values. In particular, the format is "#define mnemonic value", as in:

#define STOP

Which will subsequently have each occurrence of "STOP" replaced with the period character (which denotes the last entry of an arbitrary list of characters). More importantly, however, it allows much more understandable information for non-7-bit ASCII values, such as the mnemonic:

#define A_GRAVE 200

for the character á. While a more sophisticated macro preprocessor could be added, there is a clear tradeoff between capability and speed. In this case, the preprocessor is used each time the database is read by the internationalization library (at startup for any program that uses the library).

Specific items are denoted by the use of a "$" as the first character, and have either a pre-defined type of value, as in the "short" and "long" format strings for currency:

$currency
%dFF
%d francs

or the more freeform formats for the date notation, where a small, but sophisticated format parser is added, allowing information database developers to define various date formats for the three types of interest: long date only ("August 4, 1991"), long date and time ("August 4, 1991 at 3:40") and abbreviated date ("8/4/91"). The notational convention is quite simple, with "D" representing the

day, "M" the month, and "Y" the year. Entries in upper case refer
to the numeric value and those in lower case refer to the word (where
appropriate). The French database defines:

$date
DmY %d %s 19%02d
DmY %d %s 19%02d à %dh%02d\n
DMY %d.%d.19%02d

This indicates that dates of the form "8 avril 1983", "8 mai 1992 à
2h43" and "8.3.1984" are the preferred notations.

Day and month names are listed with one entry per line, each
having to list all values as appropriate (7 for days, and 12 for
months). Capitalization is important, so while the English notation
is to capitalize proper nouns, many languages tend to use all lowercase. As with so many other things, ensuring validity by having
someone who is a native speaker check the material is vitally important.

Finally, numbers are defined by two quantities; the radix point
(separating whole from fractional values) and the separator (breaking large quantities into smaller groupings, as in "1,000"), each of
which appears subsequent to the numbers indicator:

$numbers
radix

,
separator

11.1 The Library

Based on the information presented thus far in the book, much of
the functionality of the internationalization library should be obvious. In particular, previous chapters have shown versions of a
number of the subroutines needed. Before you look at them, though,
let us have a quick tour of the header file "intl.h", shared by all the
source files that comprise the library.

The first items in the file are a set of defaults which allow the file
"english.db" to be empty, defining various aspects of U.S. English:

```
#define DEFAULT_TRANSLITERATION_TABLE_SIZE      127
#define DEFAULT_ORDERING_TABLE_SIZE             255

#define DEFAULT_STANDARD_DATE_FORMAT              \
    "mDY %s %d, 19%d"
#define DEFAULT_SHORT_DATE_FORMAT                 \
```

```
    "MDY %d/%d/19%d"
#define DEFAULT_DATE_WTIME_FORMAT                              \
    "MdY %d %s, 19%d at %d:%02d"

#define DEFAULT_SHORT_CURRENCY      "$%d"
#define DEFAULT_LONG_CURRENCY       "%d dollars"
#define DEFAULT_TIME_FORMAT         "%d:%02d"
#define DEFAULT_RADIX               '.'
#define DEFAULT_SEPARATOR           '\0'
```

There are clearly some constraints in this approach that are worth considering, if they have not already become obvious. The first we will discuss is the considerable limitations in the way that time presentation formats are denoted in this library; you assume 24-hour time, only hours and minutes displayed, yet many locales use 12-hour notation, often with a before-noon/after-noon delimiter ("4:00 pm"), and other locales include seconds as well as hours and minutes ("11:30:45"). Again, for production, shipment quality code, these variations must be accounted for and allowed.

The next set of defines in the include file denote where international locale library files (henceforth "library files") and the notational convention for naming each file, both library files and individual program message catalogs:

```
#define INT_LIBRARY       "/usr/int_lib/library/%s.db"
#define INT_DIR           "/usr/int_lib"
#define CATALOG_SUFFIX    ".cat"
```

Various systems might well place this information in different locations. For example, a Unix system might have this in the directory "/usr/int_lib", and a regular MS-DOS PC could have everything located in "C:\INTL-LIB" with different suffixes.

To allow for more readable source code, the next set of defines assigns mnemonic names to various characters and numeric values used throughout the package:

```
#define MACRO          '#'
#define COMMENT        '#'    /* in message catalogs */
#define TAB            '\t'
#define SET_MARK       '$'    /* sets in msg catalogs */
#define END_OF_DATA    '.'

#define F_EXISTS    00    /* see access() */

#define SLEN        80
```

```
#ifndef TRUE
# define TRUE          1
# define FALSE         0
#endif
```

The next routine compensates for a peculiarity of many versions of the C standard input/output library, wherein the routine *gets()* returns a line entered by the user with "carriage return" characters stripped, but the same routine reading a file—*fgets()*—includes the return, or line feed character. To make removal simple, the program includes the in-line macro function *remove_return()*:

```
#define remove_return(s) { int i = strlen(s)-1;          \
                  if (s[i] == '\n' || s[i] == '\r')      \
                  s[i] = '\0';                           \
                  }
```

With all the macro definitions done, the next section of the include file defines various data structures and then actually allocates specific variables of those types:

```
struct char_order {
      unsigned char       key;   /* the character in question  */
      int                 value; /* and it is value            */
 };

struct char_map {
      unsigned char lowercase; /* character in lowercase */
      unsigned char uppercase; /* character in uppercase */
 };

#ifdef _MAIN_
 struct char_map                     \
 transliteration_table[DEFAULT_TRANSLITERATION_TABLE_SIZE];
 struct char_order                   \
 character_ordering[DEFAULT_ORDERING_TABLE_SIZE];
#else
 extern struct char_map transliteration_table[];
 extern struct char_order character_ordering[];
#endif
```

Again, the main routine here will define "_MAIN_", allowing it to use the actual definitions, while all other files including this simply get the external definition.

External variable definitions cannot have default values specified, so the set of global identifiers used in the internationalization library perforce must have, again, two different set of definitions:

```
#ifdef _MAIN_
char *time_format                  = NULL;
char *short_currency_format        = NULL;
char *long_currency_format         = NULL;
char *standard_date_format         = NULL;
char *date_wtime_format            = NULL;
char *short_date_format            = NULL;

unsigned char radix_character = DEFAULT_RADIX;
unsigned char separator_character = DEFAULT_SEPARATOR;

char *dayname[7] = { "Sunday", "Monday", "Tuesday",
                "Wednesday", "Thursday", "Friday",
                "Saturday" };
char *monthname[12] = { "January", "February", "March", "April",
                "May", "June", "July", "August",
                "September", "October",
                "November", "December" };
#else
extern char *time_format;
extern char *short_currency_format;
extern char *long_currency_format;
extern char *standard_date_format;
extern char *date_wtime_format;
extern char *short_date_format;
extern unsigned char radix_character;
extern unsigned char separator_character;

extern char *dayname[7];
extern char *monthname[12];
#endif
```

By specifying unsigned character values for the radix_character and separator_character you can ensure that if the library information specifies, say, a character with the value 208, it does not cause difficulties (since many versions of the C standard input/output library expect 7-bit ASCII and will strip the high bit on input).

11.1.1 The Macro Preprocessor

To allow programmers more flexibility in defining and maintaining the library files, the program includes a simple macro preprocessor that is a small subset of the C macro preprocessor, allowing for the use of a single type of macro, equating a single-word mnemonic with an arbitrary set of information, as in:

#define BIGNUMBER   9944958

Macros encountered are stored in a simple linked list:

```
struct macro_entry {
            char  *name;
            char  *value;
            struct macro_entry *next;
} *macro_table = NULL;
```

where "name" is the mnemonic, and "value" is the associated value of that mnemonic.

11.1.1.1 GET_MACRO—Add Definitions to Table

The macro preprocessor has two main functions; parsing and adding new macros to the list, and then scanning arbitrary lines of text, replacing all macros with their values. This is the first of these two routines:

```
void get_macro(char *buffer)
{
    /** read a buffer in, adding it to the translation table **/

    /* format for these is '#define token<tab>other information'
      but '##' can be used to delimit a full line comment too */

    struct macro_entry *new_entry;
    char name[40], *value;
    int i = 0;

    if (buffer[1] == MACRO)     return;  /* two "#" in a row */

    while (*buffer && ! whitespace(*buffer)) buffer++;

    if (! *buffer) return;              /* no data on line: done! */

    while (*buffer && whitespace(*buffer))
     buffer++; /* skip white space */

    while (*buffer && ! whitespace(*buffer))
     name[i++] = *buffer++;
    name[i] = 0;
```

```
     while (*buffer && whitespace(*buffer))
     buffer++; /* skip white space */

     /** now let us save it all... **/

     new_entry = (struct macro_entry *)
                    malloc(sizeof(struct macro_entry *));

     new_entry->name = (char *) malloc(i);
     new_entry->value = (char *) malloc(strlen(buffer));

     strcpy(new_entry->name, name);
     strcpy(new_entry->value, buffer);
     new_entry->next = macro_table;

     macro_table = new_entry;
}
```

Rather than spend the processing time to sort the definitions alphabetically (allowing the search routine to ascertain more quickly
when a word is not a macro), this algorithm simply prepends each
entry to the front of the list, continually growing the list as needed.
In essence, the list ends up in reverse order to its ordering in the
file.

11.1.1.2 IS_A_MACRO—Look Through Table, Returning Value

A simple partner for the routine above that builds the linked list,
this routine skims through the list looking for the specified mnemonic. If found, it will return the value associated with that entry,
and if not found, it will return a NULL:

```
char *is_a_macro(char *word)
{
     /** look for word in the macro table, and if found return
       the macro value. Otherwise return NULL **/

     struct macro_entry *entry;

     entry = macro_table;

     while (entry != NULL) {
     if (strcmp(entry->name, word) == 0)
```

```
    return( (char *) entry->value );
    entry = entry->next;
    }

    return( (char *) NULL);
}
```

11.1.1.3 EXPAND_MACROS—Replace Mnemonics in String

The second of the two basic routines in the macro preprocessor, this one steps through the given string buffer checking each word to see if it is a mnemonic, and replacing any encountered with their appropriate value, as per the *is_a_macro()* subroutine:

```
void expand_macros(char *buffer)
{
    /** given the string, step through all words to see if any are
       actually macros previously defined. If they are, replace
       them with the value of that macro.
    **/

    char *ptr, *word, *value, new_buffer[512], *strtok();

    ptr = buffer;
    new_buffer[0] = '\0';

    while ((word = strtok(ptr, " \t")) != (char *) NULL) {
    if ((value = is_a_macro(word)) != NULL)
     strcat(new_buffer, value);
    else
     strcat(new_buffer, word);
    strcat(new_buffer, " ");        /* space field separators */

    ptr = (char *) NULL;
    }
    new_buffer[strlen(new_buffer)-1] = '\0'; /* rm trailing space */
    strcpy(buffer, new_buffer);
}
```

One subtle problem with this routine is that lines that may have an arbitrary number of spaces between tokens are rewritten to have only a single space between each field. While this actually eases the subsequent parsing job, it does mean that this macro preprocessor would require modification before being more generally useable.

11.1.2 Catalog Access Routines

As you will recall from the previous chapter, run-time internationalization allows each program to have a set of simple message catalogs, each of which is organized by set and messages within each
set. The set of routines which allows access to the message catalogs
is straightforward, with them all sharing a single global variable:

FILE *catalog = NULL;

which holds a pointer to the particular catalog file record that the
program is accessing.

11.1.2.1 OPEN_MESSAGE_CATALOG—Open Catalog, if Available

The first task for the catalog access routines is to be able to find and
open the message catalog itself. *open_message_catalog()* tries to open
a message catalog of the language specified for the given program,
returning TRUE if it succeeds, FALSE otherwise. The first directory
consulted is the current working directory (the first call to *access()*),
and if that fails, then the main internationalization directory is
checked:

```
int open_message_catalog(char *program, char *language)
{
    /** Look for the specified message catalog, and open it if
        possible, returning TRUE if successful. **/

    char filename[SLEN];

    sprintf(filename, "%s%s", language, CATALOG_SUFFIX);

    if (access(filename, F_EXISTS) != 0) {

        sprintf(filename, "%s/%s/%s%s", INT_DIR, program, language,
            CATALOG_SUFFIX);

        if (access(filename, F_EXISTS) != 0)
            return(FALSE);
        else if ((catalog = fopen(filename, "r")) == NULL)
            return(FALSE);
        else
            return(TRUE);                    /* opened central catalog */
    }
    else if ((catalog = fopen(filename, "r")) == NULL)
```

```
        return(FALSE);
    else
        return(TRUE);                   /* opened central catalog */
}
```

Upon receipt of a failure notice, programs are expected to output an appropriate error message rather than continue, therefore other routines that access the global "catalog" variable do not check for valid values.

11.1.2.2 GET_MSG—Extract Specified Message from Catalog

Get_msg is the heart of the entire internationalization library and scans through the message catalog looking for the specified message in the specified message set. If found, the routine not only returns the message as the return value (allowing get_msg() to be used as "printf(get_msg(1,2, NULL))") but also stores that value in the optional character buffer argument.

```
char * get_msg(int msg_set, int msg_index, char *buffer)
{
    /** Look for the specified msg_index in the specified msg_set
        and load the value into "buffer" if found. If found, the
        message is saved in buffer (if not NULL), and returned as
        the result of this system call. Failure return = NULL
    **/

    static char linebuffer[SLEN];
    char *ptr;
    int index, current_set = -1, looking = FALSE;

    rewind(catalog);

    while (fgets(linebuffer, SLEN, catalog) != NULL) {
    if (linebuffer[0] == COMMENT) continue;
    remove_return(linebuffer);

    ptr = (char *) linebuffer;      /* reset pointer */

    if (linebuffer[0] == SET_MARK) {
    if (current_set == msg_set)
     return((char *) NULL); /* cannot split sets up */
    current_set = atoi((char *) ptr + 4);
```

```
    if (current_set == msg_set) looking = TRUE;
  }
  else if (looking) {
   index = atoi(ptr);            /* ignore rest of line */
   if (index == msg_index) {
   while (*ptr != TAB && *ptr) ptr++;
   if (buffer != NULL) {
        strcpy(buffer, linebuffer);
   translate_slash_cmds(buffer, ++ptr); /* skip the TAB too */
   return((char *) buffer);
   }
   translate_slash_cmds(linebuffer, ++ptr); /* skip the TAB */
   return((char *) linebuffer);
   }
  }
 }
 return((char *) NULL);
}
```

There are some approaches to designing a message catalog that would allow faster access, notably giving each message a unique index—throwing away the entire set concept—and having the format specify two-line pairings; the unique index value on the first, and the message itself on the second. However, the improvement in performance is not sufficient to justify the additional obfuscation in the message catalog and user program.

11.1.2.3 CLOSE_MESSAGE_CATALOG—Close Catalog

A simple routine that allows the programmer to gracefully close the message catalog as they finish use of the internationalization library.

```
void close_message_catalog(void)
{
    /** close the open message catalog **/

    (void) fclose(catalog);
}
```

11.1.2.4 TRANSLATE_SLASH_CMDS—
for Backslash Sequences

One of the surprising features of the C standard input/output library is that while the *printf()* routine interprets its format string on-the-fly at run-time, the backslash sequences are actually translated into the appropriate values by the C preprocessor at compile-time. That is, when a program contains a line:

printf("hello\tthere %s\n", name);

The preprocessor rewrites it in a format similar to:

    printf("hello   there %s
", name);

which is then stored in memory during link time. The run-time interpretation of the format string then needs merely to substitute the value for each of the variables referenced.

Because of this, to allow programmers the ability to have sophisticated formats specified in the message catalogs, you must translate the backslash formats directly, and that is exactly what this routine does. It understands the following formats:

FORMAT	MEANING
\b	backspace
\f	formfeed
\n	carriage return
\r	line feed
\t	tab
\\	a backslash

Pleasantly, the routine is quite easy to understand because the switch statement used to map values exploits the preprocessor, as can be seen in the listing:

```
void translate_slash_cmds(char *target, char *source)
{
    /** Copy source to target, translating all backslash
       sequences into the actual escape sequence on the fly. **/
    int i=0, j=0;

    while (source[i] != '\0') {
    if (source[i] == '\\') {
    switch (source[++i]) {
      case 'b' : target[j++] = '\b';             break;
      case 'f' : target[j++] = '\f';             break;
      case 'n' : target[j++] = '\n';             break;
      case 'r' : target[j++] = '\r';             break;
      case 't' : target[j++] = '\t';             break;
      case '\\' : target[j++] = '\\';            break;
      default : target[j++] = '\\';
```

```
                    target[j++] = source[i];              break;
        }
        i++;            /* and skip the character */
        }
        else
         target[j++] = source[i++];
        }
        target[j] = '\0';               /* close the string */
}
```

11.1.3 Read Locale Database

The next piece of the puzzle is the set of routines that scan through
and load the international informational databases for each of the
locales. In particular, these read files like "french.db" presented earlier, storing each item of information into memory.

11.1.3.1 INTERNATIONAL_SUPPORT—Open and Read Locale

The entire set of routines to locate, open, scan, and store the information for the appropriate language is invoked by the user calling
the single routine "international_support".

```
int international_support(char *language)
{
        /** look for, open, and read in the locale-specific support data.
        Returns FALSE on error, TRUE otherwise.
        **/

        char filename[SLEN];
        FILE *fd;

        if (! *language) return(TRUE); /* no need to look */

        sprintf(filename, INT_LIBRARY, language);

        if (access(filename, 00) != 0) {
        fprintf(stderr, "No support available for language '%s'\n",
                language);
        return(FALSE);
        }

        if ((fd = fopen(filename, "r")) == NULL) {
```

```
        fprintf(stderr, "Cannot open language data for '%s'\n", language);
        return(FALSE);
    }

    /* initialize language database elements, as needed */

    transliteration_table[0].uppercase = END_OF_DATA;
    transliteration_table[0].lowercase = END_OF_DATA;

    character_ordering[0].key = END_OF_DATA;

    /* and read the information itself in to the database */

    if (read_in_data(fd) == 0) {
        fprintf(stderr,
                "Insufficient information to support language '%s'\n",
                language);
        return(FALSE);
    }

    (void) fclose(fd);
    return(TRUE);                    /* got it set up! */
}
```

The program will output error messages of its own, rather than allowing the calling program to handle all possible errors. Because there are three possible error messages, returning and having the user cope with the four different possible states (each error and a no-error state) seems overly complicated. Further, there are really a greater number of errors possible too; many of the separate routines that parse individual modules of the database files can encounter format errors, requiring meaningful error messages.

Note that since the default is U.S. English, cases where there is no language specified at all (e.g., "language" is NULL) result in a success of the routine, not failure. This is to allow the system to behave rationally in default situations, rather than leaving users with the frustration of "Language 'English' not supported" upon invocation.

11.1.3.2 READ_IN_DATA—Extract Locale Information

While the previous routine finds and opens the database file for the specific language, this routine actually scans through the individual database file, invoking the various subsidiary modules to read in specific sets of information. The format of the file itself is predicated on the same layout as other data and informational files in the package; lines beginning with "#" can be either macro definitions or, if the second character is not "d" for "define", a comment. Blank lines are ignored, and lines starting with a "$" denote the beginning of specific sections of information, as follows:

Delimiter	Meaning
$c	Currency information
$d	Date information
$f	Full day names
$m	Month names
$n	Numeric information
$s	Sorting/Collation information
$t	Time display information
$u	Upper-Lower/Transliteration

The routine only checks the first two characters to ascertain which delimiter is being used, so developers are free to actually use more mnemonic names to denote each of the different sections in the locale information database file, as can be seen in the earlier examples in this chapter.

```
int read_in_data(FILE *fd)
{
    /** Read through the language-specific data, storing it in the
       data structures as appropriate. We will read in the collation
       data, transliteration data, various notational conventions
       (including currency, numbers, date and time), and specific
       constant values (month names, day names, etc).

       If any of this information is missing from the file, we will
       flag an error and return FALSE, otherwise TRUE indicates
       that all information has been successfully read from the file.
       **/

    char buffer[SLEN];

    while (get_next_line(buffer, fd) != EOF) {

        if (buffer[0] == '$') {
            switch(buffer[1]) {
                case 'c' : currency(fd);                    break;
                case 'd' : date_format(fd);                 break;
```

```
            case 'f' : fulldaynames(fd);           break;
            case 'm' : months(fd);                 break;
            case 'n' : numbers(fd);                break;
            case 's' : sorting_data(fd);           break;
            case 't' : time_data(fd);              break;
            case 'u' : upper_lower_data(fd);       break;
        default : error(1, buffer);       break;
        }
    }
    else
    error(2, buffer);
    }
    return(1);
}
```

This routine aptly demonstrates the value of mnemonic routine naming, as well as the value of simplification through use of subroutines;
the actual lines of code above could almost be an actual presentation
of the algorithm rather than working code.

11.1.3.3 ERROR—Output Appropriate Error Message

To allow for expansion of error messages, as well as to streamline
the code and avoid significant duplication of error messages within
the program, this routine offers a simple approach to sharing a couple of common errors through the different routines.

```
void error(int num, char *arg)
{
    /** output an error and exit the program **/

    char *err;

    switch (num) {
    case 1 : err = "Unknown data section delimiter\n> %s\n"
            break;
    case 2 : err = "Unknown line in language data file\n> %s\n"
            break;
    }
    fprintf(stderr, err, arg);
    exit(1);
}
```

Since this routine will cause the entire program to quit after it has
presented the error message, these errors are known as "fatal" errors.

Both cases denote situations where the program has ended up out
of synchronization while reading the data file, and while it can
probably be recovered (skip lines until the next "$" delimited line
is found) exiting the program ensures that any problems encountered
in the datafile are promptly corrected.

11.1.3.4 GET_NEXT_LINE—Read Next Line of Data File

As already noted in the macro library definition, the *printf()* function
interprets format strings at run-time, but translation of backslash
sequences (such as "\n") are done at compile time by the C preprocessor. Therefore, to allow use of backslash sequences in the
format strings we will find in the locale information database, the
strings need to be translated by the program itself:

```
int get_next_line(char *buffer, FILE *fd)
{
    /** Get next line from the database file, expanding macros we
        encounter, as buffer. Returns EOF if hit. This routine is
        also responsible for translating backslash sequences into
        actual escape sequences.
    **/

    char our_buffer[2*SLEN];
    int i=0, j=0;

    do {
     if (fgets(buffer, SLEN, fd) != NULL) {
      remove_return(buffer);

      if (buffer[0] == MACRO)
       get_macro(buffer);
     }
     else
      return(EOF);

    } while ((strlen(buffer) == 0) || (buffer[0] == MACRO));

    expand_macros(buffer);

    /* now expand backslash characters in the string */

    strcpy(our_buffer, buffer);              /* dest = buffer */
```

```
    while (our_buffer[i] != '\0') {
    if (our_buffer[i] == '\\') {
    switch (our_buffer[++i]) {
     case 'b' : buffer[j++] = '\b;';                        break;
     case 'f' : buffer[j++] = '\f;';                        break;
     case 'r' : buffer[j++] = '\r';                         break;
     case 'n' : buffer[j++] = '\n';                         break;
     case 't' : buffer[j++] = '\t';                         break;
     case '\\' : buffer[j++] = '\\';                        break;
     default : buffer[j++] = '\\';
                       buffer[j++] = our_buffer[i];         break;
    }
    i++;             /* and skip the character */
    }
    else
     buffer[j++] = our_buffer[i++];
    }

    buffer[j] = '\0';              /* close the string */
}
```

By scanning and processing macro definition lines and comments
at this point, the developer of a locale database file is freed to have
comments and definitions absolutely anywhere in the program. If
a particular section requires two format definitions, for example, they
can appear either as:

$currency
%dFF
%d Francs

Or with significant commentary interspersed:

The currency notations, both abbreviated and full, appear here:
$currency
#define MONEY_NAME   Franc
First the shorthand notation for charts, tables, etc:
%dFF
and then the full name of the currency
%d MONEY_NAME

While you could also define a mnemonic for the "%d" integer format
string, this could backfire; the macro preprocessor requires that all
mnemonics be surrounded by spaces or tabs, so "NUMBERFF" as
a replacement for "%dFF" would fail to be correctly translated.

11.1.3.5 CURRENCY—Read Locale-Specific Currency Information

The first of a number of functions to read in a specific set of values into the program, this one reads the two currency values.

```
void currency(FILE *fd)
{
    /** get the currency presentation information for the language */
    char buffer[SLEN];

    if (get_next_line(buffer, fd) == EOF) return;
    short_currency_format = (char *) malloc(strlen(buffer)+2);
    strcpy(short_currency_format, buffer);
    if (get_next_line(buffer, fd) == EOF) return;
    long_currency_format = (char *) malloc(strlen(buffer)+2);
    strcpy(long_currency_format, buffer);
}
```

Rather than having statically allocated buffers for this type of information, the approach used is to have the character buffers dynamically allocated as each field is read and its length ascertained. In particular the *malloc()* (memory allocation) calls refer to the length of the string plus two to ensure that there's space for the string termination character and another byte as a separator (Admittedly, this is somewhat akin to the rule for making a good pot of tea; one teaspoon for each cup and "one for the pot." Well, the "+2" is one for the termination byte, and "one for the pot").

11.1.3.6 DATE_FORMAT—Locale-Specific Date Information

Recall that there is a further level of indirection in the format strings for the date; the first few characters indicate the type and order of the three items of information needed: month, day and year. To improve clarity, the macro *load_value* is defined:

```
#define load_value(item){\
        if (get_next_line(buffer, fd) += EOF)\
            return;\
        item = (char *) malloc(strlen(buffer)+2);\
            strcpy(item, buffer)\
```

Leading to the succinct routine:

```
void date_format(FILE *fd)
{
```

/** Get the date formats. The database specifies them in
standard, standard+time and short notation, with the
first few characters indicating what order month, day
and year should be presented. This information is
retained, and will have to be processed on-the-fly by
the show-date routines **/
char buffer[SLEN];

load_value(standard_date_format);
load_value(date_wtime_format);
load_value(short_date_format);
}

11.1.3.7 FULLDAYNAMES—Read Locale-Specific Day Names

While not actually used in the date format strings that the library
can currently understand and build, this is an important piece of
information needed for future expansion of the library.

void fulldaynames(FILE *fd)
{
    /** read in the seven day names from the database **/
    char buffer[SLEN];
    int i;

    for (i=0; i < 7; i++) {
    if (get_next_line(buffer, fd) == EOF) return;
    dayname[i] = (char *) malloc(strlen(buffer)+2);
    strcpy(dayname[i], buffer);
    }
}

While this routine expects to read seven separate entries (Sunday
through Saturday), if fewer are encountered because the file ends,
it will return without an error—the remaining undefined dates will
be left as their English defaults. If a new format delimiter is encountered, however, such as "$c", it will be read as one of the day
names without any error seen. Having the correct number of fields
in this module of the locale database, therefore, is essential for the
correct functioning of the program.

11.1.3.8 MONTHS—Read in Locale-Specific Month Names

Similar to day names, this routine scans in the names of each of the
twelve months of the year.

```
void months(FILE *fd)
{
    /** read in the twelve month names from the database **/
    char buffer[SLEN];
    int i;

    for (i=0; i < 12; i++) {
    if (get_next_line(buffer, fd) == EOF) return;
    monthname[i] = (char *) malloc(strlen(buffer)+2);
    strcpy(monthname[i], buffer);
    }
}
```

This implies, correctly, that calendars with other than twelve months cannot be easily handled by this routine nor, really, by the entire internationalization library. Because computers work with Western dates a change of this nature is particularly challenging and has rarely, if ever, been attempted in software.

11.1.3.9 NUMBERS—Locale-Specific Numeric Format Information

Defines radix point and separator character, if any.

```
void numbers(FILE *fd)
{
    /** read in the radix point, then the separator character **/
    char buffer[SLEN];
    if (get_next_line(buffer, fd) == EOF) return;
    radix_character = buffer[0];
    if (get_next_line(buffer, fd) == EOF) return;
    separator_character = buffer[0];
}
```

Since these are expected to be single characters, they simply store the first character of each line. Therefore, attempts to keep the locale database attractive by indenting values can have grievous consequences here, as the leading tab or space will be read and stored as the radix point and separator, rather than the character in question. Yet this is reasonable behaviour, since it allows localization experts to specify numeric formats where a separator character is not used at all.

11.1.3.10 TIME_DATA—Locale-Specific Time Presentation Format

How to present hours and minutes.

```
void time_data(FILE *fd)
{
    /** time data: format for HHMM time display **/
    char buffer[SLEN];

    if (get_next_line(buffer, fd) == EOF) return;
    time_format = (char *) malloc(strlen(buffer)+2);
    strcpy(time_format, buffer);
}
```

11.1.3.11 UPPER_LOWER_DATA—Transliteration Information

Unlike the previous functions, where the sections have a specific number of fields expected, *upper_lower_data()* and *sorting_data()* can be presented with an arbitrary amount of information for storage. As a result, the algorithm is slightly modified, and the routine will read transliteration pairs until a line is encountered with a single dot, or ".", therein.

```
void upper_lower_data(FILE *fd)
{
    /** read in the transliteration data. This will be in the
        format of uppercase <space> lowercase, with special
        characters optionally indicated by numeric values.
    **/
    char buffer[SLEN], field1[40], field2[40];
    int value1, value2, entry = 0;

    while (get_next_line(buffer, fd) != EOF) {

    sscanf(buffer, "%s %s", field1, field2);

    value1 = strlen(field1) > 1 ? atoi(field1) : field1[0];
    value2 = strlen(field2) > 1 ? atoi(field2) : field2[0];

    transliteration_table[entry].lowercase = value1;
    transliteration_table[entry++].uppercase = value2;

    if (buffer[0] == END_OF_DATA)
     return;
    }
}
```

This routine can be speeded up considerably by replacing the CPU-expensive call to *sscanf()* with a custom function written to separate the two values out, but since the database is only read once, the savings in time on most machines is not worth the effort.

11.1.3.12 SORTING_DATA—Locale Collation Information

Reading pairs of "character numeric-sorting-value" rather than transliteration data, this routine is nonetheless almost identical to *upper_lower_data()*. The greatest difference is that the second field is expected to be a numeric value.

```
void sorting_data(FILE *fd)
{
    /** read in the collation data. This will be in the format
      of character <space> numeric value, with special
      characters optionally indicated by numeric value. **/
    char buffer[SLEN], field1[40], field2[40];
    int value1, value2, entry = 0;

    while (get_next_line(buffer, fd) != EOF) {
    sscanf(buffer, "%s %s", field1, field2);
    value1 = strlen(field1) > 1 ? atoi(field1) : field1[0];
    value2 = atoi(field2);
    character_ordering[entry].key = value1;
    character_ordering[entry++].value = value2;
    if (buffer[0] == END_OF_DATA) return;
    }
}
```

Another down side with the use of *sscanf()* is that some implementations have difficulty retaining information alignment when reading numeric values. As a result, you use a two-step approach of reading both values as character strings, then using the simple C function *atoi()* to translate the value field into a numeric quantity.

11.1.4 The Internationalized Library Routines

With all these support sections written, the functions remaining are the actual routines that utilize the international locale database information.

11.1.4.1 OUR_STRNCMP—Compare Two Strings

Identical in function to the standard C *strncmp()* function, this routine compares two strings lexically, for up to "len" characters, returning -1 if the first string appears earlier than the second, 0 if they are identical, and 1 if the first string appears later.

```
int our_strncmp(char *str1, char *str2, int len)
{
    /** Given two strings, compare them (for a max of len chars,
        if specified) and return <0 if str1 < str2, =0 str1 = str2,
        or >0 if str1 > str2
    **/

    int diff;

    if (character_ordering[0].key == END_OF_DATA)
     return ( len < 0 ? strcmp(str1, str2) : strncmp(str1, str2, len) );

    if (len < 0) len = maximum(strlen(str1), strlen(str2));

    while ( len && *str1 && *str2) {
     if ((diff = (valueof(*str1) - valueof(*str2))) != 0)
      return(diff);
     str1++; str2++;
    }

    return(valueof(*str1) - valueof(*str2));
}
```

The first check is to ascertain if there is any locale-specific lexical information; if not, the built in *strncmp()* routine is used for improved performance. Unlike the standard *strncmp()* routine, this function will allow users to specify "-1" as the length, which results in the function performing identically to the *strcmp()* function.

11.1.4.2 VALUEOF—Return Numeric Value of Given Character

A low level routine for character mapping, this returns the value out of the character mapping table if present, or the straight ASCII value otherwise.

```
int valueof(unsigned char ch)
{
    /** return the value of the specified character from the
     lookup table, or, if not therein, the ASCII value. **/
    int i;

    for (i=0; character_ordering[i].key != END_OF_DATA; i++)
     if (character_ordering[i].key == ch) {
```

```
        return(character_ordering[i].value);
    }
    return( (int) ch);
}
```

11.1.4.3 ISLOWER—Return True if Given Character is Lowercase

Check the character in the character mapping table. If that is not defined, check the regular ASCII table, returning true if the character is a lowercase alphabetic character.

```
int islower(unsigned char ch)
{
        /** returns TRUE if character ch is lowercase. We note this
            when in a foreign language by checking the translation table
            for the presence of the character; if it is there, then return
            TRUE.
        **/
        int i;

        if (transliteration_table[0].uppercase == END_OF_DATA)
        return( ch >= 'a' && ch <= 'z' );
        for (i=0; transliteration_table[i].lowercase != END_OF_DATA;
                i++)
        if (transliteration_table[i].lowercase == ch)
         return(TRUE);
        return(FALSE);
}
```

11.1.4.4 ISUPPER—Return True if Given Character is Uppercase

Functionally opposite, but algorithmically identical to *islower()*.

```
int isupper(unsigned char ch)
{
        /** returns TRUE if character ch is uppercase. We note this
            when in a foreign language by checking the translation table
            for the presence of the character; if it is there, then return
            TRUE.
        **/
        int i;

        if (transliteration_table[0].uppercase == END_OF_DATA)
```

```
    return( ch >= 'A' && ch <= 'Z' );
    for (i=0; transliteration_table[i].uppercase != END_OF_DATA;
            i++)
    if (transliteration_table[i].uppercase == ch)
     return(TRUE);
    return(FALSE);
}
```

11.1.4.5 TOLOWER—Transliterate Characters to Lowercase

Similar to the existing C standard input/output library, this implementation of *tolower()* will attempt to shift whatever it receives into lowercase, even if it is not uppercase.

```
unsigned char tolower(unsigned char ch)
{
    /** translates the specified character to lowercase, by
     using the transliteration table for the specified language.
     We assume no error will be encountered, because we expect
     isupper() to have been called immediately prior.
     **/
    int i;

    for (i=0; transliteration_table[i].uppercase != END_OF_DATA;
            i++)
    if (transliteration_table[i].uppercase == ch)
     return(transliteration_table[i].lowercase);

    return( ch - 'A' + 'a' );
}
```

11.1.4.6 TOUPPER—Transliterate Characters to Uppercase

With an identical algorithm to *tolower()* this also has the same limitations.

```
unsigned char toupper(unsigned char ch)
{
    /** translates the specified character to uppercase, by
     using the transliteration table for the specified language.
     We assume no error will be encountered, because we expect
     islower() to have been called immediately prior.
     **/
```

```
    int i;

    for (i=0; transliteration_table[i].lowercase != END_OF_DATA;
            i++)
        if (transliteration_table[i].lowercase == ch)
        return(transliteration_table[i].uppercase);

    return( ch - 'a' + 'A' );
}
```

11.1.4.7 THE_DATE—Return Current Date and Time

Of the three date formats that are expected in the locale specific database information, the second, the long date and time format, is the one that will be used in this routine. This is also where the value of the prefix data sequence information will become valuable; this routine can not only work with arbitrary formats, but can work with formats that specify either month-day-year or day-month-year.

```
char *the_date(void)
{
    /** return the current date and time as a printable string **/

    struct tm *timeptr;
    long      thetime;
    static char buffer[SLEN];
    char      *format;

    time(&thetime);
    timeptr = localtime(&thetime);

    format = (strlen(date_wtime_format) ? date_wtime_format :
            DEFAULT_DATE_WTIME_FORMAT );

    /* prefixed with either mDY or DmY */

    if (strncmp(format, "mDY", 3) == 0)
        sprintf(buffer, format+4, monthname[timeptr->tm_mon],
            timeptr->tm_mday, timeptr->tm_year, t
            timeptr->tm_hour, timeptr->tm_min);
    else
        sprintf(buffer, format+4, timeptr->tm_mday,
            monthname[timeptr->tm_mon], timeptr->tm_year,
            timeptr->tm_hour, timeptr->tm_min);
```

```
    return( (char *) buffer);
}
```

A quick explanation on a particular preprocessor feature that is used extensively throughout the source code: the line:

```
format = (strlen(date_wtime_format) ? date_wtime_format :
        DEFAULT_DATE_WTIME_FORMAT );
```

exploits the inline expansion shorthand of "a ? b : c", which is identical to "if (a) then b else c", or:

```
if (strlen(date_wtime_format))
 format = date_wtime_format;
else
 format = DEFAULT_DATE_WTIME_FORMAT;
```

As is typical with programmers, we have opted for a more succinct notation than clearer code.

11.1.4.8 TRANSLATE_DATE—Map U.S. Date Notation to Locale

While it is clearly of value to be able to present information, including time and date data, in the appropriate language and notation of the specified locale, there is the question of how to store date information in multiculturally shared files. Clearly they cannot be specific to any one locale, because then the next user will not be able to successfully read it. The solution chosen is to have things in a succinct U.S. notation.

   To aid this, *translate_date()* maps a U.S. notation date, in the specific format MM/DD/YY, and returns it as the short-format date as specified in the locale information.

```
char *translate_date(char *date)
{
    /** given MM/DD/YY date, return it as; DD Mon, 19YY **/
    int     mon, day, year;
    static char buffer[SLEN];
    char    *format;

    sscanf(date, "%d/%d/%d", &mon, &day, &year);
    format = strlen(standard_date_format) ? standard_date_format :
            DEFAULT_STANDARD_DATE_FORMAT;

    if (strncmp(format, "DmY", 3) == 0)
     sprintf(buffer, format+4, day, monthname[mon-1], year);
```

```
    else if (strncmp(format, "mDY", 3) == 0)
    sprintf(buffer, format+4, monthname[mon-1], day, year);


    return( (char *) buffer);
}
```

11.1.4.9 SHORT_DATE—Current Date in Locale-Specific Notation

Similar to *the_date()*, this routine returns the current date in the abbreviated locale-specific notation.

```
char *short_date(void)
{
    /** return the current date in MM/DD/YY type format **/
    struct tm *timeptr;
    long      thetime;
    static char buffer[SLEN];
    char      *format;

    time(&thetime);
    timeptr = localtime(&thetime);

    format = (strlen(short_date_format) ? short_date_format :
             DEFAULT_SHORT_DATE_FORMAT );

    /* prefixed with either MDY or DMY */

    if (strncmp(format, "MDY", 3) == 0)
    sprintf(buffer, format + 4, timeptr->tm_mon+1,
            timeptr->tm_mday, timeptr->tm_year);
    else
    sprintf(buffer, format + 4, timeptr->tm_mday,
            timeptr->tm_mon+1, timeptr->tm_year);

    return( (char *) buffer);
}
```

Since there are no parameters to this routine, ANSI C notation requires that a "void", or "no argument", notation is used.

11.1.5 The Makefile

Notice with this Makefile the changes required to allow creation of a Turbo-C style library. The "-+" notation indicates that routines of the same name should be replaced, rather than appended, to the basic library file.

```
# Makefile for INTERNATIONALIZATION utilities library


CC=tcc
RM=rm -f
TLIB=tlib

main.exe : main.obj int_lib.lib
    $(CC) -L int_lib.lib main.obj

int_lib.lib : database.obj library.obj macros.obj catalog.obj
    $(TLIB) int_lib.lib -+database -+library -+macros -+catalog

main.obj: main.c
    $(CC) -c main.c

catalog.obj: catalog.c
    $(CC) -c catalog.c

database.obj: database.c
    $(CC) -c database.c

library.obj: library.c
    $(CC) -c library.c

macros.obj: macros.c
    $(CC) -c macros.c
```

11.2 Thoughts on the Internationalization Library

Many of the best films ever made have shocking, dramatic scenes that are so critical to the story line that all the footage leading up to that moment justifies the scene, and all the footage afterwards explains and expands the idea. In the brilliant Alfred Hitchcock film *Psycho*, for example, the murder of Janet Leigh is absolutely pivotal; the tone and theme of the film changes dramatically after that event.

In a similar manner, this chapter, and the internationalization library presented herein, are the most important element of this book from a programmer's point of view. Not only have you seen that there is a tremendous market for internationalized software, both foreign-created and foreign-targeted, but you have examined the various approaches to internationalizing (and subsequent localization) of software packages.

Finally, you have now seen in this chapter a general purpose library of routines that suggest how to modify your own programs to work with multiple languages, cultures, and locales. With the addition of the entire set of programs and support libraries on disk (see Appendix) you can then actually utilize this code to internationalize and localize whatever programs you might choose.

The rest of the book talks about what to do once you have figured out how to internationationalize, including expanding to allow multi-byte Asian, Arabic, and other non-Latin languages, discussing and comparing existing *de facto* standards for internationalization in the Unix workstation marketplace, and export restrictions and limitations.

12
Other Elements of Internationalization

For someone reading this straight through, the previous chapter probably seems the logical end for the book, the place where you have not only learned about why to internationalize, but had it demonstrated at length too. Yet as with many other things, internationalization is much more complex than it may seem. In fact, just as with the software marketing process itself, there are a considerable number of different aspects to consider here; graphics, documentation, customer support, packaging, marketing, sales and distribution. Further, we have only really explored Latin-based localization, completely ignoring the vastly greater complexities of so-called multi-byte languages, languages such as Japanese, where the application might be required to present characters from top to bottom, left to right, or Hebrew, where text is presented right to left and often without vowels included.

The reluctance to talk about this topic herein mirrors a feeling in the internationalization community on the subject; members of various standardization groups have even noted in private that they are "not particularly interested" in trying to standardize beyond the 8-bit domain. Why? Because the non-Latin language based computer market can be broken down into two significant segments; Arabic, representing not only the Arab nations, but also Israel, and the Pacific Rim, including Japan, China, Korea, and Taiwan. The former is a very small market, and a significant number of their technical people are comfortable working in English, and the latter is alien enough from Western culture that successful companies *must* be located in the Pacific Rim itself.

As a result, companies that have penetrated either market, such as Sun Microsystems (as examined in Chapter 2), have done so through foreign subsidiaries staffed by people local to that region, rather than U.S. corporate personnel. This had tended to result in these foreign versions being "a revision behind," since they receive the source code—sometimes internationalized, sometimes not—from the parent company, then are responsible for their own localization into the appropriate language and culture.

Of course, shrewd companies try to transfer the lessons learned at the foreign subsidiaries back to the parent, to tighten the iterative loop and allow for faster localization of their products (and perhaps more importantly, new products as they are introduced on the market) but that is a considerable challenge. One way of coping is through something we have already discussed; modular programming. Indeed, object-oriented programming, in particular C++, a direct outgrowth of the C programming language, offers considerable strength in this regard. In many ways, object-oriented programming, wherein data items become "objects", routines become "methods" and calls to routines become "invocations," represents the zenith of formalized modular programming paradigms.

Nevertheless, the significant point here is that being able to allow a program to be localized for very different languages is considerably more difficult than simply going from one Latin-based 8-bit language to another. And that difficulty directly begets two problems for a software vendor; time and complexity. And they both result in a higher priced product.

Ironically, foreign markets often are used to paying greater sums of money for software and hardware, so they then can make their own decisions regarding the tradeoff between a localized version of a particular product, or an imported, English-based version that is less expensive. While this feeds into an interesting marketing dilemma (do you push the imported version that seems to sell well and is "better value for the money" or do you push the localized version that is "what you'd like in a product," even though it is more expensive?) there are some other interesting results of this dilemma, notably that local vendors will then have an edge because they can design their competing product in the locale-specific version from the beginning.

Which then points to a truism for almost all products in the global market; there is always going to be a local competitor that can beat your price or more closely match the needs of the locale. The strength that global companies can offer with properly localized products are related to installed base: installed base generates user groups, which generates excellent customer feedback paths, which then allows for a much stronger product to be produced, itself creating a yet bigger market. Lotus 1-2-3 is an example of this cycle, as is Ventura Publisher, Microsoft MS-DOS, and many other products, each of which has an active user group that is not only involved in learning to use the product to its fullest potential, but in helping the company evolve the product to better fit the needs of the user community itself.

In addition, greater product revenue allows companies to invest more in research and development, which enables them to be at the forefront of breakthroughs, as has been the case with Sun Microsystems and the rapid acceptance of RISC-based computer systems in the Unix workstation marketplace.

The cost of entry into the non-Latin foreign markets is considerable, nonetheless, leading to two simultaneous observations; few U.S. software firms have direct presence in the Asian market, and, for that very reason, there is a potentially large market for companies that can offer the right product, properly localized, for that region.

The Middle East is yet another interesting situation. Considerably more politically volatile, and perhaps more xenophobic regarding U.S. residents and U.S. products, they nonetheless often have massive budgets for quick-turnaround technological improvements to their services, both within the government and for the major corporate concerns present. The 1991 destruction of Kuwait and subsequent damage to Iraq are examples of potentially lucrative new markets for properly localized software; when an information infrastructure must be rebuilt completely, firms offering the best solutions can find themselves big winners.

Localizing for these two very foreign cultures and language groups, however, can involve considerably more work than a simple translation of a message catalog.

12.1 Moving into Multi-Byte Locales

Perhaps the greatest challenge with multi-byte languages is that of input. For example, Japanese has over 50,000 glyphs in their language which not only presents a great challenge for displaying them, but the even greater challenge of how do users enter information? Clearly, a keyboard with 50,000 keys is completely unworkable, and overloading the keys—even at five different glyphs per key (shift, control, control-shift, meta, meta-shift, and so forth)—still requires a 10,000 key keyboard.

This challenge of input has been traditionally one of the greatest limitations in the spread of localized computer software into certain regions of the country. The situation affects more than just computer software nowadays too. Books published, newspapers written and distributed, and even signs printed for shops all must endure the same constraints.

The Japanese, perhaps the most Westernized of multi-byte locales, applied some ingenuity and have a couple of interesting solutions, specifying subsets of the language, a newer form of the written language, and even a version of Japanese that uses Western ASCII characters. The result is a bewildering array of different languages that can be used in Japan, often interspersed on the same page, as shown in Figure 12.1.

Among the different variations are:

Katakana—phonetic Japanese character set, consisting of 64 characters, including punctuation.

Kanji—the Japanese ideographic codeset based on Chinese characters. The set consists of roughly 50,000 glyphs. Traditional Japanese is ideogrammic, that is, each glyph conveys a meaning akin to separate words in English. A phonetic approach is closer to Latin-based languages, where each character instead conveys a specific sound, or phoneme, and combinations of characters jointly convey an idea or concept.

Hiragana—a set of phonetic symbols (or syllabary) used in Japanese in conjunction with Kanji and other character sets.

Romaji—a mapping of the Japanese sounds into a Roman alphabet.

Katakana is most often used to represent words of foreign origin in Japan; Hiragana, phonetic-based, is more often used to represent Japanese in printed media. Ultimately, many computer systems in Japan have traditionally stuck with Romaji (e.g., straight 7-bit ASCII) and Katakana, ironically making Japanese itself the alien language on the system (the exact opposite of the goal of localization). Newer systems include Hiragana, which then leads to the difficult mapping process required to accept input in the different character sets.

Setting the trend, as they did with many other aspects of the international computer market, Hewlett-Packard introduced their Native Language Input/Output system, essentially a layer between the user and the application, allowing input of complex multi-byte characters. Since then, many other vendors have offered a similar approach, which is typically:

1. User enters Romaji characters to denote word,
2. System translates it into Hiragana, phonetically,

コンピュータシステム標準の簡単な歴史

コンピュータ業界では数多くの標準が提唱されている。標準は、以下の項目の1つを実現することを目的としている。

・製品が比較検討できる
・データの相互交換性（コスト面での利益として）および移植性
・コミュニケーション機能と相互運用性

標準は次第に普及してきた。当初は、各コンピュータメーカーの製品はユニークであったため、互いに比較することができず、データの相互交換もできなかった。通信と相互運用性の実現も不可能だった。アプリケーション・プログラムはプロセッサに依存するアセンブリ言語で作成されていたが、ソフトウェアとハードウェアの相互交換性は、あるベンダーの同じ製品に関してのみ可能だった。

標準化に関しての最初の画期的な作業は、IBM360の製品ファミリで行なわれた。IBMの製品ライン全体で相互交換性が実現されたのである。そして、複数ベンダーの製品を含むより複雑な相互交換性と相互運用性の実現は、2つの両極端の分野で始まった。その2つの分野とは、集積回路の普及によるハードウェア・コンポーネントと、FORTRANのような標準のプログラミング言語インタフェースによるアプリケーション開発である。しかし、コンピュータシステム自体は、各メーカーによって付加価値をつけられ、依然として非・標準の道を歩み続けた。

実は、標準化のプロセスはコンピュータ業界が最初に始めたものではない。半導体部品の標準化は、大手ユーザーと米国政府の圧力に促された半導体メーカーが行なったのだ。また、プログラミング言語（COBOLやADAなど）の標準化は、政府の後援と業界の専門協会（ANSI、ISO、IEEE）によって進められた。OSやCPUアーキテクチャ、ネットワーキングの機器やソフトウェアなどのコンピュータベンダーによって提供される付加価値が、標準インタフェースを取り入れるようになったのは、ここ10年ほどのことなのである。　　　　　　　　―C.T.

Figure 12.1. Passage from *SunWorld Magazine* (Japan).

3. Once that is acknowledged as correct, the system finds and presents a range of different kanji glyphs, allowing the user to choose which is correct.

Not surprisingly given the complexity and steps involved here, many programmers and developers in Japan prefer to use Romaji or Katakana to interact with computer systems.

Arabic languages have intriguing variations of their own, adding still more to the complexity of multi-byte support. In particular, the characters portrayed on the screen vary not only based on which character (as would be expected), but based on what characters are adjacent to them. Arabic characters have an attribute known as "shape" which describes this variation, and each character can have up to four different shapes, denoting whether the character is first, middle, end or isolated on the line. The process of ascertaining which shape to use for Arabic characters is known as "shape determination."

One of the challenges in the entire internationalization world is to be able to not only work within a specific locale, but to allow easy interchange of information between locales. That is, if someone in the United States types in 50¢ in a document, a user in Yugoslavia should be able to have it displayed as 50¢ rather than another character, due to remapping of characters.

What this implies is that there be a single character set used for all languages throughout the world, to encompass Chinese, Arabic, Hebrew, Slavic, and more, in addition to all the Latin-based languages. This is an excellent approach to the problem, but one that is, predictably, very difficult to actually implement. The most promising effort as of this writing is the Unicode Project, sponsored by a number of corporations and initially devised by Apple and Xerox Corporation.

Joseph Becker of Xerox, a key member of the project, describes; "Unicode is a proposal for a fixed-width multi-byte multilingual character encoding. The time has come to recognize that 16 bits are necessary and sufficient to represent all of the world's normal text characters, so there needs to be a single "wide" character type representing an unambiguous assignment of multi-byte character codes. Unicode is proposed to be that encoding."

The Unicode project design is almost complete, including input from representatives of Apple, Claris, Metaphor, Microsoft, NeXT, Research Libraries Group, Sun, and Xerox. While the participation of individuals does not necessarily imply a priori endorsement by their companies, the members represent a community of engineers that have substantial experience with multilingual computer software and hardware products. Further, each company represented also has a vital interest in multilingual and international compatibility of not only computer systems but also the data itself.

The role model for Unicode is the ASCII system, and the ISO 8859-1 Latin-1 8-bit character set, with its simple unambiguous fixed-width characters. Becker computes that the world of computing now includes over 25,000 "useful" characters, and perhaps an equal number of arcane ones, necessitating an expansion of ASCII to multi-bytes; Unicode.

One of the obstacles in this effort is the anglocentric view in the United States that a step to multi-byte characters is inappropriate, and wastes too much storage space. In particular, if only 7 bits of information are required to denote all English characters, then why pay the price of an additional 9 bits for each character, doubling the size of all text storage and programs?

The answer should be obvious; as the world makes the transition from national communities and economies to global trade zones and marketplaces, countries are forced to change in order to cope. Doubling the space required for textual information seems a small price to pay for the subsequent ability to have arbitrarily mixed languages in any document. While input is still a considerable challenge, especially if users desire to switch between languages on-the-fly (mostly due to vendors offering localized keyboards for each specific language), the added capabilities are tremendous, and can go a long way towards shrinking the planet and globalizing the information infrastructure of the world.

It is ironic to note, by the way, that the English character set cannot, in fact, be conveyed in 7-bit ASCII anyway. In particular, well typeset documents will include umlauts, such as over the 'i' in the word naïve, dipthongs such as the 'æ' in dictionære, and will be able to include foreign words using the appropriate characters (such as "ñ" for Spanish, "ß" for German, and so on).

A further complication with the internationalization aspects of multi-byte languages is due to the variation in the starting and ending point of the eye on lines of information. In particular, many Arabic languages, including Hebrew, are read from the right to the left, and some Asian languages are presented in lines, being read top to bottom.

If you are working on a program that prompts users for input, for example, should the prompts be right flush, with the cursor to the left of the prompt in Arabic?

12.2 Use of Color

One of the most interesting differences found localizing software is that colors convey different meanings in different cultures. While this may seem an oddity, not particularly of interest to those inter-nationalizing software, the growth of color displays, and color usage in software, suggests otherwise.

In U.S. culture, for example, green denotes growth and nature, white denotes purity and cleanliness, black denotes death and the unknown, yellow denotes cowardice and warning, and red denotes danger. Examination of street signs demonstrates this; stop signs are red, yield signs are yellow, wedding dresses are white, and funeral wreaths are in black.

Software designers, then, might have a desire to utilize color as a way to convey information to the user with error messages appearing in red, text in white, warning messages in yellow, and so on. Indeed, many PC applications—particularly (and ironically) those from HP's PC software group—are a veritable rainbow of varied color text.

These applications, however, are more difficult to localize for other cultures than monocolor applications. For example, in most Asian cultures, red denotes happiness and good luck, hardly the right choice for an error message! Even worse, white is the color denoting death in Japanese cultures. Green isn't always the right color either; in countries possessing dense jungles green often is associated with diseases. In some African countries, red is considered blasphemous—dark red is even the color of mourning on the Ivory Coast of Africa, in fact.

The color of flowers can indicate different meanings in different cultures too; France, Britain, and the U.S. use the white lily in funerals, yet in Mexico, lilies are used to lift spells by those that are superstitious. Purple flowers symbolize death in Brazil, but yellow flowers represent death in Mexico. The same color flower, however, signifies infidelity in France and the Soviet Union.

12.3 Appropriateness of Graphics

In Chapter 1, it was noted how illustrations vary dramatically from culture to culture. In particular, we saw that the Japanese love of comics and "animé" (cartoon style graphics) results in many of their documents containing graphics that are viewed as insulting or condescending in other cultures. Just as there are differences in the use of, and appropriateness of, color, so can simple graphical elements result in the customer being offended or insulted.

In the Middle East, for example, it is considered quite rude to show another the soles of your feet, so illustrations that are acceptable in the U.S., showing an executive with their feet up on a desk, could be quite rude elsewhere in the world.

Subtle variations can cause problems too: a red circle with a slash through it is the internationally recognized symbol for "do not".

But, quickly, does the slash go from the top left to the bottom right, or the top right to the bottom left? It should go from the top left to the bottom right. Indeed, having the slash oriented incorrectly is also an international symbol: "end of".

In the same way subtle graphical elements can become obstacles in selling products. One company relates the tale of how their graphic for a canned product included a six-pointed star. It was only after putting it on the market in the Middle East that they learned it was viewed as representing Israel (the Israeli flag has a six-pointed Star of David on it) and therefore customers avoided purchasing the product. Another firm designed a graphic that contained a solid red circle on a white background. Marketing the product in Asia proved quite difficult, however, because the locals believed it was a Japanese product and therefore would not purchase it.

One undercurrent throughout the entire topic of internationalization is that people do not get along very well. Indeed, international marketing is full of xenophobic and ethnocentric tales of woe, with companies from a particular region failing in a foreign clime simply because they were not local merchants. While one certainly looks forward to the day when we are a global village, it is not here yet, so great caution must be exercised when choosing foreign partners as well as foreign markets.

12.4 Documentation

Not surprisingly, one of the most important tasks of translation, perhaps even more important than translating the software into the local language, is the correct, appropriate, and professional translation of all accompanying documentation into the local language and culture.

This is just as much a challenge for foreign companies importing products into the United States as it is for U.S. companies exporting overseas. There are, however, few simple solutions to this challenge; people fluent in the appropriate language, familiar with the local cultural mores, must be engaged to at least assist in the translation efforts.

Actually, for the last thirty years there has been significant effort underway in the computer science community, notably in the field of artificial intelligence, to create automatic language translation systems. Known now as "Computer Assisted Translation" (CAT), the latest approach has been for the system to attempt to ascertain the contextual meaning of words and sentences, then offer possible translations to the user, allowing them to choose the one that most properly reflects the meaning of the original. While likely to speed up the translation effort, the requirement for a human fluent in the target language is still of vital importance.

12.5 Customer Support

Slightly more abstract a challenge, yet one that can, again, really determine the success of a foreign venture, is ensuring that the overseas customer support is at least as good as that of the competition, if not better. Some countries, for example, require that vendors have free phone support and money back guarantees, and others allow vendors to stick with the often dubious promises made on the shrink-wrap of the product, including such popular items as billed-by-time phone support and requiring separate finite-duration support contracts.

Fundamentally, though, for almost all software, customer support is vitally important, and indeed, the frustration that customer feel when they first encounter a feature that does not work as they had anticipated represents a critical juncture in the success of the product: if the company can help them understand and succeed at their task, they are a customer for life. If, however, they have a frustrating, or worse yet, fruitless time trying to solve their problem they might well discard or return the product. Worse yet, the frustrated customers might relate their experience to others.

As a result, customer support is a critical element in the overall "software experience", what might be called the angst of the program. Indeed, in Japan, for example, customers are not only familiar with a very high level of customer support, but they are also very sensitive to improper behavior in this area.

12.6 Packaging

Just as important as customer support, packages must be appropriately packaged for the locale. Consider the aforementioned tales regarding inadvertent inclusion of taboo graphical designs in packaging; in the Middle East products did not sell because their packaging included a six-pointed star, and in the Far East, products remained unpurchased because of the presence of a solid red circle on a white background.

Just as importantly, the photographs and phrases that appear on a package must be appropriate too. A graphics program that includes an illustration of a bikini-clad woman might be successful in the United States and United Kingdom, where that type of graphic is commonplace, but that same package in the Middle East would almost cause rebellion and rioting for its flagrant violation of local cultural taboos.

A new type of packaging may include quoted passages from popular reviewers with their candid opinions on the program. This can prove a problem too; first off, it will need to be translated, with the target audience perhaps unfamiliar with the reviewers and publications, but more importantly, there might well be publications cited, from particular countries, that are inappropriate for the target locale. An example that springs to mind is that many films cite reviews in *Playboy* magazine, which would clearly be inappropriate and counterproductive in countries where that magazine is not distributed.

Additionally, packages often contain screen shots, to allow the prospective buyer to get an idea of what the package does and how it appears on the screen. While a good marketing tool, this type of packaging can be quite difficult to successfully translate, as it necessitates either the overseas group localizing the product to find a suitable professional photographer (finding a photographer familiar with the challenges of shooting a CRT screen in São Paulo can be considerably more difficult than in San Francisco).

Finally, shrink-wrap is much more common in the United States than elsewhere in the world. Nintendo game cartridges, for example, are securely shrink-wrapped before sale in the United States, with many shops refusing to accept return of a game that has been opened. In Japan, however, cartridges are never shrinkwrapped, and returning packages is accepted without difficulty. Not shrinkwrapping, of course, also allows the vendor to immediately put the product back on the shelf.

12.7 Other Factors

Just as customer support, packaging, and translation play an important role in the success or failure of a global software venture, so do other traditional aspects of marketing, including advertising, sales, and distribution. In particular, advertisements placed in magazines, newspapers, heard on the radio, and so forth, should be appropriate for that culture, and remember that billboards can be read right to left in some countries.

Further, the best product in the business, with excellent advertising and terrific customer support, can still fail if the customer cannot get it. Sales and distribution are very important, even more so in countries where software shops are uncommon.

Unfortunately, as in the domestic software marketplace, success requires much more than just a brilliant idea or sparkling piece of software. It takes packaging, documentation, marketing, sales, service, and a prompt and efficient distribution channel. And sometimes just a bit of luck.

Section Three

Existing Tools and Organizations

Comprising:

Chapter 13: Hewlett-Packard's Native Language Support System

Chapter 14: International Standards Organizations

With billions of dollars available through the international market for software and computer products, it is not surprising that quite a few vendors have put significant effort into developing flexible and powerful internationalization tools. Further, at least in the Unix marketplace, the pressure to standardize on functionality is as tremendous for this niche as elsewhere, notably with the work done by the X/Open Consortium and the UniForum Association.

In this section you will first consider the exemplary Hewlett-Packard Native Language Support (NLS) system in significant detail, then compare it with the work done by the X/Open Consortium. Finally, you will be presented a roadmap of different standards organizations, including the Institute for Electronic and Electronic Engineers (IEEE), the X/Open Consortium, and the Electronic Components and Manufacturing Association (ECMA).

13

Hewlett-Packard's Native Language Support System

Of the computer vendors in the market, none have been as aggressive in their expansion into the global marketplace as Hewlett-Packard. With solid and steady growth in their overseas market for over a decade, HP early recognized the importance of a library to aid programmers and developers in internationalizing, and later localizing, programs. Known as the Native Language Support system (NLS), it has been the basis of their multi-locale software offerings for quite a few years.

A clear inspiration for the run-time internationalization library presented in this book, NLS includes not only a set of routines to replace standard C libraries, but also a set of tools to aid in the construction and maintenance of message catalogs and locale databases. One significant difference between the design herein and that of the NLS system, however, is that NLS requires that message catalogs and locale databases be compiled into an intermediate format, to speed up access by the programs. There is an obvious tradeoff here; however the slight performance impact of having the program parse through a human-readable, commented file is negligible and the value of being able to easily modify the catalogs without having intermediate files justifies the cost. There is, of course, another reason to have message catalogs translated into an intermediate format too; security. To ensure that message catalogs are only modified by qualified NLS administrators, the company can limit distribution of the human-readable message catalogs, with customer sites receiving only the machine readable format instead. If that constraint is important, then the modifications required to expand the run-time li-

brary herein to work with a compressed or otherwise enciphered*
file should be straightforward (HP does also include a program called
"dumpmsg" which will take a compiled message catalog and rewrite
it in human readable form, decompiled).

There are two steps involved in internationalizing a program using
the NLS routines: mapping of standard routines into NLS-ized routines, and extraction and generation of message catalogs.

One feature of the NLS routines that should come as no surprise
is that they work with 8-bit, rather than 7-bit ASCII. In addition,
the NLS collation routines sort information according to the locale.

Collation also takes into account other complexities of foreign
languages, including the "ch" and "ll" characters in Spanish, the
placement of characters with diacriticals, and so on.

HP's Unix system, HP-UX, also allows locale-knowledgeable regular expressions, used as search patterns and the like. For example,
to search for the sequence of characters "bed", the regular expression
would be "bed". This will not, however, match the characters if the
"e" has a diacritical, as in "béd". To allow that, HP has—in accordance with X/Open specifications—extended regular expressions
to allow users to search ignoring diacriticals; in the previous example, the correct regular expression is "b[[=e=]]d".

13.1 Modifying Programs to Work With NLS

Many of the routines used in C programs are NLS knowledgeable
on HP systems, including all character classification and translation
routines (*islower, toupper,* and so on), many of the numeric and string
translation routines (e.g., *ecvt, atof*) and many of the structured input
and output routines (*printf, scanf*). Other routines used by the programmer must be updated to the newer, NLS-aware, system calls
as noted in Table 13.1.

While there are some utilities included with the NLS package to
ease the translation of existing programs to an NLS format, much
of the work required to use the NLS information is left to the programmer. For example, HP presents the following demonstration of

---

*An interesting internationalization note: security experts are trying to move
away from use of the word "encryption" due to international difficulties.
In particular, while in English the word refers to changing something for
security reasons, "encrypt" in French means "to put into a crypt or tomb",
rather a more negative connotation.

Table 13.1. Mapping of C Routines to HP NLS Routines.

C Version	NLS Version
ctime()	nl_cxtime()
asctime()	nl_ascxtime()
	strftime()
strcmp()	strcoll()
strncmp()	strcoll()

code that can print monetary values with the correct currency notation:

```
#include <locale.h>
struct lconv *lcs;
float number;
char *prefix, *suffix;
{
  lcs = localeconv();   /* get locale information */

/* only allow prefix notation if the numeric value is
  greater than zero and the currency symbol precedes
  the numeric quantity (as in the U.S. $5), or if
  the number is less than zero and the currency symbol
  precedes negative quantities (which isn't true in
  America: -$5 indicates negative five dollars). */

if ((number >= 0 && lcs->p_cs_precedes == '1') ||
  (number < 0 && lcs->n_cs_precedes == '1')) {
 prefix = lcs->currency_symbol;
 suffix = "";
}
else {
 prefix = "";
 suffix = lcs->currency_symbol;
}
printf("%s %6.2f %s\n", prefix, number, suffix);
}
```

This routine is clearly a small subset of the code required to work
properly with various currency notations. Indeed, the -$5 noted in
the comment cannot be properly displayed with this routine, and
would be presented as "-5 $", which is incorrect. Further, expansion
would be required to ascertain what the appropriate radix character
is (here it is left as ".", implicitly, in the *printf* format statement),
whether there is a thousands separator, and so forth.

13.2 Creating and Using a Message Catalog

HP supplies a number of useful routines to aid in the extraction of messages from existing applications. In particular the program *findstr* can be used to aid in extracting all quoted strings from program source code. The steps required to revise a program to use an NLS catalog are:

Find and extract all quoted strings (using *findstr*),
Review the list, ensuring they are all message strings,
Assign a message number to each string in the catalog, and replace
    the reference to each string in the original program with invo-
    cations of *catgets()* as appropriate (using *insertmsg*),
Add the code required to open a message catalog at the beginning
    of the program,
Generate a message catalog (using *gencat*).

While the functionality of the routines *findstr* and *insertstr* are beyond the scope of this book (though functionally equivalent programs are shown in an appendix) the result is quite similar to the library created earlier.

Individual messages are extracted from the NLS message catalog through use of the NLS *catgets()* routine, which has the following calling parameters:

catgets(catd, set, message, default_msg)

where "catd" is the catalog file descriptor returned by the catopen() routine, "set" is the numeric set identifier, "message" is the numeric message identifier, and "default_msg" is the default string that is returned if the message cannot be located.

HP recommends that when a program cannot find the message catalog, the "catd" variable be left as a NULL, with subsequent calls to "catgets()" then returning the default string value. This means that code that might have originally been written :

if (value < 0)
 printf("Error: Value less than zero!\n");

would be, post NLS translation:

if (value < 0)
 printf(catgets(catd, 1, 2, "Error: Value less than zero!\n");

which is, unfortunately, much more obscure than the original. One approach to making it more readable would be to have a separate include file that defined macros similar to:

```
#define ERROR            1
#define VAL_SUBZERO      2, "Error: Value less than zero!\n"
#define getmsg(a,b)      catgets(catd,a,b)
```

which could then be used:

```
if (value < 0)
 printf(getmsg(ERROR, VAL_SUBZERO));
```

leading to a more readable program.

A more exotic approach to this entire problem would be to have a file laid out similar to:

```
set ERROR
VAL_UNKNOWN       unknown value
VAL_SUBZERO       Error: Value less than zero!
```

Which upon being fed into a program along with a source file, would result in three new files: a default message catalog, a set of mnemonic defines shared between the catalog and source files, and an include file for the program. With the addition of a simple macro preprocessor to the catalog compilation program (*gencat*), the shared mnemonic definition file could be:

```
#define ERROR              1
#define VAL_UNKNOWN        1
#define VAL_UNKNOWN_MSG    "unknown value"
#define VAL_SUBZERO        2
#define VAL_SUBZERO_MSG    "Error: Value less than zero!"
```

the message catalog would be almost identical to the original data file format:

```
$set ERROR

VAL_UNKNOWN       unknown value
VAL_SUBZERO       Error: Value less than zero!
```

and the source code that utilized the information would be written:

```
if (value < 0)
 printf(getmsg(ERROR, VAL_SUBZERO,
      VAL_SUBZERO_MSG));
```

This would free up the programmer from having to ever deal with numeric set or message identifiers, and would also make the requirement of having default messages for when a catalog cannot be opened quite a bit simpler.

In any case, the message catalog format for an NLS program is very similar to that already presented, and is exemplified:

```
$ this is a comment introducing this set of messages
$set 1

1       unknown value
2       Error: Value less than zero!
```

For simple programs, no set specification is required; the default set for messages appearing before an explicit set definition is defined in the include file "<nl_types.h>" as the identifier NL_SETD.

A comprehensive example of the NLS message catalog feature can be seen in this translation of a basic "hello.c" program:

```
main()
{
    printf("hello world\n");
}
```

to the NLS version "nl_hello.c":

```
#include <nl_types.h>
main()
{
  nl_catd      catd;
  catd = catopen("hello", 0);
  printf(catgets(catd,NL_SETD,1,"hi world\n"));
}
```

with the message catalog "hello.msg":

```
$ sample message catalog: set is NL_SETD
1       hello world\n
```

To build this, the program would be compiled using the command:

```
cc -o nl_hello nl_hello.c
```

and the message catalog ("hello.cat") would be built with

```
gencat hello.cat hello.msg
```

NLS defaults to looking for a compiled catalog in the current directory, with the default LANG of "C"; U.S. English sans currency and thousands separator.

One subtle problem with NLS catalogs, as with any approach that has information split into multiple files, is that they can end up out of synchronization; the message catalog might be as written for version "1.2" of the program, but the application itself could be at version "1.3," possibly generating significant errors. A possible way to avoid this is to have a version number as one of the messages in the catalog, then check this value within the program to ensure that the catalog is current and correct.

13.3 Initializing the NLS Library

In addition to having the correct locale library available, and having created the appropriate message catalogs, programs that are internationalized using NLS require an initialization section:

```
#include <nl_types.h>        /* defines NLS constants */
#include <locale.h>          /* locale specific information */
nl_catd catd;                /* catalog pointer */
```

and in the program itself, near the beginning of the executable section of the program:

```
if ( ! setlocale(LC_ALL, "") ) {
 fputs("setlocale failed: continuing with \"C\" locale.", stderr);
 catd = (nl_catd) -1;
}
else
 catd = catopen (PROGRAMNAME, 0);
```

Early versions of the NLS package, amusingly enough, defined the default language of the system as "n-computer", or "native computer". Presumably, someone pointed out that assuming that the native language of computers was U.S. English was a bit too ethnocentric, hence the change to "c".

The programmer is also required to track and maintain the catalog file pointer ("nl_catd" is an "int" as used by lower level file input and output routines; it is declared in the included system file "nl_types.h") rather than simply having the library routine allocate space for an internal pointer.

Somewhat of a surprise is that the single call to *setlocale()* above not only results in it checking for a LANG environment variable, but, because of the LC_ALL argument, also checking for each of the many specific NLS variables that are possible. This means that if the user had a specification of:

LANG=english
LC_TIME=swahili
program

where they wanted to use English, but have time formats in Swahili, if available, they might well receive the error upon invoking the program:

Warning! The following language(s) are not available:
    LC_TIME=swahili
Continuing processing using the language "C".

That error message, however, is not really what you want; the text should note that LANG=english was acceptable and that the program will continue with "english," not "C" as the locale. Certainly allowing for individual portions of the locale to be specified via environment variables and then not having appropriate error messages not only confuses the user needlessly, but also limits the programmer. In particular, programmers should be able to get more meaningful results from the *setlocale()* routine, allowing code more of the nature:

if ((value = setlocale(LC_ALL, "")) != 0) {
switch (value) {
  case 1: "LC_TIME specification failed";
  case 2: "LC_MONETARY specification failed";

and so on.

13.4 Using the NLS System

Unlike the single LANG identifier used in the run-time internationalization library presented herein, NLS has a bewildering variety of different environmental options that can be specified, as shown in Table 13.2.

Why these are useful is not immediately obvious, but imagine if you are a bank in the United States and you do considerable business with a French firm. Displaying currency in a French notation might be invaluable, and would certainly make transactions easier to understand. More generally, this capability does give you the option of having a program work with an English message catalog, for example, while presenting currency and dates in a French format, and numbers in German:

LANG=english
LC_TIME=french

Table 13.2. HP NLS Environment Variables.

LANG	specifies which language/region
LANGOPTS	specifies data directionality (left-right/right-left text)
LC_COLLATE	specifies string collation
LC_CTYPE	specifies character classification and case conversion
LC_MONETARY	specifies currency symbol and monetary value format
LC_NUMERIC	specifies decimal number format
LC_TIME	specifies date and time format and the names of days and months
NLSPATH	specifies search path for message catalogs

Table 13.3. NLSPATH Notational Shorthand.

%L	replaced by the value of LANG
%N	replaced by the name of the application
%l	replaced by the language element of LANG
%t	replaced by the territory element of LANG
%c	replaced by the codeset element of LANG

LC_MONETARY=french
LC_NUMERIC=german
program

Again, if this feature were desired, the run time library presented in this book could be easily modified.

NLSPATH allows users to specify not only where to look for message catalog files, but also what type of file naming convention is used in addition. Specifically, the notations indicated in Table 13.3 are recognized.

Within the NLS environment, LANG is allowed to have various specifiers to help developers organize the international information. Rather than have "uk-english", for example, the system might specify "english.uk", leading to %l = english, and %t = uk. The path and naming convention presented earlier could be coded as:

NLSPATH=/usr/int_lib/%N/%L.cat

Indeed, the default NLSPATH for HP's Unix operating system is the complex looking path:

NLSPATH=/usr/lib/nls/%l/%t/%c/%N.cat

13.5 Helpful Hints from HP

In their excellent tutorial on the Native Language Support system, HP includes a number of helpful suggestions regarding the creation and commenting of message catalogs:

—Provide a "cookbook" for the translator which contains the numbered messages and, carefully separated, any additional explanatory information they may need. A message that is obvious to you may be a mystery to a translator. You should assume that the translator has a different native language than you, is thousands of kilometers away, and is doing the translation months or years after you have completed the program.

—All text that needs to be localized should be put in the message catalog, including prompts, help text, error messages, format strings, function key definitions, and command names. Text that is not to be translated should remain in the program so as not to confuse the translation team.

—Provide a unique, unambiguous message for each situation. A single message in your own language may appear to cover several different situations, yet when the message is translated into another language, each different situation may require a different local language translation.

—Allow for at least 60% extra space in text buffers and screen layouts to allow for text expansion when messages are translated.

13.6 Other Features of NLS

In addition to supporting the creation and manipulation of message catalogs, and supplying a library of routines that are knowledgeable of a variety of different locales, HP also includes a number of features to allow for more sophisticated internationalization of software, including:

13.6.1 Codeset Conversion

Earlier, the problems of having different character sets was considered. Specifically, should the cents character in a U.S. character set be displayed as the same character if the user were in France? Well, in situations where two different character sets, or code sets, are in use, NLS supplies a utility—*iconv*—to allow conversion in either direction. "Iconv" also can work with locally defined codesets too, as well as translating between HP defined code sets and non-HP defined codesets.

13.6.2 Processing Right to Left Languages

Another challenge that NLS assists programmers in tackling is processing languages that work right-to-left, rather than the more common Western left-to-right. For example, a file written in Hebrew and stored in that order on the disk would be impossible to sort using the *sort* program, even though *sort* can utilize the NLS language information available. Instead, the program *forder* is used to reverse the order of characters on each line:

forder data | sort | forder > data.sorted

would correctly sort the file for right-to-left languages.

13.6.3 Adding New Locales

There are various utilities available to aid in defining new locales, including *buildlang*, which can extract existing locale information as well as compile new information. For example, here is a portion of the French locale definition, obtained through use of the command "buildlang -d french":

```
###################################################
# LC_MONETARY category

LC_MONETARY
int_curr_symbol           "FRF "
currency_symbol           "FF"
mon_decimal_point         ","
mon_thousands_sep         " "
mon_grouping              "\003"
positive_sign             ""
negative_sign             "-"
int_frac_digits           "2"
frac_digits               "2"
p_cs_precedes             "0"
p_sep_by_space            "1"
n_cs_precedes             "0"
n_sep_by_space            "1"
p_sign_posn               "1"
n_sign_posn               "1"
crncystr                  "+ FF"
END_LC


###################################################
# LC_NUMERIC category

LC_NUMERIC
decimal_point ","
thousands_sep " "
```

```
grouping "\003"
alt_digit  ""
END_LC
```

```
###############################################
# LC_TIME category

LC_TIME
d_t_fmt "%A %.1d %B %Y %H:%M:%S"
d_fmt "%A %.1d %B %Y"
t_fmt "%H:%M:%S"
```

Unlike the locale definitions presented earlier, the HP NLS notation is not only more complex, but also much more difficult to understand. For example, consider the date and time format from the U.S. locale definition:

```
d_t_fmt "%a, %.1d %b, %Y %I:%M:%S %p"
```

which generates dates exemplified by:

Fri, 28 Mar, 1991 09:23:34 AM

Note the differences between this and the d_t_fmt shown in the French locale above. To change this information for another locale could be quite difficult, especially without the table of equivalences, as defined in, of all surprising places, the manual entry for the *date* command (see Table 13.4).

With added complexity, however, comes more flexibility and power. Through use of an NLS locale definition, programs can work correctly with multi-byte characters, right-to-left languages, and specific locales within a larger geopolitical area.

To get a further idea of the complexity involved with the HP Native Language Support package, consider the following fields included in their specification of currency notation:

int_curr_symbol—four character string specifying the international currency symbol; first three are alphabetic specifying the international currency symbol. The fourth is the character used to separate the currency symbol from the numeric quantity.
currency_symbol—the applicable currency symbol
mon_decimal_point—radix point for formatting monetary quantities
mon_thousands_sep—separator for grouping digits
mon_grouping—value indicating number of digits grouped together by separator in monetary quantities
positive_sign—character used to indicate positive monetary quantities

Table 13.4. Format Entries, NLS Date Specification String.

%A	full weekday name—Sunday to Saturday
%a	abbreviated weekday name—Sun to Sat
%B	full month name in locale-specific language and format
%b	abbreviated month name in locale-specific language and format
%D	date as mm/dd/yy
%d	day of month—01 to 31
%E	combined Emperor/Era year and name
%F	full month name—January to December
%H	hour—00 to 23
%h	abbreviated month—Jan to Dec
%I	meridian hour (1-12)
%j	day of year—001 to 366
%M	minute—00 to 59
%m	month of year—01 to 12
%N	Emperor/Era name
%n	insert a new-line character
%o	Emperor/Era year
%p	local equivalent of AM/PM
%r	time in hh:mm:ss AM/PM notation
%S	second—00 to 59
%T	time as HH:MM:SS
%t	insert a tab character
%w	day of week—Sunday = 0
%y	last 2 digits of year—00 to 99
%z	time zone name from TZ variable in user's environment

negative_sign—character used for negative monetary quantities

int_frac_digits—number of fractional digits for internationally formatted quantity

frac_digits—number of fractional digits for locally formatted monetary quantity

p_cs_precedes—specifies if currency symbol precedes or follows a non-negative formatted quantity: 1=precedes

n_sep_by_space—specifies if currency symbol is separated by a space from a non-negative formatted value: 1=yes

p_sign_posn—indicates position of positive sign for non-negative monetary quantity as follows:

   0   parentheses surround quantity and currency symbol
   1   sign string precedes quantity & currency symbol
   2   sign succeeds quantity & currency symbol
   3   sign immediately precedes currency symbol
   4   sign immediately succeeds currency symbol

n_sign_posn—position of negative sign; specified in notation identical to p_sign_posn

crncystr—symbol for currency, preceded by:

- if it precedes monetary value
+ if it follows the monetary value
. if it replaces the radix symbol

Clearly, the currency notation introduced earlier in the book for your own internationalization library covers only a subset of the variations needed to support all the different notations used throughout the world. Before you leave this, a quick look at the LC_MONETARY category definition for U.S. English:

```
# LC_MONETARY CATEGORY
LC_MONETARY
int_curr_symbol                         "USD "
currency_symbol                         "$"
mon_decimal_point                       "."
mon_thousands_sep                       ","
mon_grouping                            \003
positive_sign                           ""
negative_sign                           "-"
int_frac_digits                         "2"
frac_digits                             "2"
p_cs_precedes                           "1"
p_sep_by_space                          "0"
n_cs_precedes                           "1"
n_sep_by_space                          "0"
p_sign_posn                             "1"
n_sign_posn                             "1"
crncystr                                "-US$"
END_LC
```

13.7 Supported Languages and Locales

The HP Native Language Support system currently includes support for almost fifty different locales, including Arabic, Western Arabic, Hebrew, Chinese, Czechoslovakian, Finnish, Hungarian, Icelandic, Japanese (and Katakana), Korean, Norwegian, Polish, Rumanian, Russian, Serbo-Coatian, Thai, and Turkish.

To aid customers in using NLS and with the localization process overall, HP currently also has over 20 different Localization Centers, including in Amsterdam, Athens, Beijing, Geneva, Helsinki, Madrid, Mexico City, Milan, Reykjavik, Seoul, Stockholm, Taipei and Tokyo.

In addition, as will be obvious when the X/Open standard for internationalization is considered, NLS has proven an important contribution to the state of the art in internationalization.

13.8 Thoughts on HP's NLS

The history of internationalization is rather surprisingly brief, with much of the significant foundation laid by the Xerox Palo Alto Research Center, then HP expanding upon it with the Native Language Support System. Since then, a variety of different companies have expanded the concepts, including most notably the X/Open Corporation, a consortium examined further in the following chapter. Fundamentally, however, NLS remains the best, de-facto standard approach for internationalization.

And therein lies its greatest problem; succinctly, HP retains the legal rights to the NLS system, including ownership of the code, the programming library, and the design. Although they are members of X/Open, and have had a significant impact on the design of the X/Open Portability Guide section on internationalization, HP has kept NLS as a proprietary package. Clearly, there are some significant ramifications on global competitiveness, one of the basic themes of this book, since the line between competitive advantage and hoarding vital technology can be rather a fine one. Nonetheless, by keeping NLS proprietary, HP has not only limited the growth of the package—since NLS becoming a genuine standard would help the industry as a whole—but of the industry itself, for the same reasons.

Licensing NLS in a manner similar to how Sun Microsystems created, then licensed and "standardized" their Network File System, would be a tremendous boon to the international community, as well as Hewlett-Packard. Or, better yet, simply offering the entire package, including source code, to a neutral third party organization or consortium could speed up evolution of the niche dramatically.

Indeed, in this age of revolutionary changes and improvements in almost all aspects of software design, from the editor used to write the program, to the language the program is written in, to the interface tools available to help design and implement powerful and friendly interfaces, it is shocking just how primitive all the internationalization and localization tools remain. Even on the Apple Macintosh, with its state-of-the-art graphical interface, programmers who want to internationalize their applications must do so from within a difficult-to-use "resource editor," modifying cryptic snippets of their program and hoping things work correctly.

There are no easy solutions to the challenges of creating global software, but having the community working on, and evolving, existing systems could go a long way to starting that change. And that would be a plus for everyone, including programmers and users.

14

International Standards
Organizations

Much of the original work in the area of internationalization was done by Xerox Corporation, notably in their Palo Alto Research Center in California. With that as an inspiration, HP developed their Native Language Support system, as shown in the previous chapter. With those graphic examples showing not only the feasibility of internationalizing software, but the tremendous advantage of doing so, many other companies took the idea and expanded upon it themselves. Notable in this list are three of the biggest minicomputer vendors in the computer industry; AT&T, Digital and IBM.

AT&T took many of the ideas inherent in NLS, pushed further in the direction of supporting multiple languages at once, arriving at their MultiNational Language Support system, or MNLS. IBM created a system of their own too, as did Digital. With the influence of the X/Open standards organization however, the ultimate result was that the various internationalization systems look startlingly similar. Compare the following code example from an IBM document to the previous NLS example, and the run-time internationalization library implementation of a localized "hello world" program:

"First you define a header file to initialize file names referring to a message catalog:

CatalogSetup.h
.
#define catname   "hello.cat"
.

Then you include the header file in whatever program needs it, and
use a variable "catname" instead of the literal "Hello World":

```
#include <CatalogSetup.h>          /* include header file */
#include <nl_types.h>              /* typedefs, etc   */
#include "locale.h"                /* local declarations */
main()
{
nl_catd cd;          /* catalog descriptor   */
cd = catopen(catname)      /* use variable, not literal */
printf("%s", catgets(cd,set_id01, msg_id01,"")); /* ptrs */
catclose(cd);
}
```

IBM National Language Design Guide, Volume 1

Rather than being surprising that the IBM and HP examples are so
similar, it is instead not only unsurprising, but quite a positive sign,
one that bodes very well for future computer users. Indeed, IBM,
DEC, AT&T and HP are all members of the X/Open Company, the
consortium most responsible for the standardization of international
libraries and utilities.

14.1 The X/Open Company

With the goal of encouraging application portability across different
operating systems and different platforms, X/Open has been defining a Common Application Environment (CAE), which is built on
the IEEE Posix standard, and covers areas required for a comprehensive applications interface.

The key document from X/Open is the Portability Guide (XPG),
which contains an evolving set of practical standards ensuring application portability. A seven part document published internationally by Prentice-Hall, it is comprised of:

Vol 1: XSI Commands and Utilities
Vol 2: XSI System Interface and Headers
Vol 3: XSI Supplementary Definitions
Vol 4: Programming Languages
Vol 5: Data Management
Vol 6: Window Management
Vol 7: Networking Services

Similar to many other standards efforts, XPG promises a more
varied selection of applications, growing portability for each application, independence from a single source, international support for

the CAE, and, as a result, better investment security for software purchases. A subtle point regarding X/Open is that it is not a standards organization, per se, but rather a joint initiative by the various member organizations to define and integrate evolving standards into a common, beneficial and continuing strategy.

Before considering the XPG internationalization system, a quick digression to define some of the other standards organizations and their relationships is in order.

14.2 ISO

The International Organization for Standardization is a predominantly European consortium devising various standards to allow for easier interchange of data between member countries. In particular, the ISO standards have successfully pushed beyond many of the original 7- and 8-bit ASCII limitations in high speed networking (notably the TCP/IP protocol) with the X.25 public network definition. In the same way, the organization has defined and implemented software that extends file transfer (with "FTAM"), electronic mail (with X.400), and distributed resource identification access (X.500). One significant difference between ISO and most of the other standards organizations is that ISO members represent their countries, rather than their companies. When votes are tallied, each country gets one vote.

ISO has also defined the widely accepted 8-bit character set table, allowing for all European languages to be included: ISO 8859-1.

Working at a relatively low level, most ISO standards have defined specific data formats, such as character sets, network packets, and so on. Little of their work directly addresses programmatic software internationalization, and they have a clear focus on telecommunications.

14.3 ANSI

The American National Standards Institute is a national standards body, with many groups working on standardization of all types. ANSI membership is open to any company or organization in the United States, with each member allowed one vote. ANSI is involved in a tremendous number of different standardization efforts, including standardization of all the various computer programming languages (notably X3J11, the C Programming Language). Indeed, the C examples presented in this book are all ANSI C rather than

Table 14.1. 8-Bit Section of ISO 8859-1 Character Set.*

0	nul	1	soh	2	stx	3	etx
4	eot	5	enq	6	ack	7	bel
8	bs	9	ht	10	nl	11	vt
12	np	13	cr	14	so	15	si
16	dle	17	dc1	18	dc2	19	dc3
20	dc4	21	nak	22	syn	23	etb
24	can	25	em	26	sub	27	esc
28	fs	29	gs	30	rs	31	us
32	sp	33	!	34	"	35	#
36	$	37	%	38	&	39	'
40	(	41	)	42	*	43	+
44	,	45	-	46	.	47	/
48	0	49	1	50	2	51	3
52	4	53	5	54	6	55	7
56	8	57	9	58	:	59	;
60	<	61	=	62	>	63	?
64	@	65	A	66	B	67	C
68	D	69	E	70	F	71	G
72	H	73	I	74	J	75	K
76	L	77	M	78	N	79	O
80	P	81	Q	82	R	83	S
84	T	85	U	86	V	87	W
88	X	89	Y	90	Z	91	[
92	\	93	]	94	^	95	_
96	`	97	a	98	b	99	c
100	d	101	e	102	f	103	g
104	h	105	i	106	j	107	k
108	l	109	m	110	n	111	o
112	p	113	q	114	r	115	s
116	t	117	u	118	v	119	w
120	x	121	y	122	z	123	{
124	|	125	}	126	~	127	del

. . .

160		161	À	162	Â	163	È
164	Ê	165	Ë	166	Î	167	Ï
168	´	169	`	170	^	171	¨
172	~	173	Ù	174	Û	175	£
176	‾	177	Y	178	y	179	°
180	Ç	181	ç	182	Ñ	183	ñ
184	¡	185	¿	186		187	£
188	¥	189	§	190	f	191	¢
192	â	193	ê	194	ô	195	û
196	á	197	é	198	ó	199	ú
200	à	201	è	202	ò	203	ù
204	ä	205	ë	206	ö	207	ü
208	Å	209	î	210	Ø	211	Æ
212	å	213	í	214	ø	215	æ

Continued

Table 14.1. 8-Bit Section of ISO 8859-1 Character Set.* (Continued)

216 Ä	217 ì	218 Ö	219 Ü
220 É	221 ï	222 ß	223 Ô
224 Á	225 Ã	226 ã	227 Ð
228 đ	229 Í	230 Î	231 Ó
232 Ò	233 Õ	234 õ	235 Š
236 š	237 Ú	238 Ÿ	239 ÿ
240 Φ	241 φ	242 •	243 μ
244	245 ¾	246 _	247 ¼
248 ½	249 ª	250 °	251 «
252 •	253 »	254 ±	255

*Slots 128 through 160 are not used in the ISO definition.

the original C language as defined by Brian Kernighan and Dennis Ritchie.

14.4 NIST

The National Institute of Science and Technology, formerly the National Bureau of Standards, is a member of ANSI and essentially represents the United States Government. In addition, NIST legislates to the government what standards will be required for software and hardware purchasing.

14.5 IEEE

The Institute of Electrical and Electronic Engineers has traditionally been involved in hardware standardization. In the past few years, however, the organization has undergone a distinct transition, becoming considerably more software oriented. One result is that the premier programmatic interface definition and standardization work ongoing in the global computer industry is a part of the IEEE standardization group: Posix, the Portable Operating System Interface for Unix.

Spanning more than just Unix systems, Posix compliance has been announced by a number of vendors for completely different operating systems, notably Digital's VMS, HP's MPE and Unisys' CTOS proprietary operating system environments. In combination with the X/Open Common Application Environment, Posix will likely prove a critical foundation for the entire computer industry for the next generation.

14.6 ECMA

The European Computer Manufacturers' Association is dedicated to standardization of hardware-oriented facets of computers, with significant overlap with the ANSI on such items as the physical characteristics of floppy disks and cartridge tape systems, as well as sizes and acceptable thicknesses for printer paper.

14.7 Unicode

Initially devised by Apple Computer and Xerox Corporation, the Unicode project includes a number of smaller vendors, notably Claris, Microsoft, NeXT, Metaphor and Sun Microsystems. The project goal is to define an acceptable multi-byte standard character set for the international community, including Pacific Rim countries. The model is the ISO 8859-1 Latin-1 character set, which has become the standard 8-bit character set for the Western world. While there are far too many entries in the current draft standard to include a comprehensive listing, the following tables give an idea of what type of information is being included in the new standard.

Table 14.2. Basic layout of Unicode.

Address	What zone contains
0000	alphabets
	space for archaic writing systems
2000	symbols
3000	CJK phonetics, symbols and syllabaries
4000	CJK ideographs
	unified Han character set subsuming all characters from the national standards for Japan, Korea, China and Taiwan
F000	user space
FE00	compatibility zone

Table 14.3. East Asian Standard Characterset Sizes, Unicode.

Country	Standard	Year	Characters
China	GB 2312	1980	6,763
Japan	JIS X0208	1983	6,349
Korea	KS C5601	1987	4,888
Taiwan	CNS 11643	1986	13,051
	Total		31,051

Table 14.4. Blocks of Space for Specific Scripts, Unicode.

Script	Slots	Used in
Greek	144	Greece, etc.
Cyrillic	256	Russia, etc.
Armenian	96	Armenian SSR
Hebrew	112	Israel, etc.
Arabic	256	Mideast, etc.
Ethiopian	512	Ethiopia
Devanagari	128	Northern India, Nepal
Bengali	128	West Bengal, Assam, Bangladesh
Gurmukhi	128	Punjab (India), Pakistan
Gujarati	128	Gujarat (W India)
Oriya	128	Orissa (E India)
Tamil	128	Sri Lanka, Tamil Nadu (SE India)
Teugu	128	Southern India
Kannada	128	Karnataka (S India)
Malayalam	128	Kerala (SW India)
Sinhalese	128	Sri Lanka
Thai	128	Thailand
Lao	128	Laos
Burmese	128	Burma
Khmer	128	Cambodia
Tibetan	96	Tibet
Mongolian	64	Mongolian SSR
Georgian	96	Georgian SSR

14.8 The Uniforum Association

The International Association of Unix Users, the UniForum Association was one of the first user groups to become interested in internationalization. Since then, it has worked closely with the Posix committees and the X/Open Company on developing standards that are workable in the everyday computing environment.

14.9 The X/Open Portability Guide

As described earlier, the XPG is based on work done by the Posix group, as well as the ANSI C specification and other standards as appropriate. XPG describes a considerable body of software library functions, essentially a complete operating system interface. The particular library we are interested in, however, is the X/Open Native Language System (also called NLS), which specifies a standard interface for the following facilities: message catalogs, a so-called announcement feature (the "LANG" environment variable and its brethren as explained in the chapter on HP NLS), internationalized

C library functions, additional functions allowing the programmer to determine culture and language, as well as information relating to a given locale, and a library of regular expression routines.

XPG3, the third and most recent revision of the XPG, specifies that the character set used be ISO 8859-1 for compatibility purposes. Ensuring compliance with the new ANSI C standard (X3J11), the XPG3 specifies a number of ANSI compatible functions.

A few of these, notably the *printf()* family, have been further extended by the X/Open group, in ways compatible with the original definition by the ANSI standardization group. XPG3 also defines a number of other routines to aid in regular expression parsing, message catalog interaction, and similar activities.

Within XPG3, locales are defined, via the LANG environment variable, as having three possible parts: language, territory, and an explicit codeset. For example, the default is "LANG=C.8859", specifying the language and the ISO 8859-1 codeset. A language with significant regional variation, French, as used in Switzerland, could be denoted with the ISO 6937 codeset as "LANG=french_ch.6937". When the locale is defined within the program using *setlocale()*, the

Table 14.5. ANSI Compatible Functions in XPG3.

atof()	fprintf()
	fscanf()
	isalnum()
isalpha()	isgraph()
	islower()
	isprint()
ispunct()	isspace()
	isupper()
	printf()
scanf()	setlocale()
	sprintf()
	sscanf()
strcoll()	strerror()
	strftime()
	strtod()
strxfrm()	tolower()
	toupper()

Table 14.6. Additional Functions Available within XPG3.

catclose()	catgets()	catopen()
nl_langinfo()	perror()	regexp()
vfprintf()	vprintf()	vsprintf()

possible categories defined are LC_ALL, LC_CTYPE, LC_COLLATE, LC_TIME, LC_NUMERIC, and LC_MONETARY, with identical meaning to HP NLS.

Message catalogs within XPG3 have a new feature added to the now standard "$set", "$" message prefix, and numerically prefixed message text. The new feature is a "$delset" instruction, which allows specific message sets to be deleted from an existing message catalog. To allow for clearer spacing in individual messages, the XPG3 specification includes the NLS "$quote" feature, allowing catalogs similar to:

```
$ sample XPG3 compatible message catalog
$set 1
$quote "
1      " message, quotes will be removed"
```

In addition, messages can have a variety of different escape sequences, including "\n", "\t", "\f", "\b" as well as the less common "\v" vertical tab, and "\ddd", where specific octal characters can be defined (e.g., to get decimal character 214, it would have to be recast as the octal, or base-8, number 326, then included in the message as "\326"). Another useful extension is that having a slash as the last character of a line denotes continuation onto the next line, as in:

```
$ sample XPG3 compatible message catalog
$set 2
13      This is message thirteen and continues \
onto the next line for ease of formatting.
```

Once the message catalog is properly written, it is compiled into an intermediate format using *gencat*, as if it were within the HP NLS system.

Accessing the XPG3 message catalog is almost identical to what has already been shown—this example is another visitation to the oft-used "hello world" program:

```
#include <stdio.h>
#include <nl_types.h>
#define NL_SETN            1
#define HELLO_MSG          1
main()
{
 nl_catd catd = catopen("prog", 0);
```

```
printf("%s\n", catgets(catd, NL_SETN, HELLO_MSG,
    "hello world"));
catclose(catd);
}
```

The most significant change is that the "catd" identifier is defined and initialized as a single statement ("nl_catd catd = catopen(. . .").

The XPG3 interface also expands greatly upon the definition of regular expressions, adding many features to allow them to be used for other languages and locales. Regular expressions are used in a surprising number of different commands, especially within the context of the Unix operating system. XPG3 notes two different type of regular expressions: simple, and extended, and expands upon these to create a list of commands that are required to support internationalized regular expressions for X/Open endorsement.

14.10 Thoughts on Internationalization Standards

In general, the use of the word "standardization" is rather curious in this context. As Scott McNealey, Chief Executive Officer of Sun Microsystems, is fond of pointing out, standards arise from common usage and best applicability to the specific problem domain. Yet many of these groups, especially Unicode, seek to define a standard without any iterative field experience. They bring their collective experiences to the negotiating table, of course, but it is difficult to ascertain whether something can be successful without use.

The ISO standards are another example of this quirky approach to standardization; with the membership reflecting a wide variety of European and international corporations, ISO standards are defined over years of negotiation with many draft versions sent out for formal review, then, once they are agreed upon, are essentially cast in stone. The problem is, it is at that point that companies put any serious effort into implementing the standards (and often find just how poorly thought out they are) from an implementation standpoint. As an example of this, the ISO X.400 standard for message handling systems allows transfer of arbitrarily complex electronic mail messages—including voice, multiple languages, graphics, and more—across compliant networks. Unfortunately, when companies tried to implement the original, 1984 standard, it proved to be too ambiguous, had nonsensical information, and even had conflicting specifications. The end result was that it was years before reliable implementations were available, and those didn't interact gracefully, although that was the entire goal of the X.400 standard in the first place. In 1988 ISO issued a considerably revised standard for message handling systems.

The evolution of the global computer software market has happened at a sufficiently reasonable pace that this type of frantic premature standardization has not occurred. Indeed, the growth has been a terrific example of market evolution: originally each country had their own completely proprietary systems, with little interest in global interaction. Gradually business travellers found appealing applications overseas and brought them into the local market, encouraging standardization of hardware. At the same time, the software was still limited to those that spoke the foreign language required. Finally, some firms began to offer localized versions of their products, with that gradually becoming the vehicle of choice for breaking into the international marketplace. The dichotomy between exports and overseas sales for Microsoft Corporation in the last five years, as shown in Chapter 2, is an example of how this process gradually bears fruit.

In parallel to this global software evolution, approaches to the internationalization of software have grown too. There has been an evolution from ad hoc compile time modifications by overseas programmers to vendor-specific solutions using vendor-specific character sets, to vendor-specific programming libraries utilizing standard character set definitions to standard libraries using standard character sets.

Undoubtedly the wave of the future is going to be software development environments where all library routines will be able to work with international data—perhaps transparently—and the tools for extracting message catalogs (indeed the entire message catalog paradigm) will have evolved to a more sophisticated level. At that point the global software market will have become a reality, and vendors developing applications anywhere in the world will be able to offer their wares in any other part of the world without any software modifications at all.

Section Four
The Politics of Global Software

Comprising:

Chapter 15: The Politics of Global Software

Chapter 16: The Future of Global Software

Selling a product overseas involves more than having it work in the correct language and properly translated documentation. It requires a fundamental understanding of the foreign culture. More, it requires an understanding of the United States Government, and its criteria for what can be legally exported.

In this final section, we will look at the complex U.S. export restrictions on encipherment code, as well as other types of software and hardware restrictions. With the Global Agreement on Trades and Tariffs (GATT), as well as the Coordinating Committee for Multilateral Export Controls (COCOM), many of the restrictions we will examine are true for multiple nations, including the entire European Community.

Following that discussion, a step back to look at the future of the global software market; what is it going to be like? What countries are really going to be the most likely for significant growth in the next few years? How to keep track of the market, and where to go from here?

15
The Politics of Global Software

Up to this point, we have been discussing the value and importance of the global software marketplace, without any consideration of the political and socio-economic constraints involved. While there is significant movement towards internationalizing economies, and the commensurate lessening of nationalistic protectionist policies and attitudes, there is still a distance to travel before open free market economies function on a global scale.

Balancing ideas of a global economy and global marketplace are protectionist attitudes of various countries, where they shun foreign imports in favor of (often more expensive and lower quality) domestic products. Indeed, it is the rare country that is willing to trade with foreign manufacturers without checks and balances. To achieve this control over import and export, governments utilize two primary tools: quotas and tariffs.

Quotas define what quantity of a commodity is legally allowed to be imported or exported, both for an individual supplier and for the market overall. *Tariffs* are taxes levied on the manufacturer both as a revenue generator and also as a way to balance foreign and domestic prices. In particular, tariffs are most often placed on imports to ensure that foreign products are not "dumped" into the domestic market at unreasonably cheap prices.

Actually, the world of international marketing is full of stories about protectionist attitudes, purely political and often completely inappropriate quotas, and ridiculous tariffs. Often, too, this is a response to the relatively recent business tactic of dumping, or deliberately underpricing a commodity in a foreign market, to undercut domestic manufacturers. Within the high technology niche, U.S. vendors have more than once accused Japanese firms of offering integrated circuits (e.g., memory chips) in the United States at below production cost, the sole purpose being to prevent the domestic firms from competing effectively. The result? Quotas on products, sanctions on trading that type of product, and tariffs imposed to ensure that the imported products are priced acceptably.

Another tool used by countries to monitor imports and exports is the "balance of trade", where governments try to ensure that as they open their borders to foreign competitors, the foreign competitors also open their borders to domestically produced commodities. Imbalance of trade is one of the most common sources of arguments in the international market, and resolving imbalances is one of the primary responsibilities of the ongoing Global Agreement on Trade and Tariff (GATT).

GATT is one of the primary governing bodies in this international chess game, where almost all the Western nations agree upon rational import and export policy for all manner of commodity, from wheat and grain to supercomputers and airplanes. While GATT seeks to define a well-balanced global marketplace, specific disputes between member nations are almost always resolved by the individual nations. For example, the U.S. Congress and the Japanese DIET (their congressional body) have held extensive investigations on whether the Japanese were dumping IC's into the U.S. market inappropriately or whether the U.S. manufacturers were simply unable to compete effectively.

Clearly, then, there is more to global software marketing than simply having the program work in the local language. This has only scratched the surface of what is involved with international trade, and indeed the bulk of the restrictions and limitations on computer-related products are regarding export limitations rather than import restrictions overseas.

In particular, a primary responsibility of the U.S. Government is monitoring, authorizing, and endorsing exports from U.S. companies to the rest of the world, whether a free trading partner nation or a hostile super power. In addition to the national agencies such as those in the U.S. Government, there are also international organizations with shared responsibilities for all Western nations, most notable being the Coordinating Committee for Multilateral Export Controls (COCOM), which reviews export license applications for strategic commodities from member nations: Australia, Belgium, Canada, Luxembourg, the Netherlands, Norway, Denmark, France, Germany, United Kingdom, USA, Portugal, Spain, Turkey, Greece,

Italy, and Japan. Additionally, five other countries have been granted preferential licensing benefits with the United States due to their implementing some, or all aspects of COCOM-comparable export controls: Austria, Finland, Singapore, Sweden and Switzerland.

Strategic commodities include supercomputers and encipherment* implementations, among other items, so they are of great interest to many software vendors. In fact, relevance can creep in from the most surprising of places; imagine your firm has written a document retrieval system and wants to position it as useful for personal information as well as corporate documents. To do so, you include a sophisticated compression and encipherment routine, which allows users to have completely secure document storage on shared file servers, with only them being allowed access.

That seemingly innocuous technology will have to be reviewed by, minimally, the U.S. Department of State, Office of Defense Trade Controls (DTC). In addition, the Department of Commerce, Bureau of Export Administration (BXA), would serve as an overseeing office, and the U.S. National Security Agency (NSA) might be utilized to assist in evaluating the encipherment technology.

While there are a number of different software categories that are trade restricted, the primary restricted packages are those that include encipherment features, notably the Data Encryption Standard (DES) algorithms. Before you consider this, you will need to spend more time examining U.S. Export Controls; other countries have similar controls and constraints.

Note: *This data is included for information purposes only. You must rely on official government information to ascertain whether your products require export licenses, and how to obtain them.*

15.1 U.S. Export Controls

Within the United States Government, the Department of Commerce has been given statutory authority over export administration by a number of important legislative proclamations: Trading with the Enemy Act of 1917 (TWEA), the International Emergency Economic Powers Act of 1977 (IEEPA), the Comprehensive Anti-Apartheid Act of 1986 (CAAA) and the International Security and Development Cooperation Act of 1985 (ISDCA).

In addition, there are many exports that are not controlled by the

---

*As noted earlier, "encipherment" is used rather than "encryption" whenever possible, in recognition of the negative connotation of the word "encrypt" in French. Remember: think globally.

Department of Commerce. The Department of State, Office of Defense Trade Controls, monitors the export of arms, ammunitions, and implements of war and related technical data on the U.S. Munitions List. The Department of Justice, Drug Enforcement Administration, controls exports of certain narcotics and dangerous drugs, and the U.S. Maritime Administration has licensing responsibility over export of certain watercraft. The Department of Energy controls exports of natural gas and electrical power to foreign nations, the Department of Agriculture monitors export of any tobacco seed and live tobacco plants, and the Department of the Interior is empowered to control exports of endangered fish and wildlife, migratory birds, and bald and golden eagles.

Finally, the U.S. Patent and Trademark Office, a storehouse of vital national and industrial information, controls licensing exports of unclassified technical data contained in patent applications, and The Department of the Treasury, Office of Foreign Assets Control (OFAC), controls certain business dealings involving U.S. persons and embargoed countries, and all exports to S-Category controlled export countries.

Further, export controlled countries are divided into a multi-tiered export control country group list, as shown in Table 15.1.

Canada is not included in any country group as the United States

Table 15.1. U.S. Export Control country list.*

Q	Romania
S	Libya
T	*North America:* Greenland, Miquelon and St. Pierre Islands, Mexico (including Cozumel and Revilla Gigedo Islands)
	Central America and Carribean: Bahamas, Barbados, Belize, Bermuda, Costa Rica, Dominican Republic, El Salvador, French West Indies, Guatemala, Haiti, Honduras (including Bahia and Swan Islands), Jamaica, Leeward and Windward Islands, Netherlands Antilles, Nicaragua, Panama, Trinidad and Tobago.
	South America: Argentina, Bolivia, Brazil, Chile, Colombia, Ecuador (including the Galapagos Islands), Falkland Islands, French Guiana, Guyana, Paraguay, Peru, Surinam, Uruguay, Venezuela.
V	All countries not included in any other group
W	Hungary, Poland
Y	Albania, Bulgaria, Czechoslovakia, Estonia, Laos, Latvia, Lithuania, Mongolian People's Republic, the USSR.
Z	Cambodia, Cuba, North Korea, Vietnam.

*While every effort has been made to ensure this information is up-to-date, these are fluid and volatile lists. As with other information presented in this chapter, you should check with the appropriate government agencies before making any import, export, or market targeting decisions.

has a special import and export agreement with the Canadian government. For countries with unrestricted export agreements, the only export licenses required are for: commodities or technical data in transit through the country or is intended for re-export from that country; when a U.S. Commodity Control List (CCL) entry states specifically that a license is required; for technical data related to nuclear weapons development and certain sensitive nuclear uses. Countries in this category include Canada, Puerto Rico, the Commonwealth of the Northern Mariana Islands, any territory, dependency or possession of the United States, and the Trust Territory of the Pacific Islands (i.e. Palau).

There are three different types of exports that the government controls: *direct exports* from the U.S. of products or technical data, *re-exports* of products or technical data from one foreign country to another, and exports and re-exports from a foreign country of foreign-made products that *incorporate U.S.-origin parts and components* or that are the *direct product of U.S. technical data*.

But why have all this? What justifies this complex web of government offices and regulations? The Export Administration Act (EAA) explains that exports must be controlled for three vital reasons: national security, foreign policy, and supply control. Essentially, these restrictions control the export of items that could be detrimental to the national security of the United States. This control applies principally to certain exports to Eastern Europe, the USSR and the People's Republic of China (PRC), though many more countries are affected.

Additionally, export controls significantly advance the foreign policy of the U.S., and help fulfill its declared international obligations.

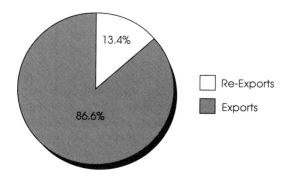

Figure 15.1. Export vs. ReExport, Cases received by the Department of Commerce, Fiscal Year 1989.

This includes commodities controlled for reasons ranging from concerns regarding regional security and military non-proliferation (missile technology and chemical weapons) to moral concerns of the United States (crime control and anti-apartheid). The special nuclear controls authorized are a combination of foreign policy and national security, and are specified in the Nuclear Non-Proliferation Act.

Finally, export controls are in place to protect the domestic economy from an excessive drain of materials that are in short supply and also to reduce the serious inflationary impact of foreign demand.

The web of departments and bureaus involved with export controls is even more complex than we have shown. In particular, when the United States has broad economic sanctions against specific countries, the Department of the Treasury Office of Foreign Assets Control (OFAC) is primarily responsible for granting export licenses for these countries. OFAC control focuses on participation by U.S. persons, including foreign subsidiaries of U.S. companies, in both import and export transactions with specific countries or nationals of such countries, notably Eastern Europe, the PRC, and the USSR.

The Trading with the Enemy Act (TWEA) also authorizes the OFAC to administer controls governing the participation of U.S. persons with the export of *foreign-produced* strategic goods to Eastern Europe, the People's Republic of China, and the Soviet Union.

Currently, OFAC administers comprehensive economic embargoes against Cuba, North Korea, Vietnam, Cambodia, and Libya, and more limited trade and economic sanctions against Iran and South Africa. The countries covered under TWEA include Cuba, North Korea, Vietnam and Cambodia, and those under the International Emergency Economic Powers Act (IEEPA) include Iran and Libya. South Africa is covered under a separate statute, the Comprehensive Anti-Apartheid Act (CAAA), and separate trade sanctions are administered against Iran under the International Security and Development Cooperation Act (ISDCA).

With multiple agencies charged with administering export licensing, there is often great confusion whether OFAC or BXA is the appropriate agency to evaluate a requested export license.

15.1.1 Cuba, North Korea, Vietnam, and Cambodia

The Office of Foreign Assets Control (OFAC) maintains broad controls on participation by U.S. persons in transactions involving country category "Z" nations, namely Cuba, North Korea, Vietnam, and Cambodia, including export transactions.

By comparison, the Bureau of Export Administration controls U.S. origin items exported or re-exported by either foreign or U.S. persons. OFAC defers to BXA on those export transactions licensed by BXA and an export license authorized by BXA is recognized by OFAC.

Jurisdictional responsibility for offshore export transactions with Trading with the Enemy Act (TWEA) countries and nationals of such countries, by U.S. persons (also including subsidiaries abroad) falls under the Department of Treasury. When dealing with these countries, companies should consult OFAC directly to determine if an OFAC or Treasury license may be needed in addition to the BXA authorization. Because OFAC's authority extends to persons acting as agents or representatives of TWEA countries (known as "specially designated nationals"), their embargo powers also apply to specific transactions in foreign countries by U.S. persons with these specially designated nationals.

15.1.2 Libya

OFAC also exercises broad authority over trade with Libya, employing both trade and financial sanctions under both the ISDCA and the IEEPA. OFAC regulates direct and indirect (or "transshipment") exports, including restricting general export licenses, while simultaneously adopting several of the BXA general licenses as its own. The Commerce Department has written a general order in its regulations deferring to OFAC in the area of export controls. However, BXA's export controls do remain in place in the event that OFAC removes its controls, and BXA continues to control re-exports to Libya.

15.1.3 Iran

OFAC administers an embargo on all imports from Iran under ISDCA; BXA regulates only exports.

15.1.4 South Africa

The Comprehensive Anti-Apartheid Act (CAAA) mandated official export sanctions against South Africa to restrict certain imports and to prohibit new loans and investments. OFAC currently administers all import and investment sanctions, while BXA administers all export sanctions and licenses.

Additionally, the Department of Commerce, International Trade

Administration group, has recently opened a new office, the Eastern European Business Information Center (EEBIC), to aid companies in learning about opportunities and restrictions in trade with Eastern Europe.

To gain an idea of how busy these offices of the U.S. government are kept, consider the illustration showing licensing activity for calendar 1989. Notice that even with all the restraints and limitations of trade with the PRC and Soviet Bloc, each had over 5000 license applications submitted that year.

The most crucial document from the U.S. Government regarding limitations and restrictions on export is the *Export Administration Regulation* (EAR), which specifies exactly which commodities and technical data require validated export licenses. This document should be obtained directly from the U.S. Government Printing Office.

In addition to specific licenses for restricted trade regions, the Department of Commerce issues what are known as General Trade Licenses, under which the majority of items leaving the United States are authorized for export, including:

G-DEST: for commodities listed on the Commodity Control List (CCL) to any destination for which a validated license (as noted in the EAR under Export Control Commodity Number or ECCN) is not required.

GIT: for export from the United States of commodities that originate in one foreign country and are destined for another foreign country. These commodities must be moved through the U.S. under

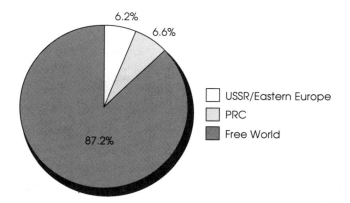

Figure 15.2. U.S. Department of Commerce,
Licensing Activity, Calendar 1989.

a "Transportation and Exportation" customs entry, or an "Immediate Exportation" customs entry as filed with the U.S. Customs Service.

GLV: for commodities to certain specified destinations that fall below a specified dollar limit (specified in the "value limit" paragraph in each CCL entry in the EAR).

GUS: commodities for the personal use of members of the U.S. Armed Forces or U.S. Government civilian personnel, and commodities consigned to, and for the official use of any agency of the U.S. Government.

GCG: commodities consigned to, and for the official use of any agency of a cooperating government (COCOM member countries and Austria, Finland, Singapore, Sweden and Switzerland).

GLR: for export of replacement parts and commodities returning from the United States to the country from which they were imported. Specifically, this covers commodities sent to the United States for servicing, unwanted foreign-origin commodities, one-for-one replacement of parts, the return of shipments refused entry, and replacements for defective or unacceptable U.S.-origin equipment.

GIFT: for export of gift parcels by an individual in the United States to an individual or religious, charitable, or educational organization located in any destination, and for the sole use of the donee or the donee's family. The item must, not surprisingly, be provided free of charge, and may not be for resale.

GTE: for export of certain commodities for temporary use abroad. They must return to the United States within one year after the

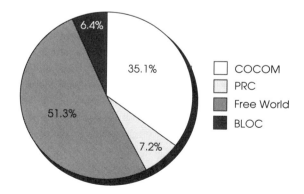

Figure 15.3. Department of Commerce, cases processed fiscal year 1989.

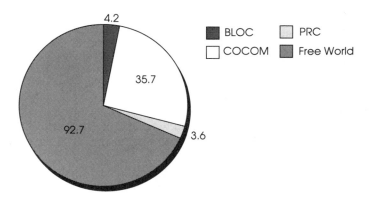

Figure 15.4. Department of Commerce,
cases processed fiscal year 1989:, value in US$ billions.

date of export, and may be used for a specific enterprise or un-
dertaking approved by the Office of Export Licensing, for exhi-
bition or demonstration country groups T (Latin American and
Cuba) and V (countries not included in any other Country Group,
including COCOM members), or for inspection, testing calibra-
tion, or repair abroad.

Baggage: for export as personal baggage to any destination by an
individual leaving the United States, comprised of personal and
household effects, certain vehicles and tools of trade, providing
that they are not intended for sale and are owned by the individual
or member of the immediate family, and are intended for use by
such.

The two licenses of most interest for software marketing are the
GTDA and GTDR. The GTDA covers information that is generally
accessible to the interested public in any form (e.g., technical lit-
erature, research projects), information resulting from fundamental
research, certain educational information, and information contained
in certain patent applications. The GTDR covers essentially all data
not exportable under a GTDA license but still eligible for export
under a general license subject to certain provisions, exclusions and
restrictions.

In general, Sections 771 through 779 of the EAR detail exactly
what is allowed in each of these general export categories, including
noting which general licenses allow the export of higher technology
products to the Free World and COCOM countries.

15.2 What License is Needed?

There is a great amount of information regarding export licensing, including validated licenses, required for all restricted export countries and commodities, and the recommended approach is to obtain the Export Administration Regulations, including supplements. Supplement No. 1 is the Commodity Control List (CCL), which categorizes commodities and indicates broadly which type of commodity is being exported. Computer software and hardware fall into "Electronics and Precision Instruments," Group 5.

Armed with the group number, the Export Control Commodity Number (ECCN) for the specific commodity must be ascertained. Each entry consists of four digits and a letter, where the first digit notes the strategic level of control (namely whether the item is unilaterally or multilaterally controlled and any country restrictions), the second digit identifies commodity group (e.g., Group 5), and the remaining digits specify the particular commodity.

Each category then specifies whether a validated license is required, the GLV dollar value limit (see GLV general license), BXA processing code, reason for control, special licenses available, and, if appropriate, special foreign policy controls, and related technical data.

While these restrictions may seem unimaginably complex, and sure to deter any but the most determined exporter, the Department of Commerce has continually modified their procedures to meet the needs of the international business market simultaneous to the security, and foreign policy requirements of the United States.

Under Secretary for Export Administration Dennis Kloske offers the following words of encouragement in a recent BXA publication: "We must strike a balance between those controls absolutely essential to national security through a strengthened multilateral control system, and the absolute necessity for U.S. exporters to be able to compete aggressively in the world market."

15.3 Export Policies on Cryptographic Products

While the majority of software can be distributed with easily obtained general export licenses, there are certain types of software, and certain types of technical information, that are constrained by the U.S. Department of State, Office of Defense Trade Controls (ODTC) (formerly the Office of Munitions Control).

The key document from the Department of State is the International Traffic in Arms Regulation (ITAR), which defines commodities and trade items on the United States Munitions List. Among the various military items—including amphibious vehicles, chemical agents, firearms, military explosives, military demolition blocks and blasting caps—are end-items, components, accessories, attachments, parts, firmware, software and systems.

The software and hardware designated as part of the Munitions List includes: weather navigation and air traffic control systems, electronic equipment specifically designed or modified for spacecraft and spaceflight, specifically designed or modified for non-military satellites, or designed for search, reconnaissance, collection, monitoring, direction-finding, display, analysis and production of information from the electromagnetic spectrum for intelligence or security purposes and electronic systems or equipment designed or modified to counteract such surveillance and monitoring.

The Munitions List continues: Very High Speed Integrated Circuit semiconductor devices that are specifically designed for military applications and which have a high-speed signal and image processing capability. In addition to these, components, parts, accessories, attachments, and associated equipment specifically designed or modified for use, or currently used with equipment in the previously specified categories are included, with the exception of items in normal commercial use.

The key category of software noted in the ITAR, however, is in Part 121.1, Category XIII, subparagraph b:

> Speech scramblers, privacy devices, cryptographic devices and software (encoding and decoding), and components specifically designed or modified therefore, ancillary equipment, and protective apparatus specifically designed or modified for such devices, components and equipment.

Further into the ITAR, there is a note that technical data relating to the defense articles listed in other categories of the Munitions List is also considered a part of the Munitions list, and therefore is also under the Department of State export restrictions.

There are more definitions required to get a full picture here: firmware, as specified earlier, includes, but is not limited to, circuits into which software has been programmed. Software includes, but is not limited to, system functional design, logic flow, algorithms, application programs, operating systems and support software for design, implementation, test, operation, diagnosis and repair. A system is a combination of end-items, components, parts, accessories, attachments, firmware or software, specifically designed, modified or adapted to operate together to perform a specialized military function.

Adding all these up seems to suggest that not only are encipherment implementations subject to export controls by the Office of Defense Trade Controls, but that any computer software or hardware associated with the implementations are subject to these restrictions too.

One of the key points in the continuing debate between the computer industry and the State department revolves around the ITAR clause in Part 125.1:

Information which is in the "public domain" is not subject to the controls of this subchapter.

In this context, public domain means information which is published and is generally accessible to the public through newsstands and bookstores, subscription magazines, or libraries open to the public.

15.3.1 Jurisdiction

In August 1989 the Bureau of Export Administration, Department of Commerce announced that they were accepting jurisdiction over certain types of encipherment software and devices from the Department of State. Three months later, in November 1989, the revised International Traffic in Arms Regulations confirmed that the Office of Defense Trade Controls still administers bidirectional encipherment software and algorithms.

Recognizing that many of the cipher programs used in computer-based industries are relatively insecure (breakable), and further acknowledging that unidirectional encoding is not useful as a military munition, the Bureau of Export Administration was granted, and now controls export licensing for the following software and devices:

Authentication: Equipment or software that calculates a message authentication code or similar result, such as digital signatures, to assure no alteration of text has taken place, or to authenticate users, but do not allow for encryption of data, text or other media other than that needed for the authentication.

Access control: Equipment or software that protects passwords or Personal Identification Numbers (PIN) or similar data to prevent unauthorized access to computer facilities.

Proprietary software protection: Decryption-only routines for encrypting proprietary software, fonts, or other computer-related proprietary information for the purpose of maintaining vendor control.

In addition, a further category of export license is subject to review by the Office of Munitions Control:

Mass market software: Software packages designed to run on micro-computers, employing non-standard cryptographic algorithms, not of strategic value—e.g., easily breakable—and for which encryption is not the primary function of the package.

This means that the document retrieval system discussed earlier, with its compression and encipherment capabilities, would require review by the Department of State and the Bureau of Export Controls to ascertain whether it could be licensed for export, and if so, to which countries. Further, in their role as expert consultants, the National Security Agency (NSA) could be called in to evaluate the level of sophistication of the algorithms.

While the fictional document retrieval system is an unlikely candidate for global marketing, some packages that include encipherment technology are on the very forefront of U.S. competitiveness in the computer marketplace. Most notably: The Unix operating system, which contains a number of applicable technologies; for user authentication, the system uses an encipherment-only scheme, where users enter their password and the enciphered version is stored. Upon subsequent login attempts, the newly entered password is also enciphered and the two are compared as a means of validation.

Underneath that, however, is a more sophisticated algorithm that implements the Data Encryption Standard (DES) as originally developed by IBM for the Department of Defense. The DES routine is used—by *makekey*—to generate a "key" which is then fed through the so-called Enigma engine, which actually does the encipherment. The programmatic access to both routines is through a library call *crypt()*, which allows encryption and decryption of data. Finally, built on top of that is a user accessible program *crypt*, which allows easy encipherment and decipherment of data.

While DES represents a cipher that is difficult to break, there are more sophisticated algorithms developed by the U.S. government for data security. Further, the DES algorithms have been widely published and not only are software implementations widely available (including through public-access dialup bulletin boards in Canada and Europe), but DES-on-a-chip solutions are available from a variety of internationally based vendors.

Yet the government, cautiously, continues to restrict export of almost all bidirectional encipherment technology, including the Unix *crypt* routines. Unix itself is available for export but overseas editions are shipped with password encoding and user authentication only: *crypt* is not included, either as a user command or as a routine that the programmer can invoke for encipherment purposes.

The crux of the matter regarding necessary export licenses is that it is best to err on the side of caution when navigating through the complex maze of standards and restrictions. Always begin by getting the most up-to-date copy of the Export Administration Regulations document from the U.S. Government Printing Office.

If you have any encipherment technology associated with your products, contact the Office of Defense Trade Control.* Finally, the Bureau of Export Administration also offers export control seminars throughout the United States; contact them for details.

---

*An interesting alternative approach is to work a joint venture with a company outside of the United States, where they could serve as a "value added reseller," actually obtaining a foreign-produced encipherment technology like DES and including it for non-U.S. customers directly.

16
The Future of Global Software

The safest way to predict the future is often to be as vague as possible. The global software market, however, has a vast body of information available that can assist in understanding how the future might appear. An important element of any prediction is to consider the historical successes and failures in the industry, as has been shown in Chapter 2 for a variety of different companies.

Analysis of the global environment in combination with historical data suggests that there are five areas of significant future growth in the high technology marketplace: Europe, Eastern Europe, Southeast Asia, the Pacific Rim, and the Middle East.

Other markets, notably Latin America and Africa, are simply too inherently unstable. Too little money for significant computer investments, currency too susceptible to the vagaries of high inflation, potentially detrimental price controls, and shortages of investment capital all contribute to the problems in these regions. Additionally, unstable governments introduce further problems, including the difficulty that as new groups take power they will often negate all previous financial and contractual obligations with foreign companies. One certainly hopes that as these regions of the world manage to stabilize they can also pull into the global market as equal players, but at this juncture it seems unwise to invest significantly in these regions.

16.1 Europe—EUR12

In 1957 two treaties, collectively known as the Treaty of Rome, were signed by France, Italy, the Netherlands, Belgium, Luxembourg, and West Germany, abolishing all quotas and tariffs between the nations. This marked the formation of the European Economic Community (EEC). Sixteen years later, in 1973, Denmark, Ireland and the United Kingdom joined, and three years after that the then-nine member EEC agreed upon a single European Currency Unit (ECU) to simplify trade between member nations. 1981 saw the addition of Greece to the EEC, and in 1985 Lord Cockfield, a British Commissioner, distributed a white paper outlining 300 measures needed to form a unified European Market. That paper was entitled *Completing the Internal Market*, and proposed December 31, 1992 as the date when all changes should be complete; creating the European Community 1992 (EC92).

These sweeping changes include the removal of physical, technical and fiscal barriers to European trade, and promise the lure of a tremendous marketplace for all goods, technical and commodity. A marketplace, however, with constraints for foreign investors and manufacturers. Chief among these restrictions, and source of much heated international debate, are the *rules of origin** that specify different quota and tariff rates for goods "primarily produced in the EC". Questions of intellectual property rights, especially as applied to copyright and trademark of computer software and hardware, are also vital on the EC92 agenda.

Market growth in the EC has been tremendous in the last decade, and continues at an even faster pace, as global corporations realize the potential of a unified European marketplace. One major reason is that while requirements for localized products will remain—due to the differing culture and language of each member nation—the technical obstacles, including network protocols, hardware standards, and so on, will be unified and *harmonised* to create a single market.

The market for high technology in billions of ECU† has grown at a comensurate rate, going from 169 billion in 1978 to over 1100 billion only eight years later, as shown in Table 16.1. Notice also

---

*The EC has stated a number of times that the *rules of origin* are targeted at limiting Japanese products and Japanese investment in European manufacturing facilities, but there are many who are doubtful that will be all that is targeted.
†Keep in mind that billions of ECU here refer to a million-million, not a thousand-million as in the U.S.

Table 16.1. Individual hi-tech products by Industry and Main Partner, Digital Computers: imports, in billions of ECU.

	1978		1982		1984		1986	
	ECU	%	ECU	%	ECU	%	ECU	%
C1*	169	98.9	521	98.3	1071	96.5	1105	79.0
C2	1.7	1.0	7.6	1.4	29.6	2.7	283	20.3
C3	0.1	0.1	0.2	0	0.2	0	0.7	0.1
USA	158	92.6	472	89	884	79.6	811	58
Japan	0.6	0.3	27.1	5.1	131	11.9	211	15.1
Korea	0	0	0	0	1.4	0.1	123	8.8
Taiwan	0	0	0.3	0.1	4.4	0.4	76.3	5.5
Hong Kong	0	0	1.4	0.3	8.9	0.8	67.7	4.8

*Class 1. Class 1 nations are those that are industrialized, Class 2 are developing nations, and Class 3 are state-trading nations.

Table 16.2. Individual hi-tech products by Industry and Main Partner, Digital Computers: exports, in billions of ECU.

	1978		1982		1984		1986	
	ECU	%	ECU	%	ECU	%	ECU	%
C1	109	61.8	208	75.5	364	74.5	509	76.1
C2	50.2	28.3	57.6	20.8	113	23.2	131	19.6
C3	17.6	9.9	9.9	3.6	11.0	2.2	28.9	4.3
Switz.	19.9	11.2	39.8	14.4	80.5	16.5	137	20.6
Sweden	17.0	9.6	25.6	9.3	54.4	11.1	84	12.5
Austria	22.1	12.4	27.0	9.8	46.2	9.3	77.9	11.6
Norway	7.0	4.0	10.3	3.7	31.4	6.4	47	7
USA	11.5	6.5	58.8	21.3	61.5	12.6	43.9	6.6

the expansion of imports by developing Class 2 nations, from 1% to over 20% in just a few years. These nations, notably those in the Pacific Rim, will be considered in more detail later in this section.

Market share of imports from the United States dropped considerably in the eight year period 1978–1986, from 92.6% to 58% of the rapidly expanding EC market, as shown in Figure 16.1. The slack was taken up by aggressive expansion in Japanese imports, from 0.3% to 15.1% over the same period. Indeed, in the European market, as elsewhere, there is a marked competitiveness between the Asian countries and the U.S. Nonetheless, one important area where the U.S. retains a greater market share is computer software.

Table 16.3 and Figure 16.2 demonstrate the change in import and export balances within the European Community as the EC has come closer and closer to the 1992 unification date. In particular, note the drop in market share by United Kingdom companies.

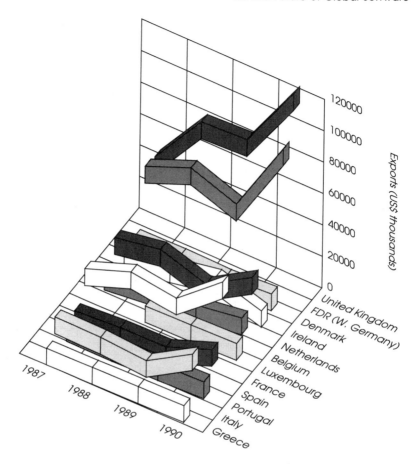

Figure 16.1. U.S. exports, in US$ thousands, to EUR12 nations.

Of the different markets, the European Community in many ways offers the best potential for growth, with its combination of existing information technology, technical knowledge, and economic growth and expansion. The greatest challenges here are to successfully localize products through internationalization and joint ventures or subsidiary operations, and to understand the shifting dynamics of the EC. It is important to remember that the primary motivation for member nations to ratify the 1992 common market proposals is to benefit themselves. EC92 is not intended to create a market for foreign goods as much as it is to create an internal market, where, for example, German companies can sell computers to English firms,

Table 16.3. Percentile share of EUR12 countries, Digital Computers.

	Imports			Exports		
	1978	1982	1986	1978	1982	1986
Belgium, & Luxembourg	5.2	3.3	2.9	2.4	2.7	2.9
Denmark	2.9	2.4	2.6	1.2	0.9	1.7
France	20.2	22.0	22.7	21.2	14.9	15.8
FR of Germany	24.1	21.1	25.5	32.3	30.1	32.9
Greece	0.2	0.2	0.2	0.0	0.0	0.0
Ireland	2.2	3.4	1.8	2.6	6.6	7.7
Italy	7.9	7.8	8.2	12.3	12.2	16.0
Netherlands	6.2	7.9	8.4	6.0	5.5	5.5
Portugal	0.0	0.6	0.5	0.0	0.8	0.2
Spain	4.4	3.8	4.1	0.4	4.4	1.8
UK	26.7	27.6	23.1	21.7	21.7	15.6

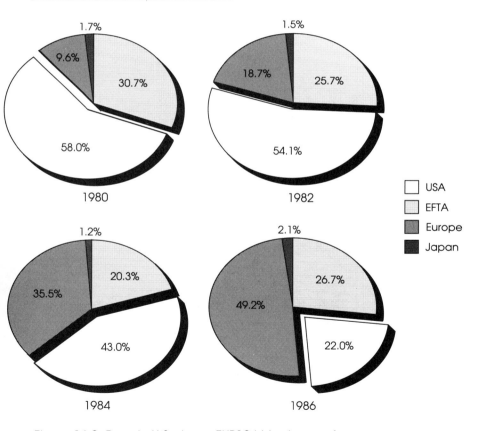

Figure 16.2. Drop in U.S. share, EUR12 hi-tech exports.

which would add their own software and market the resulting system into Italy.

16.2 Eastern Europe and the U.S.S.R.

One of the most dramatic changes in the world political balance has been the continued growth in freedom and self-determinism gained by countries in the Soviet Bloc. Freed from their extra-national rule, many of the individual Eastern European nations are questing for membership in the global market quite aggressively, as can be seen graphically in Figure 16.3.

Among the many industries that can benefit from this rapid modernization is the entire computing industry, from personal computer floppy disk manufacturers to mainframe computer software producers. The primary obstacle in Eastern Europe is one that is a constant challenge throughout the world: the need for a stable and

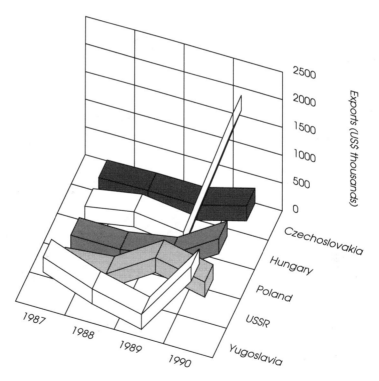

Figure 16.3. US Exports, in US$ thousands, to Eastern Europe & USSR.

exportable currency. Larger corporations, such as Digital Equipment Corporation, which has announced its expansion into Czechoslovakia, can survive a significant loss in revenues as the marketplace expands and increases in sophistication, but smaller vendors typically do not have such leeway in their financial arrangements.

A common solution to this dilemma is to create a joint venture with a foreign company, sometimes owning the foreign group and sometimes operating on the simple tenets of western capitalism, where both parties reap profit from the relationship. This aids in being able to localize and penetrate the market , but does not significantly improve the problem of how to get profits out of the country.

There are no easy solutions. The creation of the European Currency Unit (ECU) was an attempt to avoid this difficulty as the economy flourishes. The Global Agreement on Trade and Tariffs (GATT) has global trading currency on its agenda, but so far without significant results. Export of profits is probably the greatest challenge facing Eastern Europe as they move to rebuild their countries.

16.3 South America

Many analysts believe that the South American marketplace has traditionally been ignored and is ripe for growth in high technology. South America remains a difficult market to penetrate, however, with many nations having tough *local content* requirements with relatively small sales potential. Indeed, local content is an obstacle to the point where importers often must be able to demonstrate to the local government that there are no native products of any nature that might be impacted by the foreign competition, before the companies are granted import licenses.

In Figure 16.4 notice that the two leading nations are Brazil and Venezuela, yet even the best year for imports—1990—resulted in the Brazilian market accounting for a mere US$7.8 million total technology imports. This amount is insignificant when compared with the hundreds of millions exported yearly to the Pacific Rim and European nations. There remains the potential for significant growth in this area, most notably within Brazil, so keeping an eye on the South American market is a shrewd idea.

16.4 Scandinavia

The Scandinavian nations are an exceptionally homogeneous marketplace, representing a small and stable market for high technology and computer equipment, as shown in Figure 16.5. While Denmark

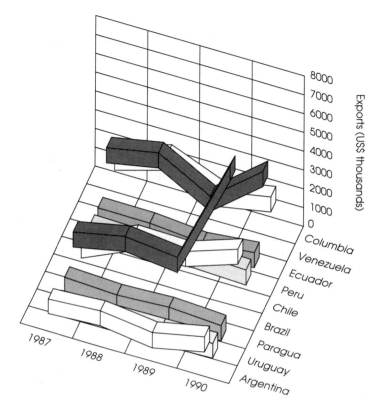

Figure 16.4. U.S. exports, in US$ thousands, to South America.

is a member of the European Community, the nation most aggressively pursuing growth in computer technology is Sweden, with 1990 imports from the U.S. in high technology of US$23.2 million, an increase of almost 300% from four years previous. Research reveals the basic problem with this area: the market is substantially closed to outside, non-Scandinavian companies. It is this same protectionist attitude that has also left most of Scandinavia as part of the European Free Trade Association (EFTA) rather than the EC itself.

Sweden is potentially the most lucrative market in this region, with projected sales of over US$50 million by 1993, and over US$100 million by the end of the century. Because of their membership in the European Community, Denmark should also prove a successful market.

A further complication is that the Scandinavian countries are

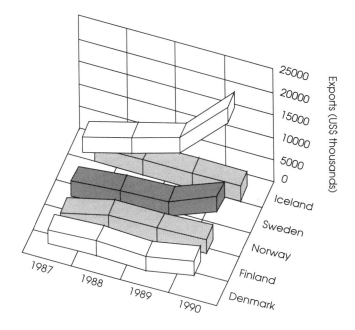

Figure 16.5. U.S. exports, in US$ thousands, to Scandinavia.

members of the EFTA which is targeting the creation of a unified European Economic Space (EEE), with a familiar target date of December 31, 1992. When that is created, it will create a market larger than that of just the EC, with, potentially, less political implications.

16.5 The Middle East

One of the most volatile regions in the world, the Middle East is also potentially one of the largest technology markets in the world. In particular, Figure 16.6 shows the effect a joint free-trade agreement between Israel and the United States has had on their imports of U.S. high technology. Further, Israel has a similar agreement with the European Community, making them a busy world trade port.

Outside of Israel, Arab expansion has been closely tied to the value of petroleum on the world market. In the late 1970's the Oil Producing and Exporting Nations (OPEC) experienced dramatic growth in petroleum revenues and used the windfall to modernize many of their public and private businesses.

The annexation of Kuwait by Iraq in 1990 and the resultant actions

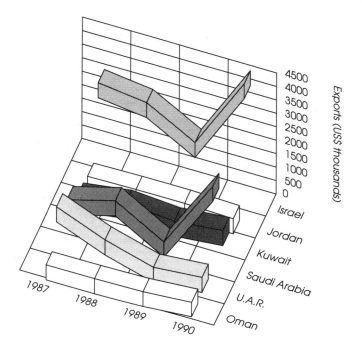

Figure 16.6. U.S. exports, in US$ thousands, to the Middle East.

will result in significant market growth for many of the Middle Eastern nations. In particular, the United States has promised significant economic aid—including high technology—most notably to Saudi Arabia, Israel, and Turkey. Further, rebuilding of Kuwait will involve a complete replacement of almost all their computer equipment, a massive "spot market" for the next few years.

Nonetheless, the long term trend is for the Middle East to be a slow market for high technology. For those products with a short time-to-market, the next few years could offer an excellent opportunity to penetrate the marketplace, particularly with products that work in the local dialects of Arabic and are culturally sensitive.

16.6 Africa

For the past few decades Africa has struggled to pull out of its status as a poor third world continent. While there have been significant improvements, the marketplace for higher technology remains small, with unimpressive growth. In 1990, the sum of all African computer-related imports from the United States was under US$11 million, as shown in Figure 16.7.

There is hope that this area can stabilize, come to terms with the continued tribal conflicts and disputes, and move into the 21st century with strong economic success, but for now it is the least profitable international computer-related market.

16.7 The Southeast Asian Nations

Changes in the world economy have time and again demonstrated the savvy of various nations, including notably the transition of Japan from third world nation to vital member of the global economic market. The tremendous growth of the Southeast Asian nations also demonstrates the importance of vision, long term planning, and a motivated work force. In 1990, total exports for the Association of Southeast Asian Nations (ASEAN) were over US$121,000 million. ASEAN is comprised of Brunei, Indonesia, Malaysia, the Philippines, Singapore and Thailand.

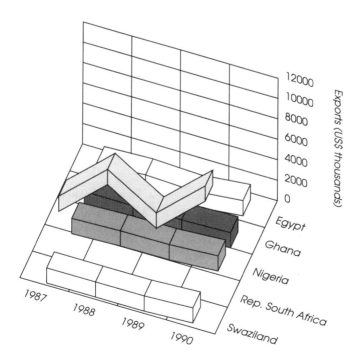

Figure 16.7. U.S. exports, in US$ thousands, to Africa.

In addition to the ASEAN nations, India, Pakistan and Nepal are also shown in Figure 16.8. India, Pakistan, Nepal, Bangladesh, Sri Lanka, the Maldives and Bhutan are all members of the South Asian Association for Regional Cooperation (SAARC). Unlike ASEAN's tremendous success, however, SAARC is most notable for its bitter political infighting and lack of actual cooperation, especially in high technology.

Note particularly in Figure 16.8 the difference between the acquisition of high technology by Singapore and the rest of the Southeast Asian nations. More importantly, notice the growth curve of the exports to Singapore, a country rapidly moving into the forefront of the global technology manufacturing market. Compared with many of the larger global markets, notably Japan, Canada, and the EC, Singapore remains a less lucrative marketplace; but with one of the most dramatic technological expansions anywhere on the globe, Singapore will undoubtedly become an excellent technology marketplace.

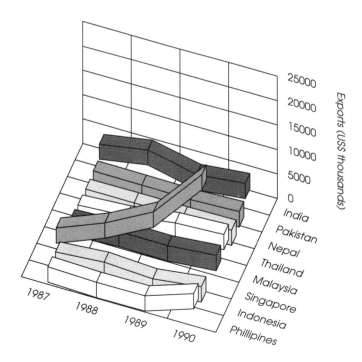

Figure 16.8. U.S. exports, in US$ thousands, to Southeast Asia.

16.8 The Pacific Rim

Geographically adjacent to the Southeast Asian nations, a distinction is drawn between nations that are members of ASEAN or SAARC and the rest of the Pacific Rim region. Counted in the Pacific Rim are China, Japan, Korea, Vietnam, Hong Kong and Taiwan, as well as Australia and New Zealand, the only two English-language markets in the Pacific Rim.

As can be seen in Figure 16.9, Australia and New Zealand represent significant, but slow growing markets for high technology.

The rest of the Pacific Rim, however, represents one of the largest and most important markets in the world. The Pacific Rim nations also represent cultures quite dissimilar to the West. Japan is the most

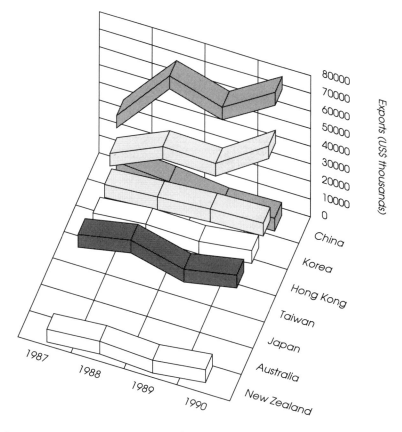

Figure 16.9. U.S. exports, in US$ thousands, to the Pacific Rim.

profitable market in the region, but Japan represents a very difficult market politically. The last few years have also seen the growth of significant anti-Japanese xenophobic sentiments throughout the Western nations, including within the context of the Global Agreement on Trade and Tariffs (GATT) Uruguay round* and in more general trade between nations. Ironically, one of the simplest commodities has become representative of the difficulties nations face importing products into the Japanese market: rice. U.S. farmers insist that they should be able to export rice into the Japanese market, and the Japanese levy an exceptionally high import tariff to ensure that the rice sold in Japan—a massive market—is Japanese.

The cultural differences in China are notable too, as is indicated by the following report from the *Wall Street Journal*:

> "Southern China's Guangdong Province is unlike the rest of China. For the past 10 years, this area has been China's doorway to the world, the hothouse where now-deposed Communist Party chief Zhao Ziyang launched his free-wheeling experimental Special Economic Zones, in a bid to modernize China. Zhao's idea was to turn China's southern coast into a laboratory for economic change by setting up a series of special zones that would cater to foreign investors. Over time, the zones were supposed to drag the entire nation towards prosperity.

> "Until the pro-democracy protests in 1989 led to Zhao's downfall, it looked as if the experiment was working. Guangdong flourished as never before, under China's "open-door" policy. In the past 10 years, the region has absorbed nearly 60% of all foreign investment in China. It has created 5 million new jobs, accounting for one-sixth of China's foreign exports and experienced economic-growth rates that exceed the best boom years in Taiwan or South Korea.

> " 'Life is so good here', boasts Zhao Jiaxiang, Guangdong's provincial director of foreign economic relations and trade, 'that even shelters for homeless garbage pickers have color television sets.'

> "Guangdong's open door has also drawn in new influences and strained old loyalties. Some observers claim that the entire province has been annexed by Hong Kong. The British colony is both teacher and banker to Guangdong, supplying it with managers, machines, and 90% of its foreign investment. Nearly 2 million people in the province are employed in Hong Kong-owned factories, while the colony's own industrial labor force totals only about 800,000 workers.

> "People in Guangdong read Hong Kong newspapers, listen to Hong Kong's Cantonese radio station, and copy Hong Kong's latest fashions. Even the province's telephone system is set up so that it is easier to call Hong Kong than Beijing. In the summer, clocks in the city of Shenzhen run a full hour behind those in the rest of China, because they stick with Hong Kong time instead of observing the mainland's daylight-saving time."

---

*GATT meetings are referred to as *rounds* with the name of the round, which can last years, denoting the name of the hosting nation. The current 1990 GATT negotiations are taking place in Uruguay, hence "Uruguay round."

16.9 The Markets of the Future

As can be seen graphically in Figure 16.10, the top markets for export are the United Kingdom, Germany, and Japan, representing between them 26% of the entire US$1,096 million in exports from the United States in 1990. Not shown in Figure 16.10 because of its size, the Canadian market has a shared language and geographic adjacency to the U.S. Canada also represents the largest single export market for the U.S.: 35.2% of overall exports, with a U.S. high technology import ledger of US$386 million dollars in 1990.

This is not the entire picture because there are a number of events that will significantly change the international marketplace; most notably, the reunification of Hong Kong with mainland China in 1997, and before that, the common market of the EEE and EC92. Combining those future markets together, the EC represents US$366 million, or 34% of the 1990 U.S. high technology export market-

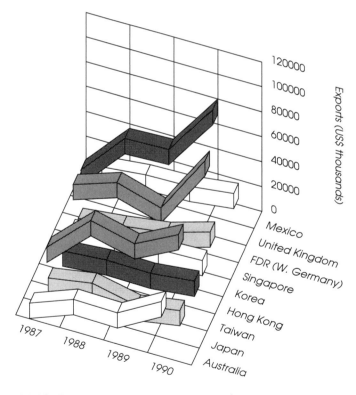

Figure 16.10. Top U.S. export nations, in US$ thousands.

place. China and Hong Kong combine for US$15 million, an almost negligible amount, except for that China will most likely go through a phase of rapid technological acquisition.

While the size of the market in Singapore is not yet significant, the aggressive expansion and growth make it a marketplace with tremendous future potential. Consider: in 1987 Singapore imported US$4.9 million worth of technology, and four years later, in 1990, the imports from the United States alone were US$24.2 million, an expansion of almost 500%. If Singapore continues at this rate, by the mid-1990's the import market for U.S. technology alone could be over US$100 million.

By contrast, Japan is a large, but fickle market. In 1990 Japan imported US$76.7 million worth of high technology. Yet, between 1988 and 1989, the imports actually dropped by over US$8 million. Japan is an important market, but one that offers many pitfalls in addition to the profit potential.

16.10 Problems in Japan and Germany

The two nations commonly viewed as poised to lead the global economy are Germany and Japan. Yet both have significant domestic economic problems that will hinder their ability to continue their rapid growth as rising international economic forces.

For formerly West Germany, the cost of bringing the now-liberated East Germany into the mainstream technologically and economically is proving extremely difficult. This economic responsibility has provoked tremendous debate within the former West Germany. The resultant nation will most likely prove a manufacturing and development hotbed, re-emerging as an important member of the global economy.

For Japan, the challenge is different; the fragile state of the Japanese economy and society will continue to become more and more difficult to ignore. The pressure to work nonstop, and to succeed at all cost is so great in Japan that "karoshi," or sudden death due to overwork, has become commonplace, and where home loans in Japan can have a life of over 75 years, and are taken by people who would like a chance at any home at all outside of the often-backward rural regions. Long-term global economic success is almost always predicated on a solid and stable national economy, and that will be the main challenge Japan will face in the last decade of this century.

16.11 Patents and Trademarks

While there are a number of obstacles preventing a single global marketplace for computer technology, none are as frustrating and financially damaging as the inability of the various nations to agree on a single, enforced, definition of copyright, patent, and trademark issues. As the European Community organization itself reports, in the important work *Patents, Trademarks and Copyright in the European Community*:

"A key area needing improvement to encourage international trade in software is the tightening of copyright, patent and trademark enforcement laws in these overseas regions. One of the fundamental questions is whether software should be copyrighted, patented, or trademarked. The differences are subtle here:

"Patents are official registrations of industrial invention or discovery, giving the author the exclusive right to use the invention for their own benefit for a specific period. (Patents can also be licensed for third parties to exploit).

"Trade Marks are intended to legally protect consumer products, ensuring that companies have a legal guarantee of uniqueness of their corporate and product names in the marketplace. Trademarks have no time limits, and many arise out of common usage, rather than being formally registered.

"Copyrights are to protect so-called works of the intellect. The EC published a paper "Copyright and the Technological Challenge" recognizing the difficulties faced in protecting software. In particular, it discusses the problems posed by unauthorized reproduction for commercial and private use of software, and related high-tech products. They note that, within the technological niche, the initial development of a sophisticated integrated circuit can require an investment of up to ECU 100 million, yet duplication of an existing circuit design can be done for ECU 50,000 to ECU 100,000.

"In the United States, the approach has been to patent inventions, including inventions as they relate to computer software (such as the "setuid" bit within Unix) and then to trademark the names of the programs (Lotus 1-2-3, Unix, MS-DOS) and copyright the programs themselves. This model is being adopted by much of the Western economic community, and the EC is working on a proposal to cover software, protecting the author's exclusive rights of reproduction, adoption and distribution for a period of fifty years."

The EC notes "Clearly, society needs industrial, commercial, and intellectual property to be protected, so as to encourage creative effort, innovation and investment. This protection has traditionally been provided by national measures, which have varied from one country to another, and each has been effective only within the territory of the State concerned. This situation has damaging consequences for intra-Community trade and for the capacity of businesses to consider the common market as a single economic environment for their activities."

16.12 Where To Go From Here

Over the next ten years, the European Community will make the transition to being a significant superpower, both militarily and economically, eclipsing the economic importance of both Japan and Germany (the latter also a member of the EC). Further, with industriousness and a zeal for modernization unmatched elsewhere in the world, the smaller Pacific Rim countries, including notably Korea, the People's Republic of China, Taiwan and Singapore, will also move to a position of greater importance.

The Middle East will remain a volatile hotbed of centuries old disputes, fueled to a great degree by the reliance of the rest of the world on fossil fuels, and the resultant massive injection of money into the Arabian economies. The money will allow individual nations to rapidly modernize, and with little, if any, domestic high technology, the possibilities for exporters in this marketplace cannot be understated.

Further, of the five areas identified, Europe, Eastern Europe, Southeast Asia, the Pacific Rim and the Middle East, all but the last have some degree of desire to assimilate aspects of Western cultures, especially the U.S., into their own, as reflected in their advertising, the products purchased, the packaging of the products, and other aspects of society. Each, however, desires to retain its own culture and values, resulting in a predictable, but no less essential, struggle between the old and the new. These countries are often easier to approach as foreign markets due to their strong growth coupled with their aggressive approach to modernization.

The Middle Eastern countries, by contrast, have a culture and society that is dramatically different from the West. While there is a strong desire to obtain all that is best from Western culture and society, including computer and high technology, the Islamic cultures are vehemently against dilution of their own values, and as a result represent a tougher, yet potentially lucrative market.

A common thread throughout all of these nations, and indeed throughout the entire global marketplace, be it for computer software or automobile steering wheel covers, is that the company absolutely must have an understanding of the target marketplace. Whether achieved through joint ventures with other companies (as is common in Eastern Europe), wholly or partially owned subsidiaries, licensing products directly, or contracting foreign agencies to act as distributors in the market, it is clearly the case that this is an essential ingredient to success.

The opportunities far, far outweigh any difficulties that might be encountered; even a company with a lackluster product in the highly competitive U.S. market can enjoy excellent growth and sales overseas. A case in point; Atari Computer, a company whose performance in the United States market is very poor, but whose performance in Latin America and Europe is tremendous, with 82% of overall net profit from foreign markets.

It seems that in some areas, one can sell almost anything to do with computers, whether localized or not. There are catches, of course, including the fact that the technology needed to utilize the application might not be available (for example, a program that requires the state-of-the-art personal computer is likely to fail in a third world nation where hardware that's five or ten years old is considered state-of-the-art).

The computer industry is a young industry, and many of the companies involved are aggressive, with fast growth and a "take no prisoners" attitude towards competitors. As the next few years open up global borders and demonstrate the unquestionably vital importance of information technologies, the market for global software and hardware will prove tremendous.

Know the territory, approach with a sense of being a traveller in a strange place, localize and target your products correctly and you will be part of a growing and successful business recognized worldwide and respected globally.

Appendix A
Organizations

International Standards Organizations

International Organization for Standardization
  1, rue de Varembé
  Case postale 56
  CH-1211 Genève 20
  Suisse/Switzerland

European Computer Manufacturers Association
  114, rue du Rhône
  CH-1204 Genève
  Suisse/Switzerland

The X/Open Company, Ltd.
  Abbots House
  Abbey Street
  Reading
  Berkshire, RG1 3BD
  United Kingdom

SHARE Europe Headquarters
  17, rue Pierres-du-Niton
  CH-1207 Geneva
  Switzerland

National Standards Organizations

Arab
  Arab Standards and Metrology Organisation
  P.O. Box 926161
  Amman, Jordan

Australia
  Standards Association of Australia
  Standards House
  80-86 Arthur Street
  North Sydney, N.S.W. 2060
  Australia

Austria
  Österreichisches Normungsinstitut
  Heinestraβe 38
  Postfach 130
  A-1021 Wien

Belgium
  Institut Belge de Normalisation
  Belgisch Instituut voor Normalisatie
  Av. de la Brabançonne—Brabançonnelaan 29
  B-1040 Bruxelles—Brussel

Canada
  Standards Council of Canada
  International Standardisation Branch
  2000 Argentia Road, Suite 2-401
  Mississauga, Ontario L5N 1V8

China
  China State Bureau of Standards
  P.O. Box 820
  Beijing
  People's Republic of China

Denmark
  Dansk Standardiseringsraad
  Aurehøjvej 12
  Postbox 77
  DK-2900 Hellerup

Finland
Suomen Standardisoimisliitto
P.O. Box 205
SF-00121 Helsinki

France
Assocation Française de Normalisation
Tour Europe, Cedex 7
F-92080 Paris

German
Deutsches Institut fü Normung
Burggrafenstraβe 6
Postfach 1107
D-1000 Berlin 30

Greece
Hellenic Organisation for Standardisation
Didotou 15
106 80 Athens

Hong Kong
Hong Kong Standards and Testing Centre
10 Dai Wang Street
Taipo Industrial Estate
Taipo, N.T.

Iceland
Technological Institute of Iceland
Standards Division
Keldnaholt
IS-112 Reykjavik

Ireland
National Standards Authority of Ireland
Ballyum Road
Dublin-9, Eire

Israel
Standards Institution of Israel
42 University Street
Tel Aviv 69977

Italy
> Ente Nazionale Italiano di Unificazione
> Piazza Armando Diaz, 2
> I-20123 Milano

Japan
> Japanese Industrial Standards Committee
> Standards Department
> Agency of Industrial Science and Technology
> Ministry of International Trade and Industry
> 1-3-1, Kasumigaseki
> Chiyoda-ku, Tokyo 100

Mexico
> Dirección General de Normas
> Calle Puente de Tecamachalco Nô 6
> Lomas de Tecamachalco
> Sección Fuentes
> Naucalpan de Juárez
> 53 950 Mexico

The Netherlands
> Nederlands Normalisatie-instituut
> Kalfjeslaan 2
> P.O. Box 5059
> 2600 GB Delft

New Zealand
> Standards Association of New Zealand
> Private Bag
> Wellington

Norway
> Norges Standardiseringsforbund
> Postboks 7020 Homansbyen
> N-0306 Oslo 3

Portugal
> Instituto Português da Qualidade
> Rua José Estêvïo, 83-A
> P-1199 Lisboa

Spain
  Instituto Español de Normalización
  Calle Fernandez de la Hoz, 52
  28010 Madrid

Sweden
  SIS—Standardiseringskommissionen i Sverige
  Box 3295
  S-103 66 Stockholm

Switzerland
  Swiss Association for Standardisation
  Kirchenweg 4, Postfach
  CH-8032 Zürich

United Kingdom
  British Standards Institute
  2 Park Street
  London, W1A 2BS

United States of America
  National Institute of Standards and Technology
  1430 Broadway
  New York, NY 10018

Other International Organizations

European Community Official Publications Office
  Office des publications offielles des
  Communautés européennes
  2, rue Mercier
  L-2985 Luxembourg

Branches of the U.S. Government

Office of Technology Assessment
  U.S. Congress
  Washington D.C. 20510

National Technical Information Servicee
  U.S. Department of Commerce
  Springfield, VA 22161

U.S. Department of State
General Counsel's Office
Bureau of Export Administration—Rm 3327
U.S. Department of Commerce
14 & Constitution NW
Washington DC 20230

U.S. Department of Commerce
Office of Technology and Policy Analysis
Bureau of Export Administration—Rm 4069A
U.S. Department of Commerce
14 & Constitution NW
Washington DC 20230

Office of Export Licensing
U.S. Department of Commerce
P.O. Box 273
Washington, DC 20044

U.S. National Institute of Standards and Technology
U.S. Department of Commerce
Bldg 225/B151
Gaithersburg, MD 20899

U.S. Bureau of Export Administration
U.S. Department of Commerce
Washington DC 20230

United States Council for International Business
1212 Avenue of the Americas
New York, NY 10036

Bureau of the Census, Foreign Trade Division
Regulations Branch, Room 2155, Building 3
Washington DC 20233

U.S. Government Printing Office
Attn: Superindent of Documents
Washington, DC 20402

Appendix B
How to Obtain
Source Code

Those interested in obtaining source code for the various programs presented herein are invited to send a check for US$25 plus a mailer with the appropriate postage to the followed address:

Global Software—Source Code
P.O. Box 4012
Menlo Park, CA 94043-4012
USA

Please include a note indicating whether you would prefer a Macintosh format or DOS format disk. The only disks available will be 3.5", 720K DOS or 800K Mac formats.

Included in the return mailing will be notes on how to work with the software in both environments, so additional space will be required in the envelope included in your mailing.

Utility Program *findstr.c*

Given a C source file, *findstr* will extract all quoted strings or messages from the program, saving them into a separate file for processing by the companion program *insertstr*. This duplicates the
functionality of the HP NLS program of the same name.

```
/*** © 1991, Dave Taylor—All Rights Reserved. ***/

#include <stdio.h>

#define SLEN            256

#define leave(a,b)   { fprintf(stderr, a, b); exit(0); }

main(argc, argv)
int argc;
char **argv;
{
    FILE *fd;
    char buffer[SLEN];

    if (argc < 2 )
     leave("Usage: findstr source file or files\n", 0);

    while (--argc) {
     if ((fd = fopen(*++argv, "r")) == NULL)
      leave("Couldn't open file '%s' for reading", *argv);
```

```
    fprintf(stderr, "(%s)\n", *argv);

    while (fgets(buffer, SLEN, fd) != NULL)
     if (has_quotes(buffer))
      extract_strings(buffer);
    }
    fprintf(stderr, "done\n");
    exit(0);
}

has_quotes(char *buffer)
{
    /** returns TRUE iff buffer has two or more double quotes **/

    int i, count = 0;

    for (i=0; buffer[i] != '\0'; i++)
     if (buffer[i] == '"') count++;

    if (count % 2 != 0)
     leave("Found line with odd number of quotes:\n\t> %s", buffer);

    return( count >= 2 );
}

extract_strings(char *buffer)
{
    /** extracts each quoted string in the line, listing each **/

    int i, j = 0, in_quote = 0;
    char   ourbuf[SLEN];

    for (i=0; buffer[i] != '\0'; i++) {
     if (buffer[i] == '"') {
      if (in_quote) {          /* done processing this quoted string */
       ourbuf[j] = '\0';
       puts(ourbuf);
       j = 0;
       in_quote = 0;
      }
      else             /* starting quote processing */
       in_quote = 1;
     }
```

```
    else if (in_quote)
     ourbuf[j++] = buffer[i];
    }
```

Utility Program *insertmsg.c*

Given a C program source file and the output of the previously executed *findstr* command, this will create two output files; an HP NLS format message catalog and a rewritten version of the source program, using the appropriate *getmsg()* calls.

The program is used as either:

    getmsg(set, message, optional_buffer_space)
or   catgets(fd, set, message, default_str)

Use of the starting option "-n" will cause the resultant C source to be translated for an NLS format function call, otherwise the default is *getmsg()* style calls with a NULL third argument.

/** © 1991, Dave Taylor—All rights reserved. **/

```
#include <stdio.h>

#define SLEN            256

#define GETMSG          "\n\t getmsg(0, %d, NULL) /* %s */\n\t "
#define NLS_GETMSG      "\n\t catgets(catd, NL_SETD, %d, \"%s\")\n\t "

#define leave(a,b)          { fprintf(stderr, a, b); exit(0); }
#define remove_return(s)    s[strlen(s)-1] = 0;

int NLS = 0;                /* use NLS format? */

struct msg_id_entry {
```

```c
        char *string;
        int id;
        struct msg_id_entry *next;
    } *message_catalog = NULL;
int maps_to_msg(char *);

main(argc, argv)
int argc;
char **argv;
{
    FILE *sourcefd, *messagefd, *outfd, *catfd;
    char buffer[SLEN];
    int id = 1;                /* message ids: starts with #1 */

    if (strcmp(*++argv, "-n") == 0) {
     argc--;
     NLS++;
    }
    else --argv;               /* back up an argument! */

    if (argc != 3 )
     leave("Usage: insertstr source-file message-file\n", 0);

    if ((sourcefd = fopen(*++argv, "r")) == NULL)
     leave("Couldn't open source file '%s' for reading\n", *argv);

    sprintf(buffer, "nl_%s", *argv);

    if ((outfd = fopen(buffer, "w")) == NULL)
     leave("Couldn't create source file '%s'\n", buffer);

    if ((messagefd = fopen(*++argv, "r")) == NULL)
     leave("Couldn't open message catalog '%s' for reading\n",
           *argv);

    sprintf(buffer, "%s.cat", *argv);
    if ((catfd = fopen(buffer, "w")) == NULL)
     leave("Couldn't create catalog '%s'\n", buffer);

    fprintf(catfd, "%c message catalog generated by insertmsg\n\n",
           NLS? '$' : '#');
    if (! NLS)
     fprintf(catfd, "$set 0\n\n"); /* known default */
```

/** First step we will want to do is to spin through all the
messages in the message file, storing them in memory and
assigning each a unique identification number.   **/

```
while (fgets(buffer, SLEN, messagefd) != NULL) {
remove_return(buffer);
new_msg(buffer, id++, catfd);
}

printf("(message catalog created . . . )\n");

fclose(messagefd);
fclose(catfd);
```

/** Next, let us go through the C source file, either replacing
all occurances of the quoted string with a reference to the
appropriate message catalog extraction routine, or prefixing
the line with an extraction function and appending the
matching quotes
**/

```
while (fgets(buffer, SLEN, sourcefd) != NULL)
if (has_quotes(buffer))
add_catalog_reference(buffer, outfd);
else
fputs(buffer, outfd);

printf("(... and new version of source file created)\n");

fclose(sourcefd);
fclose(outfd);

exit(0);
}

has_quotes(char *buffer)
{
```

/** returns TRUE iff buffer has two or more double quotes **/

```
int i, count = 0;

for (i=0; buffer[i] != '\0'; i++)
if (buffer[i] == '"') count++;
```

```
        if (count % 2 != 0)
        leave("Found line with odd number of quotes:\n\t> %s", buffer);

        return( count >= 2 );
}

add_catalog_reference(char *buffer, FILE *outfd)
{
        /** replace strings in line with catalog calls, as appropriate. **/

        int i, j = 0, k = 0;
        int   id, not_in_quote = 1;
        char   ourbuf[SLEN], quoted[SLEN];

        for (i=0; buffer[i] != '\0'; i++) {
        if (buffer[i] == '"') {
         if (not_in_quote) {                 /* starting a quote! */
          ourbuf[j] = '\0';
          fprintf(outfd, ourbuf);
          j = 0;
          not_in_quote = 0;
          }
         else {                              /* ending a quote! */
          quoted[k] = '\0';
          if (id = maps_to_msg(quoted)) /* catalog call */
          fprintf(outfd, NLS? NLS_GETMSG : GETMSG, id, quoted);
          else
          fprintf(outfd, "\"%s\"", quoted);
          k = 0;
          not_in_quote = 1;
          }
         }
        else if (not_in_quote)
         ourbuf[j++] = buffer[i];
        else
         quoted[k++] = buffer[i];
        }

        if (j > 0) {
         ourbuf[j] = 0;
         fprintf(outfd, ourbuf);
         }
}
```

```
new_msg(char *buffer, int id, FILE *catfd)
{
     /** add this message to the internal data structure, and also
        output an entry as appropriate to the 'catfd' file. **/

     struct msg_id_entry *entry;

     /** allocate a new entry **/

     entry = (struct msg_id_entry *) malloc(sizeof (struct
             msg_id_entry *));

     entry->string = (char *) malloc(strlen(buffer)+2);

     strcpy(entry->string, buffer);
     entry->id = id;
     entry->next = message_catalog;

     message_catalog = entry;

     fprintf(catfd,"%d\t%s\n", id, buffer);
}

int
maps_to_msg(char *quoted)
{
     /** look up quoted string in message catalog, returning
        its ID if found. If not, return 0 to indicate failure **/

     struct msg_id_entry *entry;

     entry = message_catalog;

     while (entry != NULL) {
     if (strcmp(entry->string, quoted) == 0) return(entry->id);
     entry = entry->next;
     }
     return(0);
}
```

References

An Annotated Bibliography

1. Adams, Douglas, *Hitchhikers Guide to the Galaxy*, Harmony Books, 1980.
2. *American Heritage Larousse Spanish Dictionary*, Houghton Mifflin, 1986.
3. Apple Computer, Inc., *Annual Report to Stockholders*, 1985–1990.
4. Apple, *A Guide to Japan for Macintosh Developers*, April, 1990. *(Distributed to Macintosh Software Developers)*.
5. "Appreciation of Cultural Differences Will Determine U.S. Success in Selling Software to Japan," *InfoWorld*, June 25, 1990.
6. "As the Iron Curtain Swings Open, Software Companies Rush in to the Soviet Market," *InfoWorld*, June 25, 1990. *(Focusing on the personal computer software market overseas)*.
7. Atari Corporation, *Annual Report to Stockholders*, 1989.
8. Ball, Donald, personal correspondence, September 27, 1990.
9. Bamford, James, *The Puzzle Palace*, Penguin, 1988. *(A fascinating, though often difficult to read, book on the history and responsibilities of the United States National Security Agency. Explains why the NSA reviews cryptographic software for the Department of State before allowing export licenses to be issued)*.
10. Becker, Joseph, personal correspondence, Sep 14, 1990.
11. Benedict, Ruth, *The Chrysanthemum and the Sword: Patterns of Japanese Culture*, Meridian, 1946. *(Though many years old, this book offers an interesting glimpse of immediately post-World War II Japan, including the rebuilding of their culture and ideology, as well as the growth of various businesses)*.
12. Brislin, Richard, Cushner, Kenneth, Cherrie, Craig, and Yong, Mahealani, *Intercultural Interaction: A Practical Guide*, Sage, 1988.

13. Carr, Richard, personal correspondence, August 27, 1990.

14. Christopher, Robert, *Second to None: American Companies in Japan*, Fawcett, 1986. *(Attempting to dispel U.S. fears regarding the Japanese, Christopher in this book ends up building many new, and equally untrue stereotypical behaviours. Nonetheless, there are some interesting case studies of various companies—notably IBM—and their success in the Japanese marketplace).*

15. Commission of the European Communities, *Esprit: Key to the Technological Awakening of Europe*, November 1989. *(Esprit is an EC funded project that has been running for years, with the express goal of making the EC more competitive in the high technology marketplace. This booklet offers a good overview of the program).*

16. Commission of the European Communities, *Patents, Trade Marks, and Copyright in the European Community*, December 1989. *(An important work detailing the main issues regarding the international aspects of U.S. patents, etc).*

17. Compaq Computer Corp, *Annual Report to Stockholders*, 1985–1989.

18. Compaq Computer Corp, *Corporate Backgrounder*.

19. Compaq Computer Corp, *Financial Fact Book 1989*.

20. Compaq Computer Corp, *International Background*, Memorandum, June 1990.

21. Compaq Computer Corp, Quarterly Analysts Meeting notes, October 30, 1990.

22. Copeland, Lennie and Griggs, Lewis, *Going International: How to Make Friends and Deal Effectively in the Global Marketplace*, Plume, 1985. *(An enjoyable book covering many aspects of global marketing, including getting started, marketing, negotiating, managing people, skills transfer, business etiquette, and more).*

23. "Current Issues in Export Control: An Interview with Under Secretary for Export Administration Dennis Kloske," *OEL Insider*, December 1989. *(A publication of the U.S. Department of Commerce Office of Export Licensing, the OEL Insider is a monthly newsletter for those interested in export licensing regulations and restrictions. Well produced, it is a refreshingly candid view of a vital office of the government, well worth reading, and full of useful and interesting information).*

24. "Data Encryption Standard," *The NCSL Bulletin*, June, 1990. *(Published by the National Institute of Standards and Technology, the NCSL bulletin advises users on computer systems technology. This particular issue discusses both the DES and specific export restrictions).*

25. Davis, Leonard, *Myths & Facts 1989: A Concise Report of the Arab-Israeli Conflict*, Near East Reports, 1989. *(An interesting, if slightly biased, view of Arab-Israeli history for the past hundred years or so, it helps explain the volatility of the Middle East, and simultaneously their aggressive drive to compete as equals in the world marketplace).*

26. "Departments of Commerce and the Treasury's Role in Licensing to Embargoed/Sanctioned Countries: The Relationship Between the Of-

fice of Foreign Assets Control and the Bureau of Export Administration," *OEL Insider*, March 1990.

27. *Digital Equipment Corporation Marketing Strategies to 1994*, Frost & Sullivan, Summer 1990.

28. Digital Equipment Corporation, *Annual Report to Stockholders*, 1985–1990.

29. *Digital Guide to Developing International User Information*, Digital Press, pre-publication review copy, 1991. *(While viewed in pre-publication form, this is a promising book that focuses on global design from the point of view that the user information is the critical key portion. Therefore, there is little discussion of methodologies, rather the focus is on concrete things such as illustrations, voice annotation, graphics, packaging, and similar, for overseas markets).*

30. *Does Your Company Make Any of These 33 Common and Costly Mistakes in Its International Marketing?*, Anderson & Lembke. *(An exceptionally witty pamphlet from a company famous for their unusual approaches to advertising, this short document also contains many insightful thoughts, including their most common international marketing mistake: Does Your Company See The Home Market As Its Real Market, and Foreign Markets as a Dumping Ground for Its Surplus?)*

31. Dunlop, Dominic, *International Standardization: An Informal View of the Formal Structures as they Apply to Posix Internationalization*, January 11, 1990. *(Informal handout from the representative of both the European Unix Users Group (EUROPEN) and the Usenix Association to the IEEE Posix internationalization subgroup).*

32. Dyson, Esther, "Micro Capitalism: Eastern Europe's Computer Future," *Harvard Business Review*, January–February 1991. *(One of the last bastions of pure market capitalism, the Harvard Business Review often features articles on international trade and international markets, as well as the problems and capabilities of foreign subsidiaries and joint ventures).*

33. "EC Moves Inexorably Toward The Single Market," *Business International Newsletter*, Fall 1989.

34. Eglash, Joanne, "HP Cheers as U.S., Allies End Ban on Most Computer Exports," *INTEREX News*, Summer 1990.

35. *European Computer Market Goes Soft*, Frost & Sullivan International Market Research Reports, April, 1990.

36. *European Market for Unix Systems*, Frost & Sullivan, Spring 1990.

37. Fields, George, *From Bonsai to Levi's*, Mentor, 1985. *(Another in the long series of books on how Japan is absorbing elements of Western culture, this is written by a U.S. citizen who lived in Japan for many years, offering insight on both the culture and business of Japan).*

38. Foy, Nancy, *The Sun Never Sets on IBM*, William Morrow & Son, 1974. *(An interesting, though very dated, look at the culture of IBM. And an ironic title two decades later, too!)*

39. Garneau, Dennis, *Keys to Sort and Search For Culturally Expected Results*, Jun 90 (IBM Publication GG24-3516-00) *(A lengthy work, this document*

is one of the most interesting from the IBM Internationalization Centre, with hundreds of tables of locale-based data).

40. Garrison, David, personal correspondence, October 3, 1990.
41. Gerasimov, Gennady, "Politics and Trade," *Business in the USSR*, February 1991.
42. Goodspeed, Peter, "The Conflict Between Reform and Repression," *World Press Review*, March 1991.
43. Government Printing Office *Style Manual*, January 1984. *(More than any other reference herein, this is a required document for anyone working in the global market. Over half the book is reference tables and descriptions of dozens of languages and locales, researched by the U.S. Government. This document is reissued every eight years).*
44. Gudykunst, William and Ting-Tooney, Stella, *Culture and Interpersonal Communication*, Sage, 1988.
45. Hall, Mark and Barry, John, *SUNBURST: The Ascent of Sun Microsystems*, Contemporary Books, 1990. *(A casual and engaging analysis of the evolution of Sun Microsystems from idea to multibillion dollar firm in less than ten years, this book has lessons for all entrepreneurs and high tech business people).*
46. Hertzfeld, Jeffrey, "Joint Ventures: Saving the Soviets from Perestroika," *Harvard Business Review*, January/February 1991.
47. Hewlett-Packard Co., *Annual Report to Stockholders*, 1985–1990.
48. Hewlett-Packard, *HP 3000 Computer Systems: Native Language Support Reference Manual*, Updated (Part 32414-90001 U1088), October 1988.
49. Hewlett-Packard, *HP-UX Concepts and Tutorials: Native Language Support*, HP 9000 series 300/800 computers (Part 97089-900058), 1989.
50. Hewlett-Packard, *Native Language Support: User's Guide*, HP 9000 Computers, (Part B1864-90003) beta documentation, January 1991. *(A promising early version of new documentation from HP on their NLS package; including many revisions indicating modifications to match the X/Open Portability Guide).*
51. Hur, Jin Ho, *Requirements and Issues for Handling Hangul in Internationalized Applications*, Human Computers, Inc., Korea, 1990.
52. IBM Corporation, *Annual Report to Stockholders*, 1986, 1988.
53. IBM, *Character Data Representation Architecture: Executive Overview*, Aug 90 (GC09-1392-00).
54. IBM, *Designing International Software*, September 90 (GX09-1220-00). *(A small fold out card summarizing a number of important points relating to internationalization and localization).*
55. IBM, *National Language Design Guide: Designing Enabled Products*, January 1991 (SE09-8001-01). *(An excellent overview of internationalization, although it is a bit slim on actual internationalization examples).*
56. IBM, *National Language Support Reference Manual*, Mar 90 (SE09-8002-01). *(Comprised almost completely of tables and other references defining dozens of languages and locales).*
57. *International Traffic in Arms Regulations (ITAR)*, United States Depart-

ment of State, November 1989. *(Defines which software and technologies are on the U.S. Defense Department restricted export list).*

58. Ishihara, Shintaro, *The Japan that Can Say No: Why Japan Will be First Among Equals*, Simon & Schuster, 1991. *(A controversial book that candidly discusses the trade imbalance between Japan and the U.S., from an unusually aggressive, pro-Japanese point of view).*

59. *Issues in Implementing Thai*, Notes for a seminar July–August 1990, Image Alpha Limited.

60. Kamioka, Kazuyoshi, *Japanese Business Pioneers*, Heian, 1988. *(An engrossing, if somewhat dry, look at the lives of various Japanese business pioneers, including the directors of Matsushita, Honda, Sony, YKK Fasteners, Sanyo and Canon).*

61. Kennelly, Cynthia Hartman, *Digital Guide to Developing International Software*, Digital, 1991. *(One of the best introductions to the mechanics of software internationalization, this book contains many pages worth of data on date formats, sorting and transliteration, forms of address, and similar, as well as an intelligent discussion of the various aspects of internationalization).*

62. Kernighan, Brian, Ritchie, Dennis, *The C Programming Language*, Second Edition, Prentice Hall, 1988. *(Includes extensions for the ANSI C standard).*

63. Kim, Young Yim, Gudykunst, William, *Theories in Intercultural Communication*, Sage Publishing, 1988.

64. KPMG, *Europe 1992 and the High Technology Industry*, 1989. *(Insightful analysis of the high tech marketplace by one of the top international marketing companies).*

65. LeDuc, A.L., personal correspondence, Sep 20, 1990.

66. Lotus Corporation, *Annual Report to Stockholders*, 1985–1989

67. Macleod, Roderick, *China Inc: How to do Business with the Chinese*, Bantam Books, 1988. *(Written in a very casual, topical style, Macleod discusses the various facets of doing business as a foreign firm in China, including joint ventures and the political challenges. Much of the book, however, focuses on cultural differences between China and the West, making it a very worthwhile read).*

68. Marcille, Kim, "Training Post," *Computer News International*, December 1990. *(Computer News International is a monthly publication from the CNI Group covering the Latin American computer marketplace, with articles presented in both English and Spanish).*

69. *Market Open For Unix Growth*, Frost & Sullivan International Market Research Reports, April, 1990.

70. Matusky, Greg, "What We Export Best," *World Trade*, March 1991.

71. Murai, Jun, *Unix Technologies of Japan*, tutorial, Winter Usenix, 1990.

72. Nash, Bruce and Zullo, Allan, *The MisFortune 500*, Pocket Books, 1988.

73. *National Trade Estimate Report on Foreign Trade Barriers*, Office of the United States Trade Representative, 1990. *(A country by country analysis of trade and import barriers, with an emphasis on high technology and*

foodstuffs. It includes discussion of copyright and intellectual property laws in each country analysed).

74. "New Europe Survey," *EuroSphere*, a publication of KPMG Peat Marwick International Practice, September/October 1990. *(EuroSphere is published quarterly by KPMG Peat Marwick and often has fascinating features on various aspects of the upcoming EC 92).*

75. Nielsen, Jakob, ed., *Designing User Interfaces for International Use*, Elsevier, 1990. *(An excellent book, this compendium includes articles on testing, user interface design, programming and more, all tied around the topic of internationalization and localization).*

76. *OECD In Figures*, a Supplement to the OECD Observer, July 1990. *(A booklet stuffed with facts and figures about all members of the Organization for Economic Co-operation and Development, including demographics, national products, education, R&D, and science and technology imports and exports).*

77. Ould, Andrew, "Can U.S. Unix Vendors Keep Their Grip on Europe?," *UnixWorld*, September, 1990.

78. Parker, Rachel, "Software Spoken Here: With the Home Market Slowing, U.S. Publishers Enjoy Strong Sales Overseas," *InfoWorld*, June 25, 1990.

79. Pfeiffer, Eckhard, untitled presentation, COMPAQ Quarterly Analysts Meeting: October 1990. *(Pfeiffer is President of Europe and International Markets for Compaq, and presents fascinating numbers regarding Compaq's growth in the global computer market).*

80. Purves, Alan, *Writing Across Languages and Cultures: Issues on Contrastive Rhetoric*, Sage, 1988.

81. Quelch, John, Buzzel, Robert, and Salama, Eric, *The Marketing Challenge of Europe 1992*, Addison Wesley, 1990. *(A reasonable introduction targeted at MBAs, this book also includes an important section on Eastern Europe, noting the possibilities for growth and the dangers therein).*

82. Ricks, David, *Big Business Blunders: Mistakes in Multinational Marketing*, Dow Jones-Irwin, 1983. *(A primary reference for Chapter Five, this book is almost an instant education in the ways companies err when targeting products for international markets. It is also very amusing).*

83. Robrock, Anna, "Test Yourself; How Much Do You Know About International Communications?," *IEEE Computer*, December 1989. *(An enjoyable self-quiz style article on international telephone number formats).*

84. Salus, Peter, "Your Standard Column: Internationalization", *SunExpert*, July 1990.

85. Schäffer, Juan Jorge, personal correspondence, December 3, 1990.

86. SHARE Europe, *White Paper: National Language Architecture*, June 1990. *(Mostly an indictment of IBM's poorly implemented internationalization featureset in their SAA architecture, it also has some interesting information on the more general topic.)*

87. "Small Business Resource Guide," *Success*, July/August 1990. *(Listing a number of worthwhile U.S. Government contacts.)*

88. "Spelling Standardized for Portuguese," *Wall Street Journal*, December

18, 1990. "There's No Truth to the Rumors of an Expanded 'Pepper ... and Salt' ", March 28, 1991. *(It goes almost without saying that the Wall Street Journal, and the Asian Wall Street Journal, are excellent sources of information as released throughout the world).*

89. Spencer, Henry, *The Visible Word: Problems of Legibility*, Royal College of Art, London, 1969. *(A classic work discussing and displaying various typefaces and discussing related aspects of legibility).*

90. *Statistical Analysis of Extra-EUR 12 Trade in Hi-Tech Products*, Eurostat, the European Communities Commission, 1990. *(Lengthy tome chock full of analysis and breakdown of trade into and out of the EUR 12 market. Difficult to understand, but fascinating and highly informative nonetheless).*

91. Sun Microsystems, *Annual Report to Stockholders*, 1986–1990.

92. Sun, Yufang, *Requirements and Issues for Handling Chinese in Internationalized Applications*, Institute of Software, Chinese Academy of Sciences, 1991.

93. Tasker, Peter, *The Japanese: A Major Exploration of Modern Japan*, Dutton, 1987. *(Not directly focused on business, either Japanese or foreign, this book is one of many offering insight into the Japanese culture, heritage, and society).*

94. Taylor, Dave, "International Unix," *Unix Review*, November 1990.

95. Taylor, Dave, "Creating International Software," *Sun Tech Journal*, Winter 1990.

96. Taylor, Dave, "The Posix Standard: What it is and what it means," *HP Design & Automation*, December, 1989.

97. Taylor, Dave, "Whither Commercial Unix?," *The Sun Observer*, June, 1989.

98. Turner, Geoffrey, *White Paper on Federal Government Export Policies for Commercial Cryptographic Products*, SRI International, April 1989. *(A sobering look at government policy regarding the Data Encryption Standard (DES), especially regarding export limitations).*

99. *Unicode 1.0, Draft Standard, Final Review Document*, The Unicode Consortium, December 1990.

100. *Unicode, a Technical Introduction*, The Unicode Consortium, January 28, 1991.

101. *Unix in Europe*, a supplement to *Unix Today!*, June 1990.

102. Waugh, Colin, "Questions and Answers on Hard Currency," *Europe*, November 1990. *(Europe: The Magazine of the European Community has consistently, month after month, contained invaluable and insightful thoughts and analysis of the EC and EUR12 countries, and their roles in the global economy. It is published bimonthly by the Delegation of the Commission of the European Communities, Washington D.C).*

103. Weltz, Richard N., *Foreign Language Typography*, from the National Composition Association, 1977. *(A classic work on setting foreign language type, though quite dated as much of it relates to movable type rather than electronic typesetting. Indeed, the National Composition Association has had to change their focus and name too, to the International Typographical Institution).*

104. Wessell, Nils, ed., *The New Europe: Revolution in East-West Relations*, Academy of Political Science, 1991. *(One of a number of books that significantly help in understanding the ramifications surrounding the end of the Cold War and simultaneous opening and closing (both due to EC92) of the European borders).*

105. White, Daryl, *Compaq: A Global Corporation*, presentation notes, September 27, 1990. *(White is Senior VP Finance and CFO, Compaq Computer Corporation).*

106. Williams, Robert, Teagan, Mark, and Beneyto, José, *The World's Largest Market: A Business Guide to Europe 1992*, Amacom, 1990. *(Comprised significantly of introductions to the EC, member countries, the political structures of the Commission, and the like, this book can serve as an excellent first step towards learning more about the upcoming European Community 1992).*

107. *X/Open Portability Guide, Vol 1: XSI Commands and Utilities*, Prentice-Hall, 1989. *(The entire X/Open Portability Guide is an absolute must-have for anyone serious about internationalization, and ensuring that the system used is X/Open Compliant is almost a necessity in addition).*

108. *X/Open Portability Guide, Vol 2: XSI System Interface and Headers*, Prentice-Hall, 1989.

109. *X/Open Portability Guide, Vol 3: XSI Supplemental Definitions*, Prentice-Hall, 1989.

110. *X/Open Portability Guide, Vol 4: Programming Languages*, Prentice-Hall, 1989.

111. *X/Open Portability Guide, Vol 5: Data Management*, Prentice-Hall, 1989.

112. Yelkin, Pavel, "Reasonably High Hopes for High-Tech," *Business in the USSR*, February 1991.

See Also

United States Government Printing Office

The United States Government Printing Office has a wealth of information, including extensive analysis of the various possible trading countries including China, Japan, each of the European countries, each of the Middle Eastern countries, and more. In addition:

1. *Assessment of the United States Competitiveness in High Technology Industries.* Examines United States high technology industries in the areas of importance, trade performance, and factors influencing their competitiveness vis-a-vis foreign competitors, U.S. GPO, 1983

2. *Business America: The Magazine of International Trade* (biweekly). Publication designed to help U.S. exporters penetrate overseas markets by providing them with timely information on oppor-

tunities for trade and methods of doing business in foreign countries. $49/year.

3. *Europe 1992: A Business Guide to United States Government Resources.* Provides an introduction to the European Community's
single market initiative and contact points for further information
and expertise in developing strategies to take full advantage of
the single European market beginning in 1993. U.S. GPO, 1990.

4. *Introductory Guide to Joint Ventures in the Soviet Union.* Discusses
how to research and establish mutually beneficial joint business
ventures with the Soviet Union. Also includes a bibliography on
the Soviet economy, perestroika, joint ventures, and countertrade.
Prepared especially for U.S. business people. U.S. GPO 1990.

5. *Overseas Business Reports.* (irregularly) Information on the economic outlook, industry trends, trade regulations, distribution and
sales channels, transportation, credit, and other facets of business
in various countries.

6. *EC 1991: Growth Markets, Export Opportunities in Europe.* Designed
to be a quick reference source on the economies of the European
Community, its 12 member nations, and other countries. Indexed
by products and by countries. U.S. GPO 1989.

7. *National Negotiating Styles.* Assesses the negotiating styles of
China, the Soviet Union, Japan, France, Egypt and Mexico. U.S.
GPO 1987.

8. *Foreign Area Studies: Persian Gulf States,* U.S. GPO 1985.

OECD

The Organization for Economic Co-Operation and Development
(OECD) also offers a wide variety of publications, with the following
of interest:

1. *Activities of the OECD,* 1988 Report by the Secretary-General
2. *China's Special Economic Zones.*
3. *Competition and Trade Policies, Their Interaction.*
4. *Countertrade, Developing Country Practices.*
5. *Technology and Global Competition, The Challenge for Newly In-
dustrialised Economies.*
6. *Appropriate Technology, Problems and Promises.*
7. *New Technology in the 1990s: A Socio-Economic Strategy.*
8. *Assessing the Impact of Technology on Society.*
9. *Technology Transfer between East and West.*
10. *The Internationalisation of Software and Computer Services.*

The OECD also has a number of publications, with back issues available. One of their most informative is the ICCP "Information, Computer and Communications Policy" Series, with two issues of particular interest:

No. 8. Exploration of Legal Issues in Information and Communication Technologies
No. 9. Software, an Emerging Industry

Additionally, the *OECD Observer, STI—Science, Technology and Industry Review, Main Science and Technology Indicators*, as well as *Annual Foreign Trade Report for the United States*, are all of interest and relevance too.

The Popular Press

There are a number of titles in the popular press also worth consulting on various topics. One warning, however; the Business and Marketing sections of the bookstores seem to be almost filled with paranoid protectionist and xenophobic titles, with everyone from the Japanese to the Italians as the bad guys out to get the poor naïve U.S. It is an unfortunate trend and does not seem likely to solve any problems. Instead, clear rational thinking is the remedy, and the following titles appear to offer just that:

1. Harrison, Bennet, and Bluestone, Barry, *The Great U-Turn: Corporate Restructuring and the Polarization of America*, Basic Books, 1991.
2. Fenwick & West, *1991 Update: International Legal Protection for Software. (Fenwick & West are a legal partnership specializing in international copyright and patent law.)*
3. Kang, T.W., *Gaishi: The Foreign Company in Japan*, Basic Books, 1990.
4. Nelson, Carl, *Import/Export: How to Get Started in International Trade*, TAB Books, 1990.
5. Prestowitz, Clyde, Jr., *Trading Places: How We Are Giving Our Future to Japan, and How to Reclaim It*, Basic Books, 1991.
6. Smith, Paul A., Jr., *On Political War*, National Defense University Press, 1989.
7. Wilson, Ralph, *Help! The Art of Computer Technical Support*, Peachpit Press, 1991.

Glossary

16-bit: character sets that require more than 200 characters, often considerably more: 16-bit character sets of 1,000 or more characters are common.

8-bit: character set that can be defined within the ANSI Latin-1 definition: usually around 200 characters total.

animé: Japanese cartoon-style graphics—from the French word "animar," to animate.

ANSI: American National Standards Institute.

ASCII: American Standard Code for Information Interchange.

AZERTY keyboard: Commonly found in France, the keys on this keyboard are arranged differently than on the common QWERTY keyboard.

bidirectional language: languages using text oriented from right to left, with numeric information included as left-to-right.

byte: an 8-bit unit of information.

CAT: Computer Assisted Translation—using a computer to aid in the translation of data from one language to another.

character set: mapping of numeric values to specific characters, as with ASCII, ISO 8859 (Latin-1), and so forth.

COCOM: Coordinating Committee for Multilateral Export Controls reviews export license applications for strategic commodities from member countries: Australia, Belgium, Canada, Luxembourg Netherlands, Norway, Denmark, France, Germany, United Kingdom, USA, Portugal, Spain, Turkey, Greece, Italy, and Japan.

codeset: a particular set of characters, see "character set."

collation ordering: information specifying the lexical ordering of specific characters and data in a particular language or locale.

collation: sorting information according to a collation ordering.

cursive script: a script that has characters connected to each other.

deshaping: returning to the base shape from one of the other forms in Arabic script languages (see also "shape determination").

diacritical: Modifying marks for a character, esp. accents.

diphthong: a pair of vowels, often from early Greek, that is printed as a single character. "Encyclopædia" is an example of this. Becoming obsolete in English.

EAR: U.S. Export Administration Regulations.

EC Class 1: All industrialized countries.

EC Class 2: All developing countries.

EC Class 3: All state-trading countries.

EC: The European Community, typically the EUR12.

ECC: European Commonwealth Community (see "EC").

ECMA: European Computer Manufacturers' Association.

ECU: European Currency Unit—a mix of various European Currencies used as a single, stable currency for intra-European trading.

EFTA: European Free Trade Association members; Austria, Finland, Iceland, Norway, Sweden, and Switzerland.

EUR12: Member states of the European Communities; Belgium, Denmark, FR of Germany, Greece, Spain, France, Ireland, Italy, Luxembourg, Netherlands, Portugal, and United Kingdom.

font: a specific instantiation of a typeface. That is, Bodoni is a typeface, but Bodoni bold 8 point is a font.

FTAM: File Transfer and Access Method, a network-based file transfer protocol and specification from ISO.

GATT: Global Agreement on Trade and Tariffs.

glyph: graphical representation of a character.

grave: a diacritical indicating a different pronunciation of the vowel in question. For example, "José" would be pronounced as in "hose" without the grave on the "e."

Hangul: script used when writing Korean characters. See also, Hanja.

Hanja: Chinese characters used when writing Korean.

Hanyu: Chinese characters as defined by Taiwanese CNS standard (as used by Digital, most notably).

Hanzi: Chinese characters as defined by PRC (mainland China) (as used by Digital, most notably).

Hiragana: a set of phonetic symbols (or syllabary) used in Japanese in conjunction with Kanji and other character sets.

HP-UX: HP's version of the Unix Operating System.

ideographic character: character that symbolizes a specific thought or idea without actually expressing the name of the thing it represents.

IEC: Information Exchange Characterset, as defined by ISO. Also International Electrotechnical Commission.

IEEE: Institute of Electrical and Electronics Engineers.

ISO: International Organization for Standardization.

ITAR: U.S. Import Tariff and Arms Regulations document.

JIS: Japanese Industrial Standards.

Kana: Syllabic Japanese set of written characters.

Kanji: the Japanese ideographic codeset based on Chinese characters. The set consists of roughly 50,000 glyphs.

Katakana: phonetic Japanese character set (traditional Japanese is ideogrammic, that is, each glyph conveys a meaning akin to separate words in English. A phonetic approach is closer to Latin-based languages, where each character instead conveys a specific sound, or phoneme, and combinations of characters jointly convey an idea or concept). This character set consists of 64 characters, including punctuation.

kerning: tucking characters together for a more pleasing appearance. Examples: "To" and, kerned: "To"; "AWAY" and, kerned: "AWAY."

ligature: typographic notation for when two adjacent characters are considered a single character, as in "fi" or "ll."

locale: the environment in which a product is used.

message catalog: a file containing program messages, command prompts and responses to prompts for a specific application.

mnemonics: techniques that use established conventions, prior training or memory aids, such as an abbreviation or symbol, to assist human memory.

MNLS: AT&T's MultiNational Language Support system.

monotoniko: simplified transliteration of Greek in which the Latin alphabet is used in conjunction with Greek diacriticals.

multi-byte: character sets that require more than a single byte to define, including 16-bit character sets (offering about 65000 characters), and various proposed 24-bit and 32-bit character sets (offering 16.7 million, and 4,294 million characters, respectively).

NBS: National Bureau of Standards—renamed NIST.

NIST: U.S. National Institute of Standards and Technology.

NLIO: HP's Native Language Input/Output subsystem.

NLS: HP's Native Language Support system or X/Open's Native Language System.

OEL: U.S. Office of Export Licensing.

OFAC: U.S. Office of Foreign Assets Control.

OSI: Open Systems Interconnect (a subset of the ISO standards).

phoneme: a particular sound used in human speech. Spoken languages are combinations of hundreds of phonemes.

polytonic: Greek writing in which a variety of diacriticals is used; diacriticals, however, only have historic meaning.

Posix: Portable Operating System Interface for Computer Environments; The IEEE Unix programmatic interface standardization group.

product dumping: A relatively cutthroat business tactic wherein a large company sells a particular product at an exceptionally low price, usually even below their cost of manufacture. The purpose behind this deliberate loss of income is to eliminate smaller competitors, who cannot be competitive because they cannot afford to lower their prices. Widely considered unethical.

quota: A set quantity of a product that cannot be exceeded when the product is imported into a country.

QWERTY keyboard: Most common keyboard layout, so called because the top left row of keys on the keyboard are "Q," "W," "E," "R," "T" and "Y."

radix: character separating the integer portion of a number from the fractional portion, as in the "." in 120.5.

remapping: translating data from one character set to another.

retrofit: Re-engineer an existing product to be internationalized.

Romaji: a mapping of the Japanese sounds into a Roman alphabet.

Romanji: see "Romaji".

screen shot: A photograph or reproduction of the actual appearance of a program on the screen.

shape determination: Process of deciding which of the possible shapes of an Arabic character is to be used in context (typically first, middle, last and alone).

shrink-wrap: a thin layer of transparent plastic covering a package, typically heat shrunk to fit the package snugly. Used to allow shops to know if customers have opened the package or not.

tariff: A form of tax levied on imported products, often used to equalize the price between the foreign import and similar domestic products.

transliteration: translation of a character from upper case to lower case. For example, "HAT" is transliterated to "hat" in English.

typeface: a family or assortment of characters in a particular style.

umlaut: a diacritical indicating a different pronunciation of the vowel in question. For example, "naïve" would be pronounced "nave" without the umlaut on the "i".

Unicode: proposal for a fixed-width 16-bit multilingual character encoding.

wide character: 16-bit characters; characters that require more than the "usual" 8-bit byte of information for storage.

X.400: Specification for international message handling systems from ISO.

X.500: ISO specification for international distributed information systems, including how to look up remote information.

X/OPEN: Consortium of vendors interested in a common application environment including an internationalization layer.

X3J11: ANSI standard specification for the C Programming Language.

XPG: X/Open Portability Guide.

Index

G

GATT (Global Agreement on Trades and Tariffs), 237, 240
GATT meetings, 268n
GCG license, 247
G-DEST license, 246
General Trade Licenses, 246-248
German message catalog, 153-155
Germany, 10, 270
GET MACRO, 169-170
GET MSG, 173-174
GET NEXT LINE, 180-181
GIFT license, 247
GIT license, 246-247
Global Agreement on Trades and Tariffs, *see* GATT *entries*
Global marketplace, ix
Global software
  future of, 255-273
  politics of, 239-253
Global trade zones, 201
Glossary, 303-306
GLR license, 247
GLV license, 247
Glyphs, Japanese, 197-199
Government Printing Office (GPO), 300-301
Graphical elements, culturally dependent, 42
Graphics
  appropriateness of, 202-203
  cartoon style, 202
Gregorian calendar, 41
GTDA license, 248
GTDR license, 248
GTE license, 247-248
GUS license, 247

H

Hebrew, 195
Hewlett-Packard Company, 22-24, 25, 26
Hewlett-Packard Localization Centers, 222
Hewlett-Packard Native Language Support system, *see* Native Language Support system
Hiragana, 198
Hong Kong, ix
Hyphenation, 37

I

Icons, 42, 49-51
IEEE (Institute of Electrical and Electronic Engineers), 229
Imperial date, 54-55
Import/export restrictions, ix
Indonesia, 15
Infix notation, 41
Inflation, 255
Institute of Electrical and Electronic Engineers (IEEE), 229
International currency symbol, 220
Internationalization
  compile-time, 63-68, 93-118
  elements of, 35-44, 77-92, 195-206
  goal of, 29
  link-time, 67, 68-71, 119-133
  localization versus, 29-33
  run-time, *see* Run-time internationalization *entries*
  three approaches to, 61-76
Internationalization standards, 234-235
Internationalized library routines, 186-192
International marketplace, 9-11, 25-26
International Organization for Standardization, *see* ISO *entries*
International software, x
International standards organizations, 225-235, 275
INTERNATIONAL SUPPORT, 176-177
International Traffic in Arms Regulation (ITAR), 250